MW01076919

Design and layout by Jason Platt

ISBN # 978-1535149556

Mister & Me

OF CASTLES & KINGS

A COMIC COLLECTION VOL 2

BY JASON PLATT

COMIC STRIPS FROM 2011-2012

INTRODUCTION BY ERIC GAPSTUR

TO MY FRIENDS

INTRODUCTION

I love the specificity in Mister and Me. Newell's love of John Williams, the Dad's failing to properly teach his son hide and seek- Jason Platt pushes past easy and gives us a strip that resonates with a rare uniqueness.

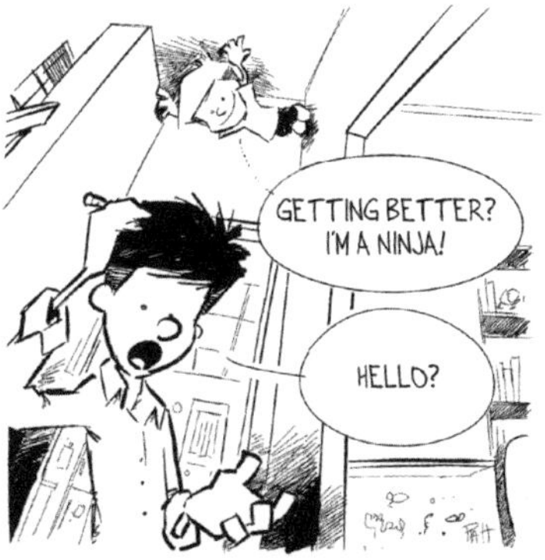
GETTING BETTER? I'M A NINJA!
HELLO?

And WOW, does this extend to the art. The slope of the stadium seating at a Star Wars premiere, the way a cereal bag explodes in pursuit of the toy- Jason gives the detail of this world an unmistakable tangibility and flavor that is so enjoyable to look at.

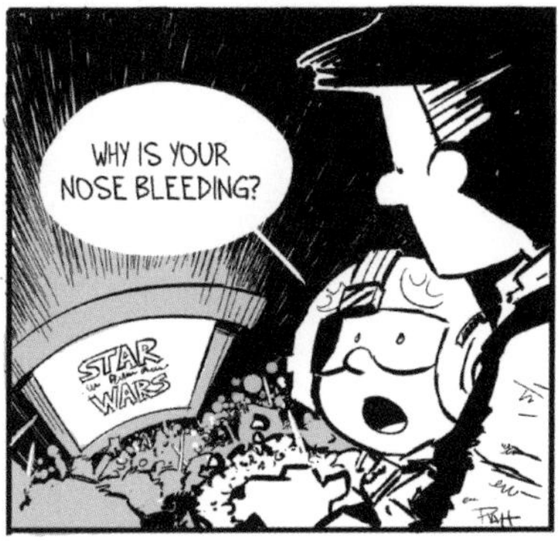
WHY IS YOUR NOSE BLEEDING?
STAR WARS

You can tell that Jason is having as much fun creating this strip as we are experiencing it.

- ERIC GAPSTUR

DC ARTIST AND CREATOR OF THE COMIC STRIP "WYATT"

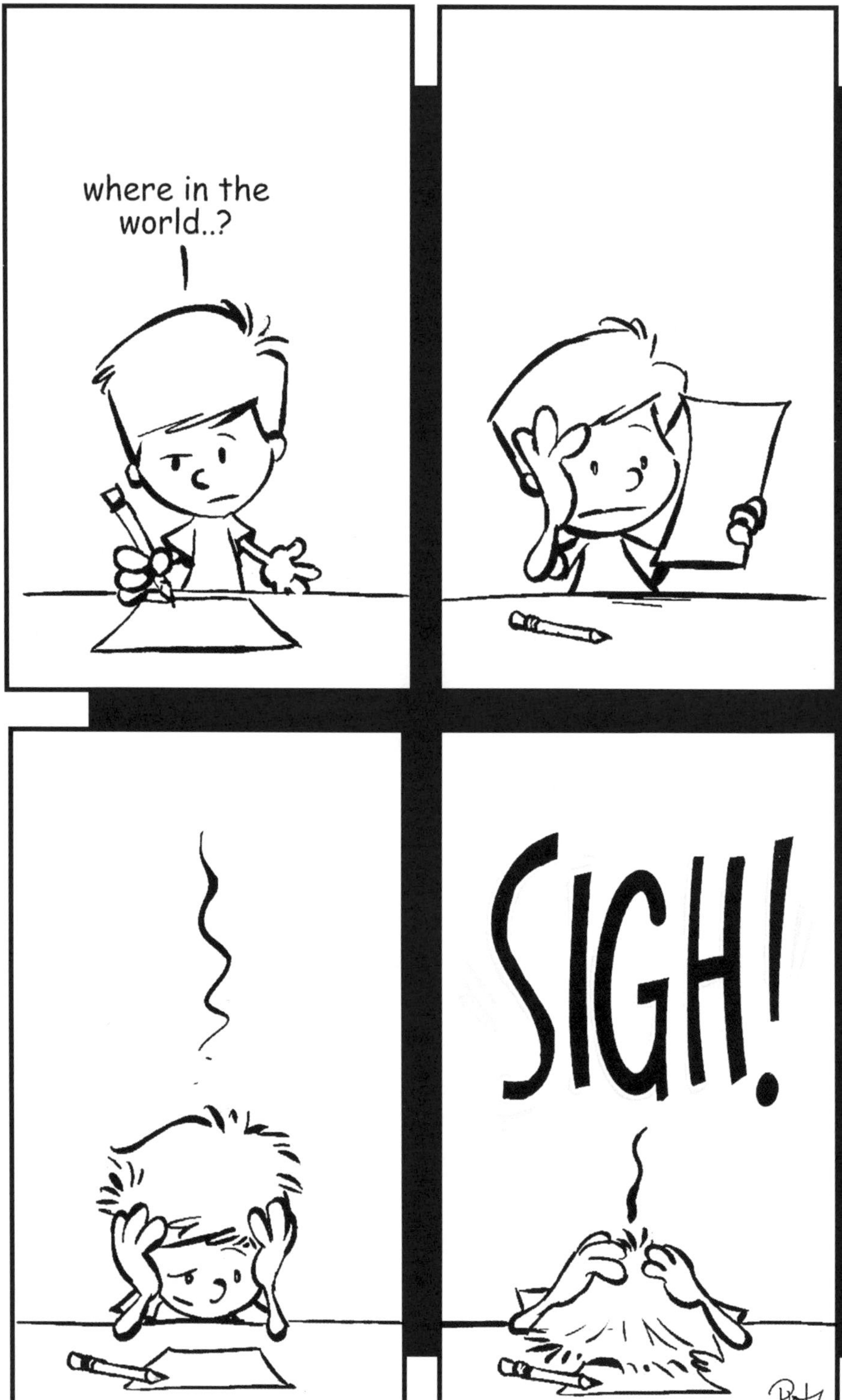
where in the world..?
SIGH!

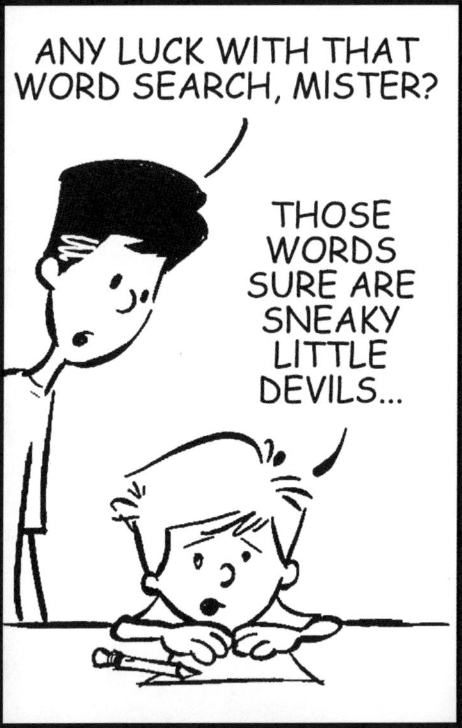
ANY LUCK WITH THAT WORD SEARCH, MISTER?
THOSE WORDS SURE ARE SNEAKY LITTLE DEVILS...

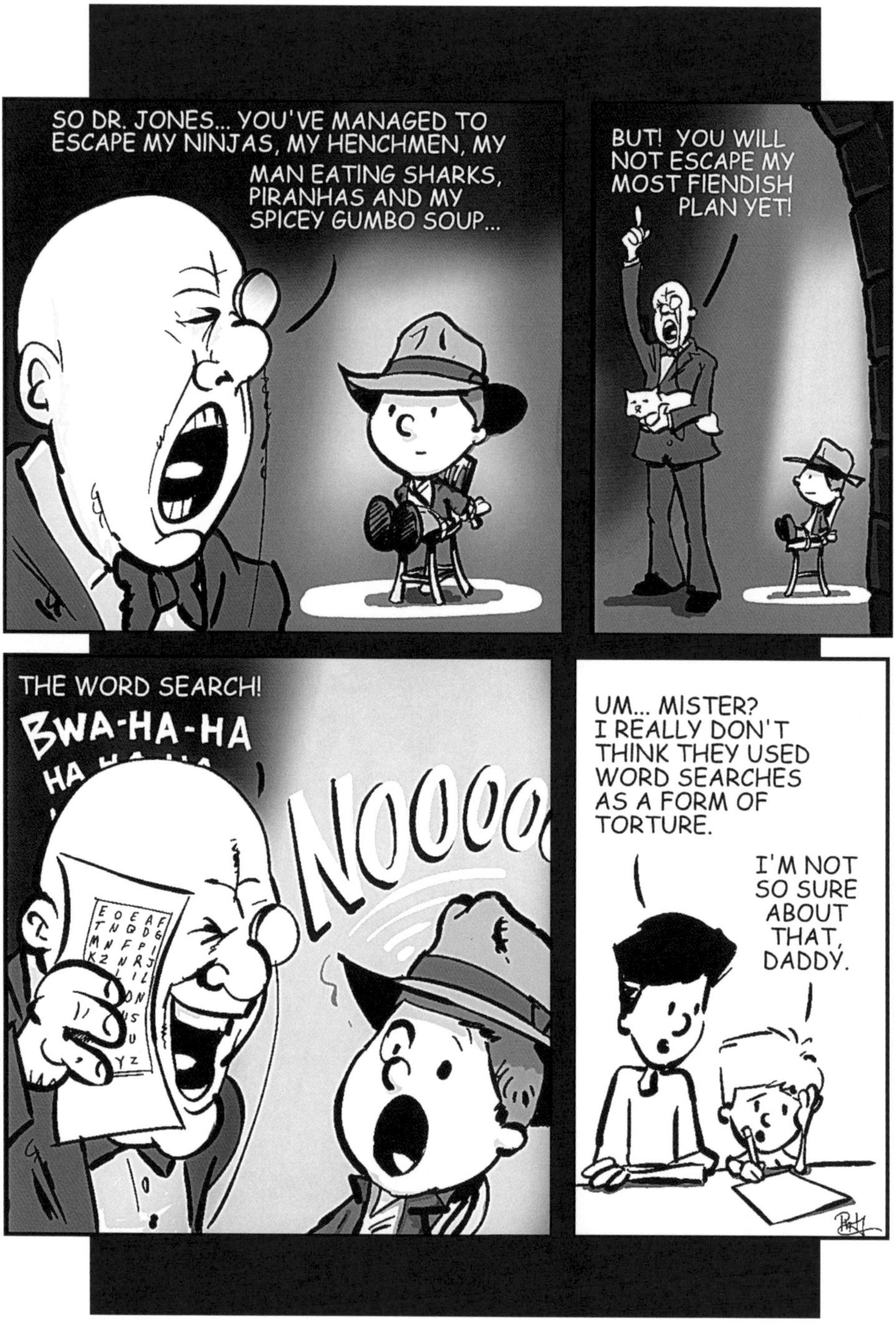
SO DR. JONES... YOU'VE MANAGED TO ESCAPE MY NINJAS, MY HENCHMEN, MY
MAN EATING SHARKS, PIRANHAS AND MY SPICEY GUMBO SOUP...
BUT! YOU WILL NOT ESCAPE MY MOST FIENDISH PLAN YET!
THE WORD SEARCH!
BWA-HA-HA
NOOOO
UM... MISTER? I REALLY DON'T THINK THEY USED WORD SEARCHES AS A FORM OF TORTURE.
I'M NOT SO SURE ABOUT THAT, DADDY.

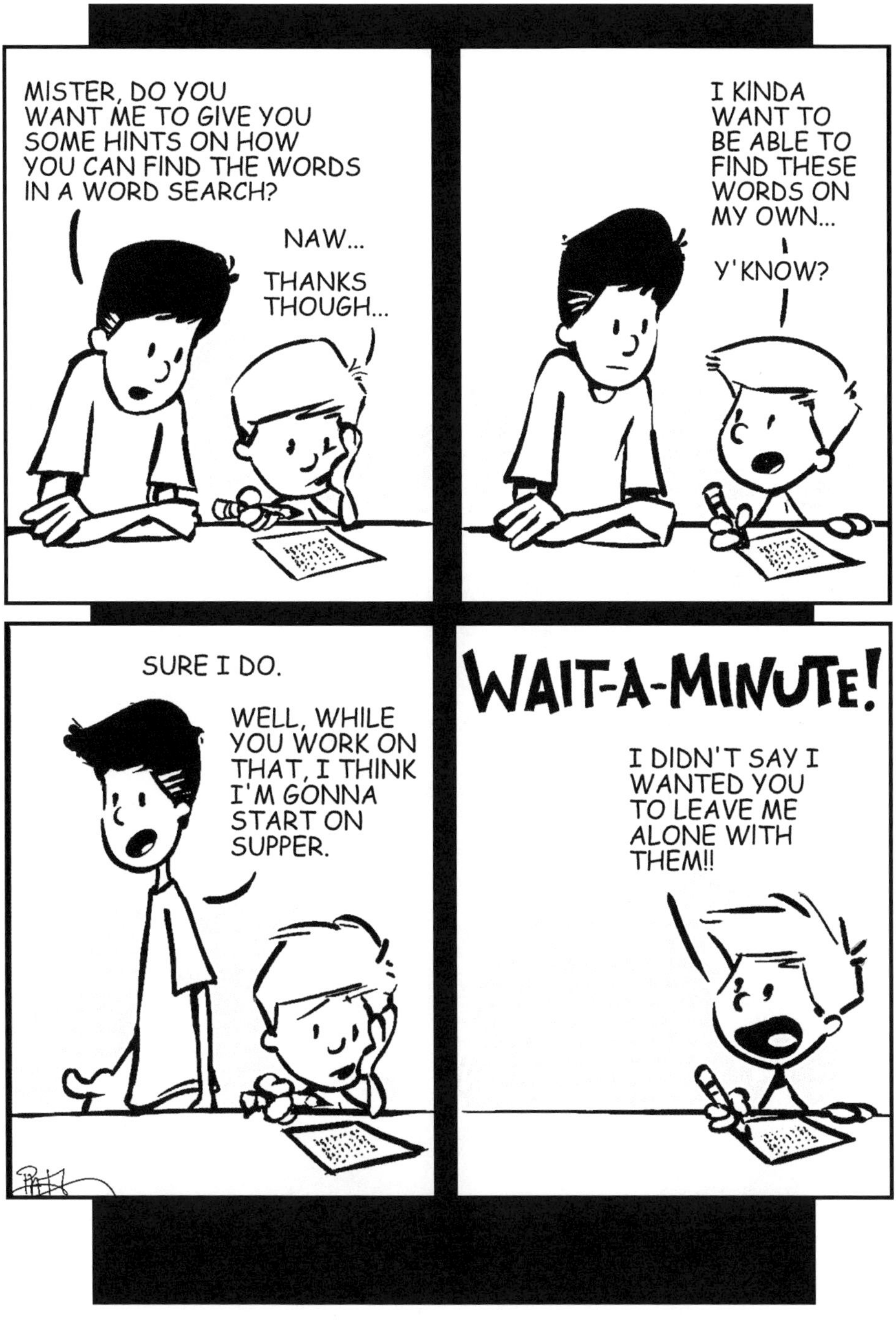
MISTER, DO YOU WANT ME TO GIVE YOU SOME HINTS ON HOW YOU CAN FIND THE WORDS IN A WORD SEARCH?
NAW...
THANKS THOUGH...
I KINDA WANT TO BE ABLE TO FIND THESE WORDS ON MY OWN...
Y'KNOW?
SURE I DO.
WELL, WHILE YOU WORK ON THAT, I THINK I'M GONNA START ON SUPPER.
WAIT-A-MINUTE!
I DIDN'T SAY I WANTED YOU TO LEAVE ME ALONE WITH THEM!!

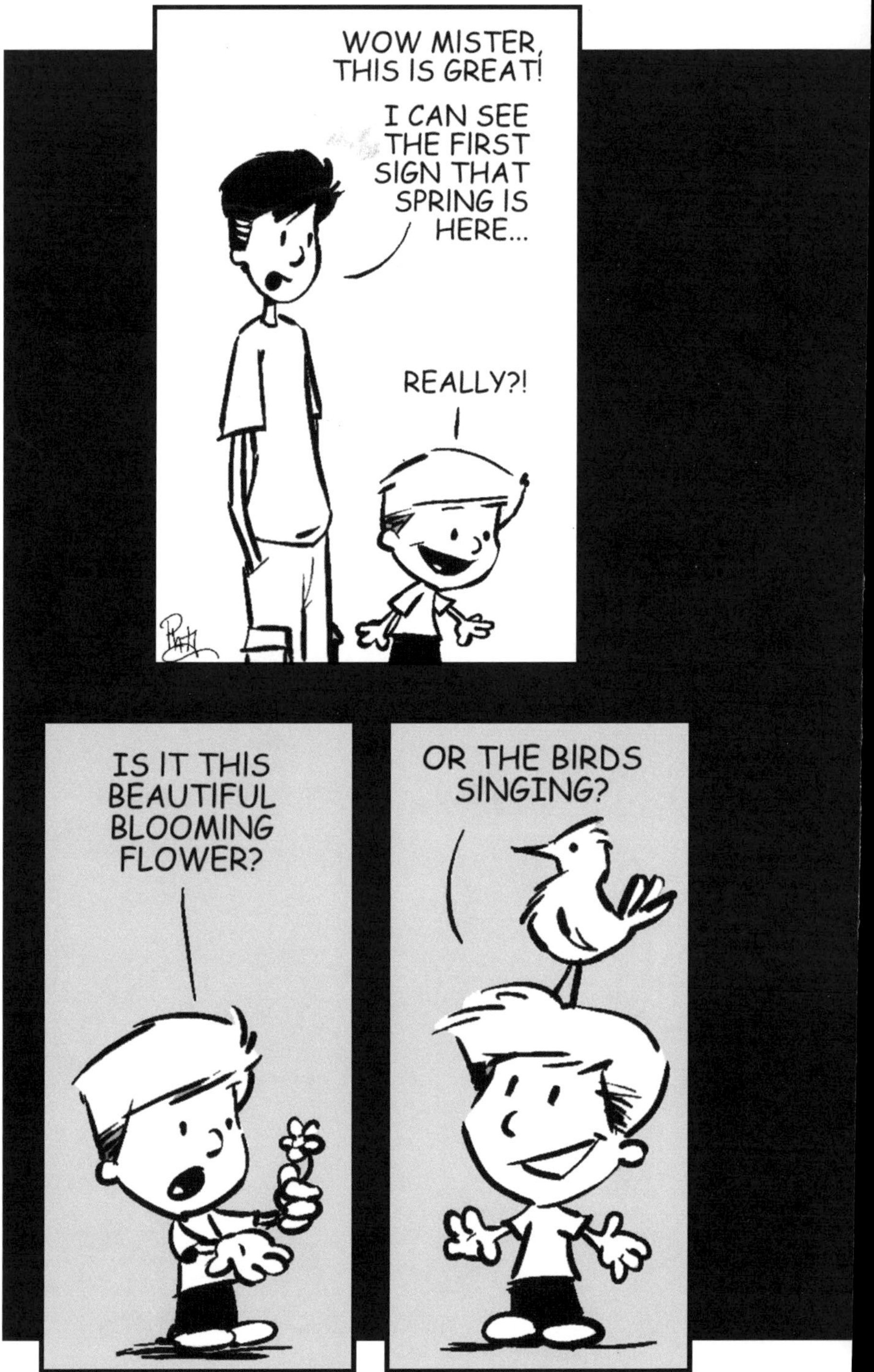
WOW MISTER, THIS IS GREAT!
I CAN SEE THE FIRST SIGN THAT SPRING IS HERE...
REALLY?!
IS IT THIS BEAUTIFUL BLOOMING FLOWER?
OR THE BIRDS SINGING?

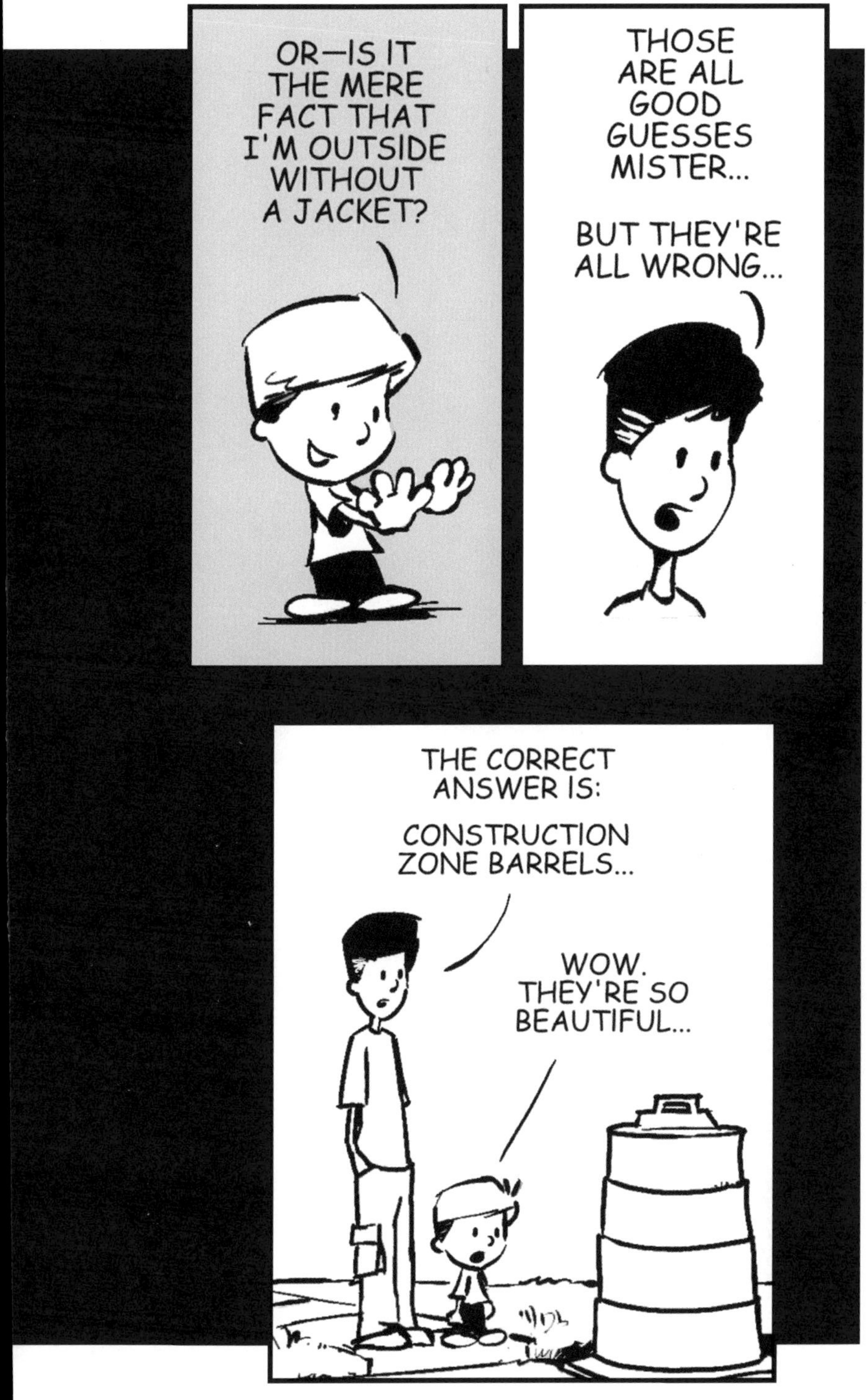
OR—IS IT THE MERE FACT THAT I'M OUTSIDE WITHOUT A JACKET?
THOSE ARE ALL GOOD GUESSES MISTER...
BUT THEY'RE ALL WRONG...
THE CORRECT ANSWER IS:
CONSTRUCTION ZONE BARRELS...
WOW. THEY'RE SO BEAUTIFUL...

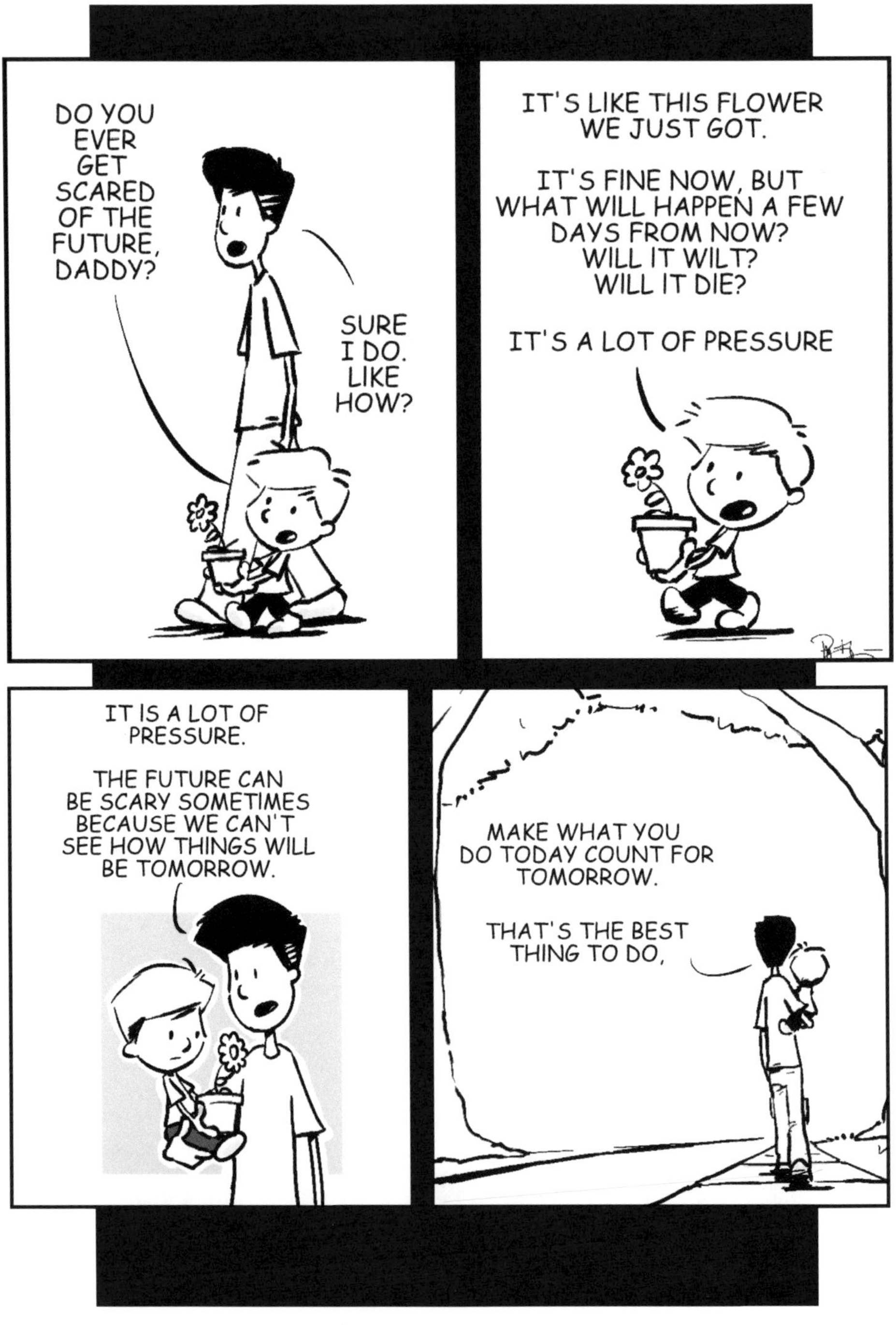
DO YOU EVER GET SCARED OF THE FUTURE, DADDY?
SURE I DO. LIKE HOW?
IT'S LIKE THIS FLOWER WE JUST GOT.
IT'S FINE NOW, BUT WHAT WILL HAPPEN A FEW DAYS FROM NOW? WILL IT WILT? WILL IT DIE?
IT'S A LOT OF PRESSURE
IT IS A LOT OF PRESSURE.
THE FUTURE CAN BE SCARY SOMETIMES BECAUSE WE CAN'T SEE HOW THINGS WILL BE TOMORROW.
MAKE WHAT YOU DO TODAY COUNT FOR TOMORROW.
THAT'S THE BEST THING TO DO,

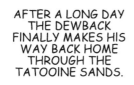

AFTER A LONG DAY THE DEWBACK FINALLY MAKES HIS WAY BACK HOME THROUGH THE TATOOINE SANDS.

WALKING AROUND ALL DAY WITH A STORMTROOPER ON HIS BACK.

LOOKING FOR SOME DROIDS OR SOMETHING...

ALL DAY.

BUT NOW HE CAN'T WAIT TO GET HOME, AND UNWIND

MEHH...

HEY, MISTER. HOW WAS SCHOOL TODAY?

MEH...

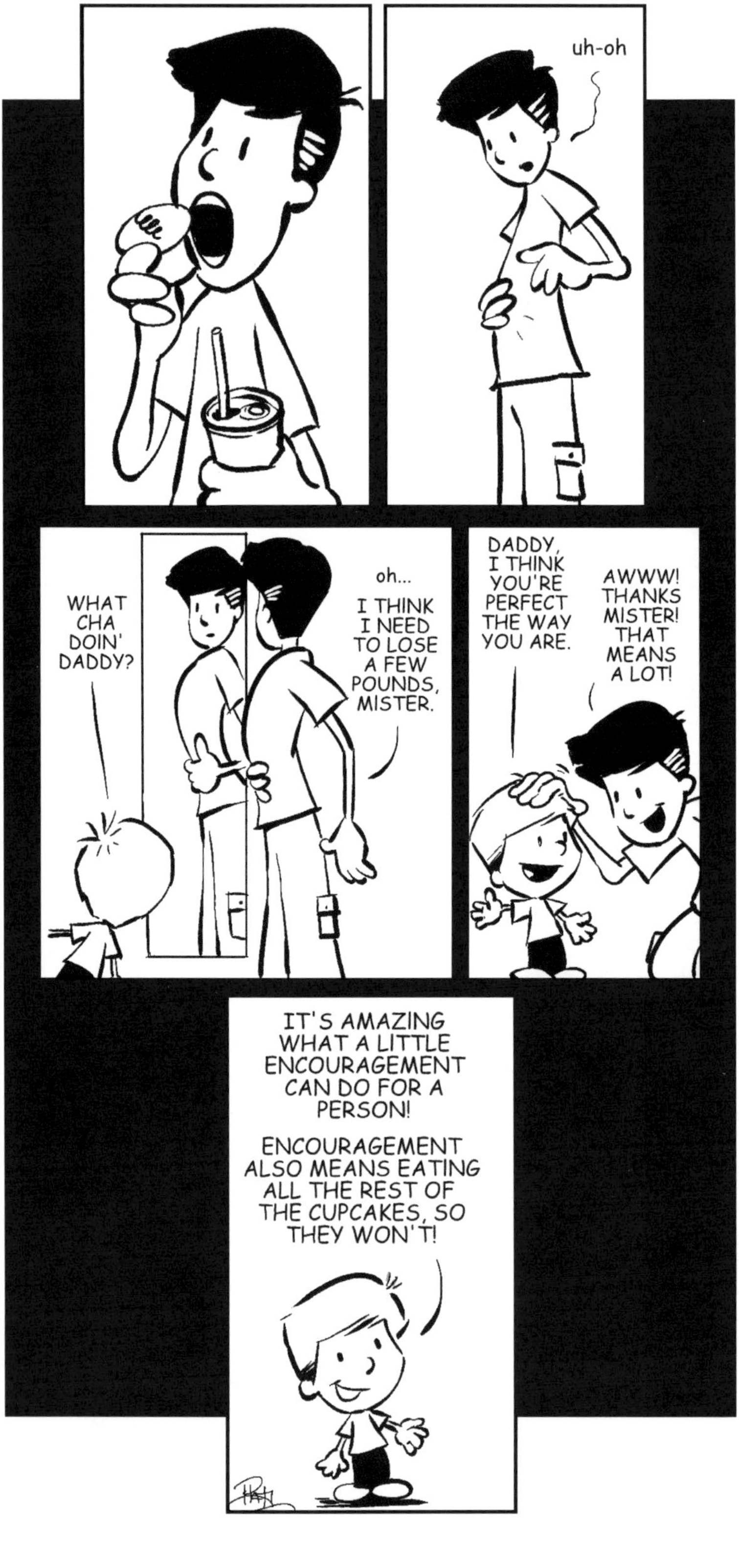
uh-oh
WHAT CHA DOIN' DADDY?
oh...
I THINK I NEED TO LOSE A FEW POUNDS, MISTER.
DADDY, I THINK YOU'RE PERFECT THE WAY YOU ARE.
AWWW! THANKS MISTER! THAT MEANS A LOT!
IT'S AMAZING WHAT A LITTLE ENCOURAGEMENT CAN DO FOR A PERSON!
ENCOURAGEMENT ALSO MEANS EATING ALL THE REST OF THE CUPCAKES, SO THEY WON'T!

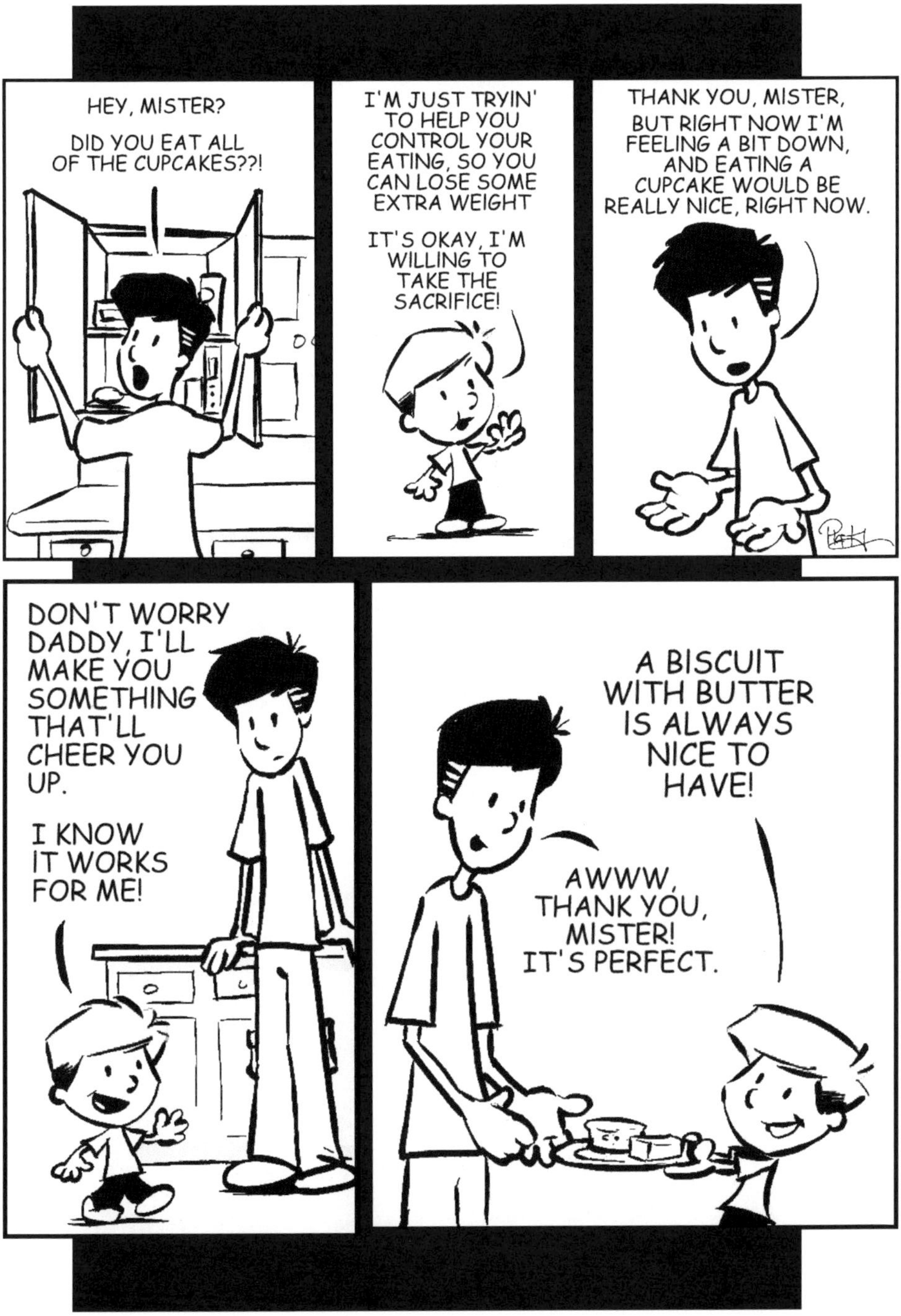
HEY, MISTER?
DID YOU EAT ALL OF THE CUPCAKES??!
I'M JUST TRYIN' TO HELP YOU CONTROL YOUR EATING, SO YOU CAN LOSE SOME EXTRA WEIGHT
IT'S OKAY, I'M WILLING TO TAKE THE SACRIFICE!
THANK YOU, MISTER, BUT RIGHT NOW I'M FEELING A BIT DOWN, AND EATING A CUPCAKE WOULD BE REALLY NICE, RIGHT NOW.
DON'T WORRY DADDY, I'LL MAKE YOU SOMETHING THAT'LL CHEER YOU UP.
I KNOW IT WORKS FOR ME!
A BISCUIT WITH BUTTER IS ALWAYS NICE TO HAVE!
AWWW, THANK YOU, MISTER! IT'S PERFECT.

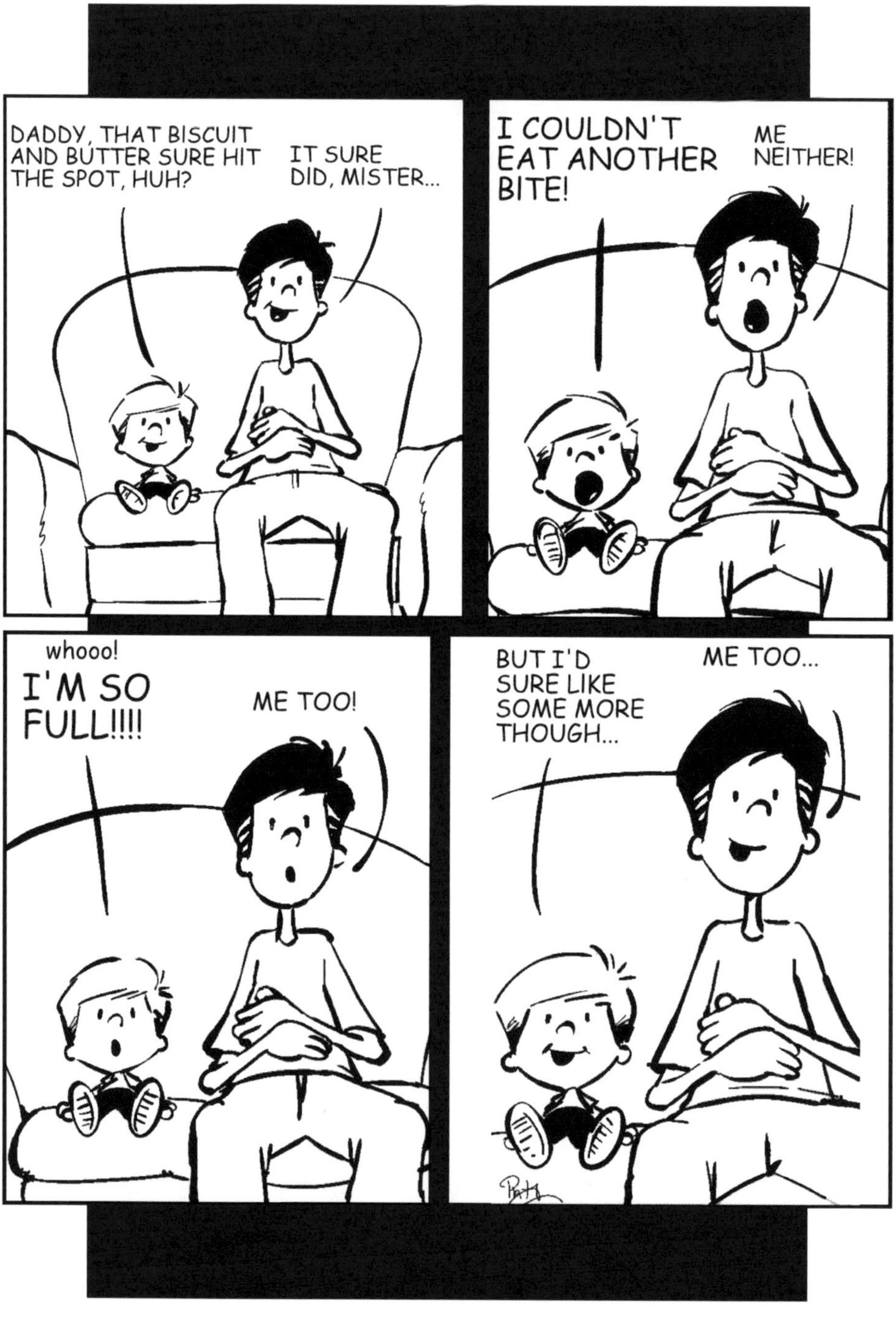
DADDY, THAT BISCUIT AND BUTTER SURE HIT THE SPOT, HUH?
IT SURE DID, MISTER...
I COULDN'T EAT ANOTHER BITE!
ME NEITHER!
whooo! I'M SO FULL!!!!
ME TOO!
BUT I'D SURE LIKE SOME MORE THOUGH...
ME TOO...

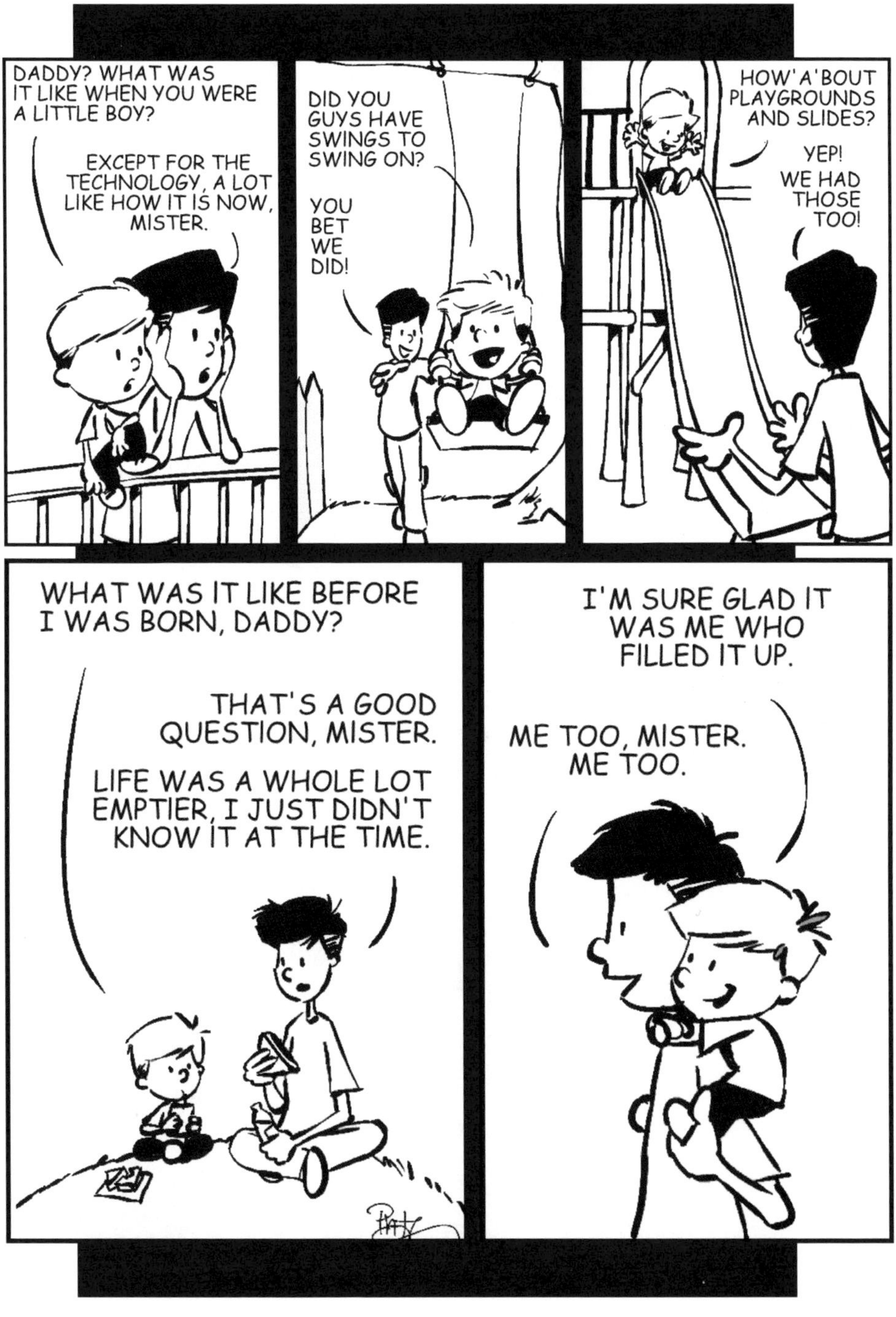
DADDY? WHAT WAS IT LIKE WHEN YOU WERE A LITTLE BOY?
EXCEPT FOR THE TECHNOLOGY, A LOT LIKE HOW IT IS NOW, MISTER.
DID YOU GUYS HAVE SWINGS TO SWING ON?
YOU BET WE DID!
HOW'A'BOUT PLAYGROUNDS AND SLIDES?
YEP! WE HAD THOSE TOO!
WHAT WAS IT LIKE BEFORE I WAS BORN, DADDY?
THAT'S A GOOD QUESTION, MISTER.
LIFE WAS A WHOLE LOT EMPTIER, I JUST DIDN'T KNOW IT AT THE TIME.
I'M SURE GLAD IT WAS ME WHO FILLED IT UP.
ME TOO, MISTER. ME TOO.

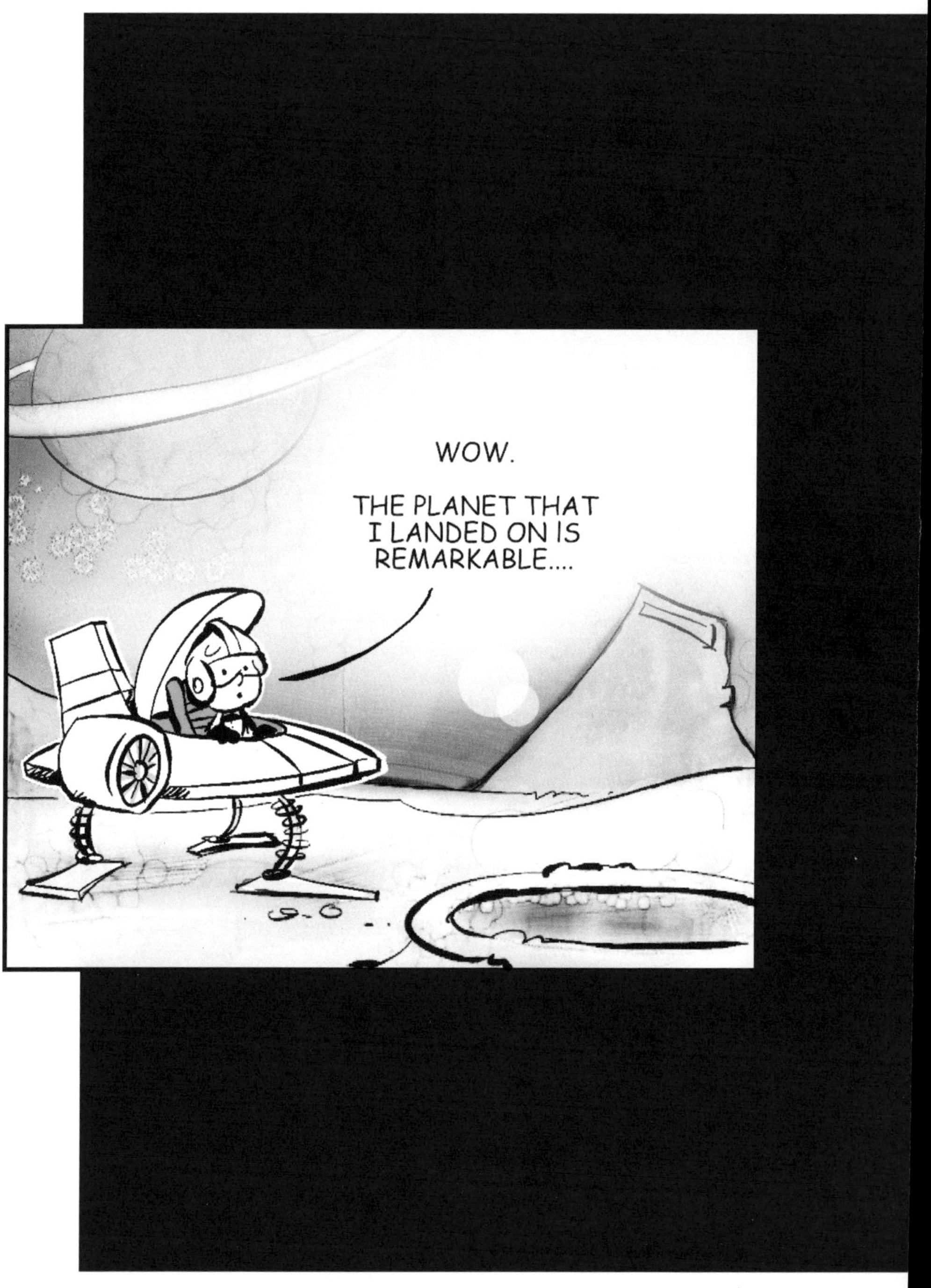
WOW.
THE PLANET THAT I LANDED ON IS REMARKABLE....

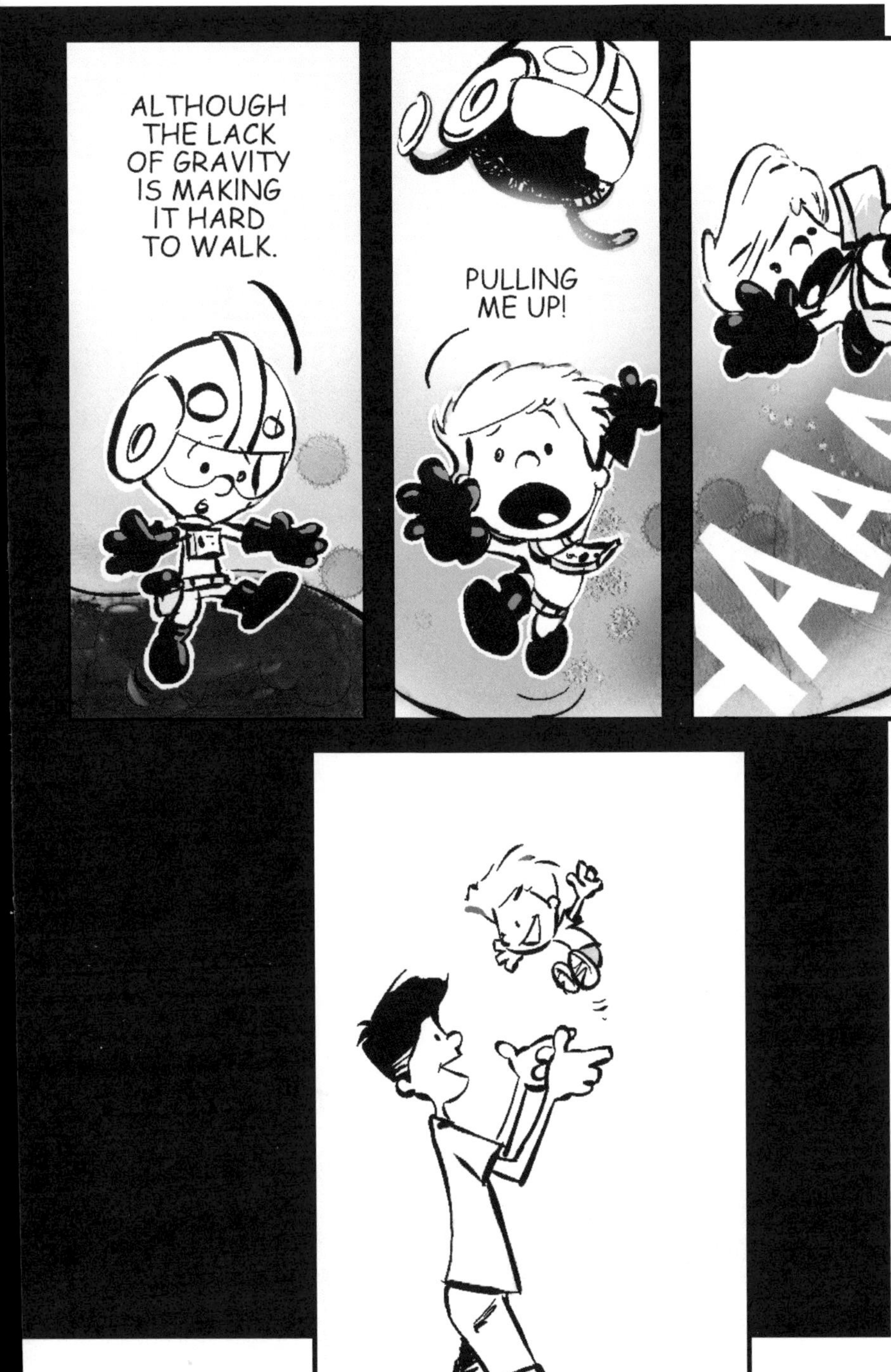
ALTHOUGH THE LACK OF GRAVITY IS MAKING IT HARD TO WALK.
PULLING ME UP!
YAAAA

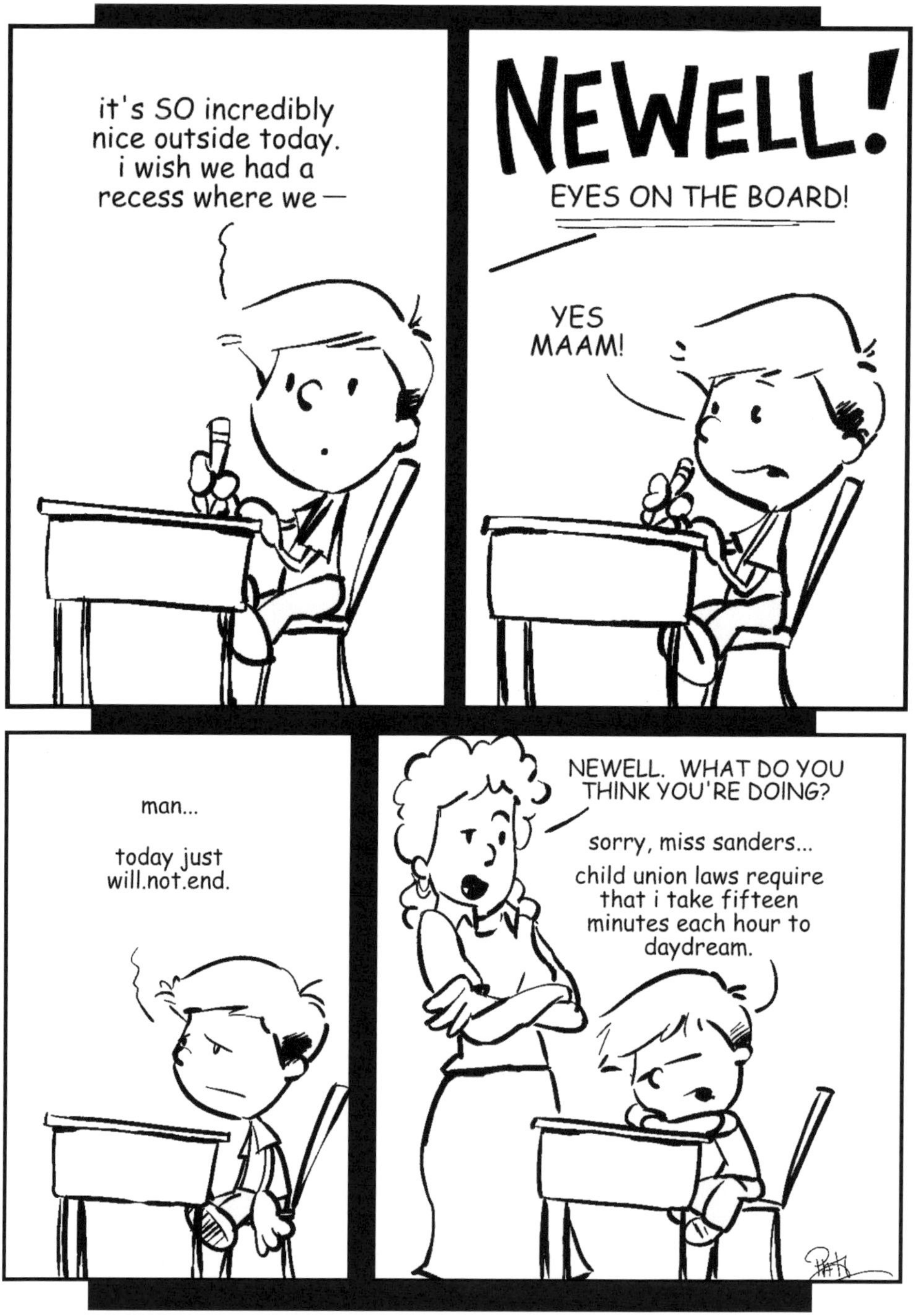
it's SO incredibly nice outside today. i wish we had a recess where we—
NEWELL!
EYES ON THE BOARD!
YES MAAM!
man...
today just will.not.end.
NEWELL. WHAT DO YOU THINK YOU'RE DOING?
sorry, miss sanders...
child union laws require that i take fifteen minutes each hour to daydream.

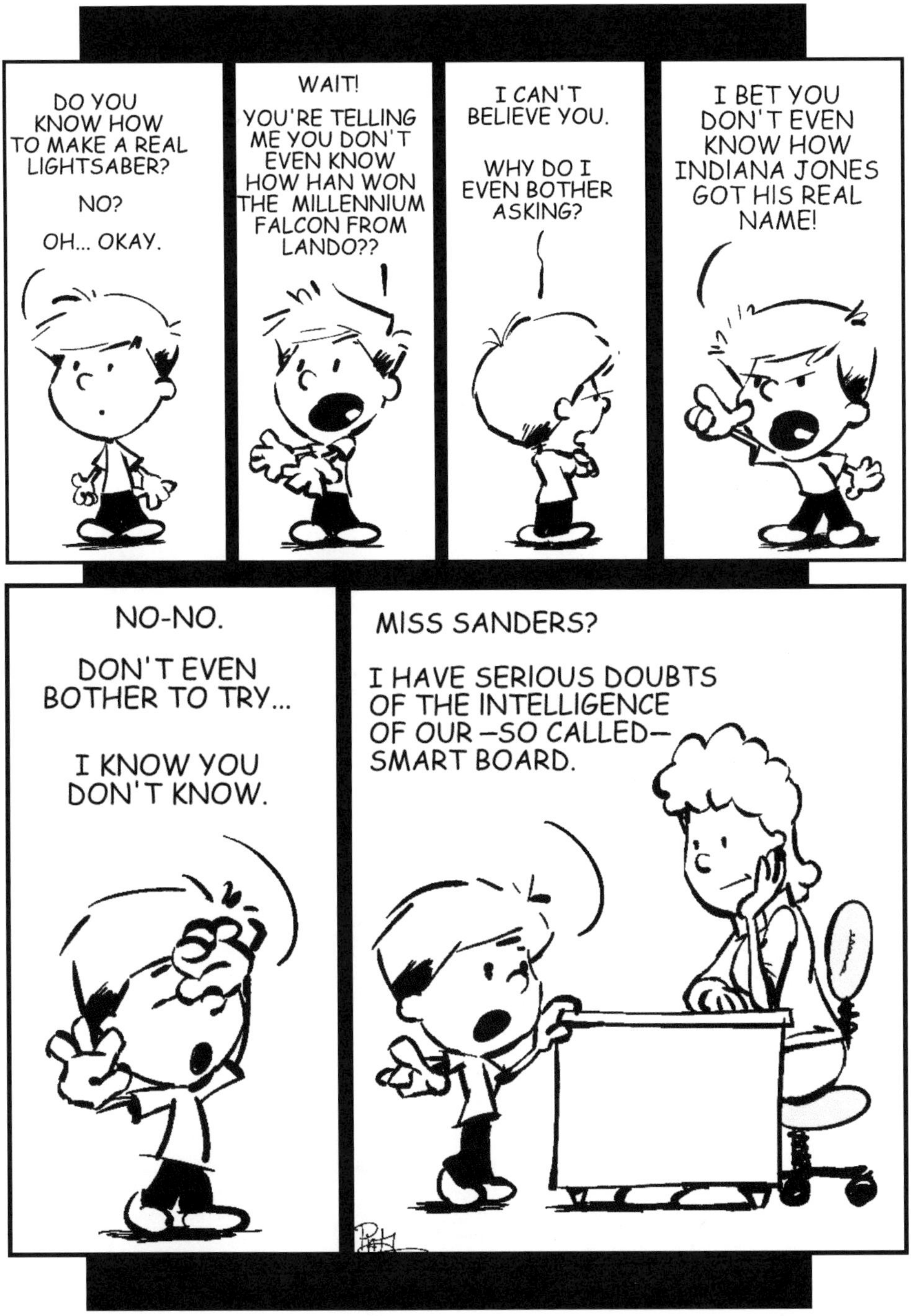
DO YOU KNOW HOW TO MAKE A REAL LIGHTSABER?
NO?
OH... OKAY.
WAIT!
YOU'RE TELLING ME YOU DON'T EVEN KNOW HOW HAN WON THE MILLENNIUM FALCON FROM LANDO??
I CAN'T BELIEVE YOU.
WHY DO I EVEN BOTHER ASKING?
I BET YOU DON'T EVEN KNOW HOW INDIANA JONES GOT HIS REAL NAME!
NO-NO.
DON'T EVEN BOTHER TO TRY...
I KNOW YOU DON'T KNOW.
MISS SANDERS?
I HAVE SERIOUS DOUBTS OF THE INTELLIGENCE OF OUR –SO CALLED– SMART BOARD.

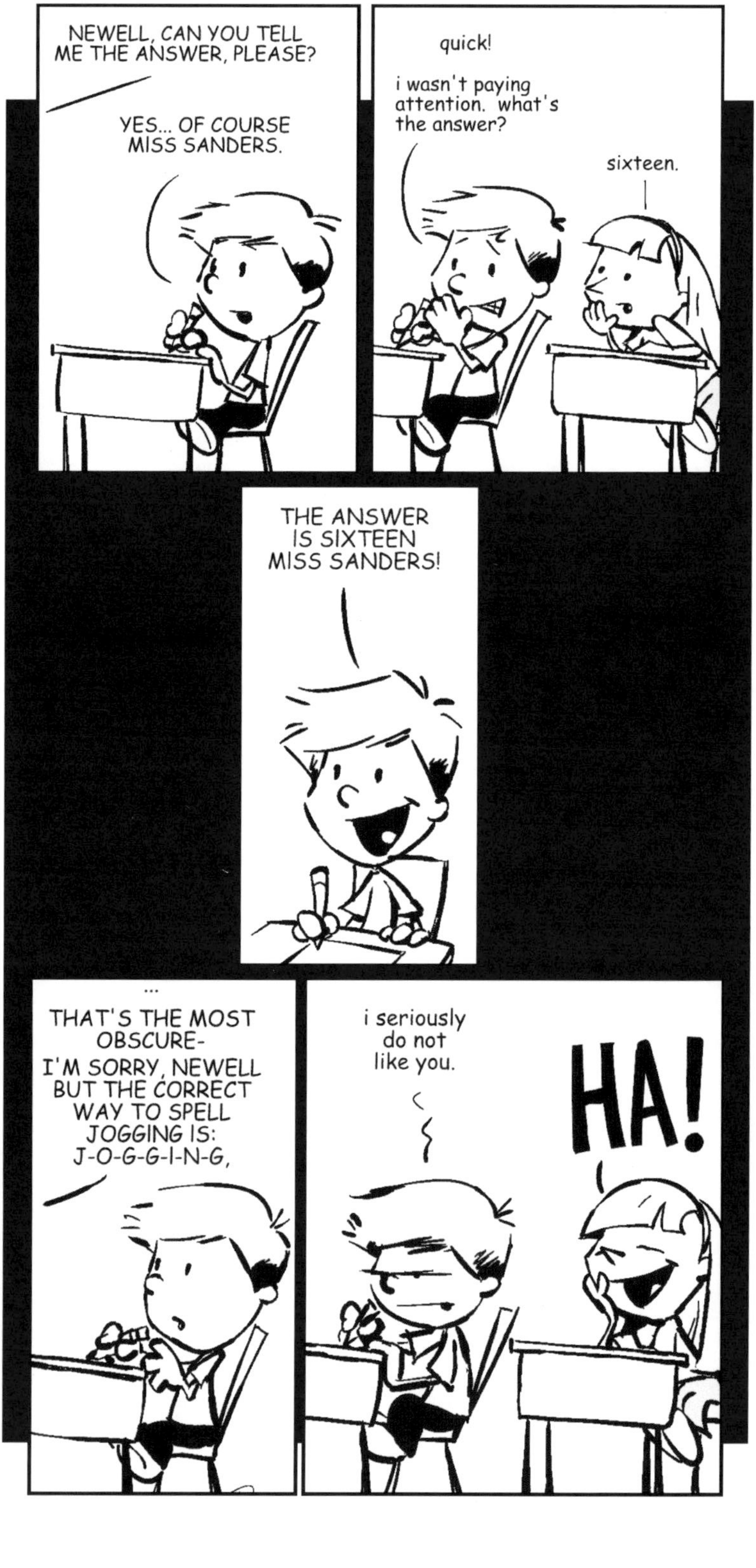
NEWELL, CAN YOU TELL ME THE ANSWER, PLEASE?
YES... OF COURSE MISS SANDERS.
quick!
i wasn't paying attention. what's the answer?
sixteen.
THE ANSWER IS SIXTEEN MISS SANDERS!
...
THAT'S THE MOST OBSCURE-
I'M SORRY, NEWELL BUT THE CORRECT WAY TO SPELL JOGGING IS: J-O-G-G-I-N-G,
i seriously do not like you.
HA!

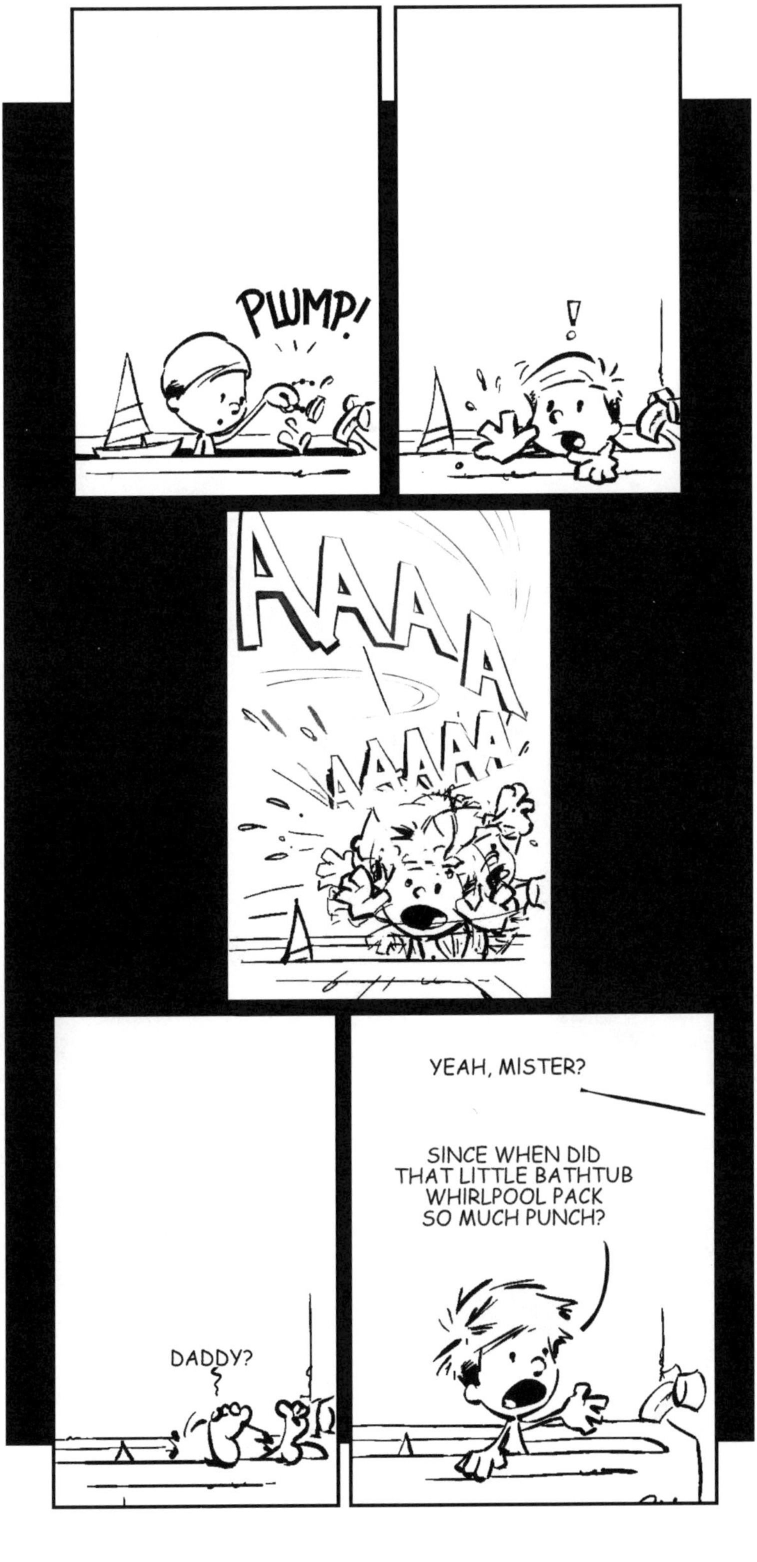
PWMP!
!
AAAAAAAAA
DADDY?
YEAH, MISTER?
SINCE WHEN DID THAT LITTLE BATHTUB WHIRLPOOL PACK SO MUCH PUNCH?

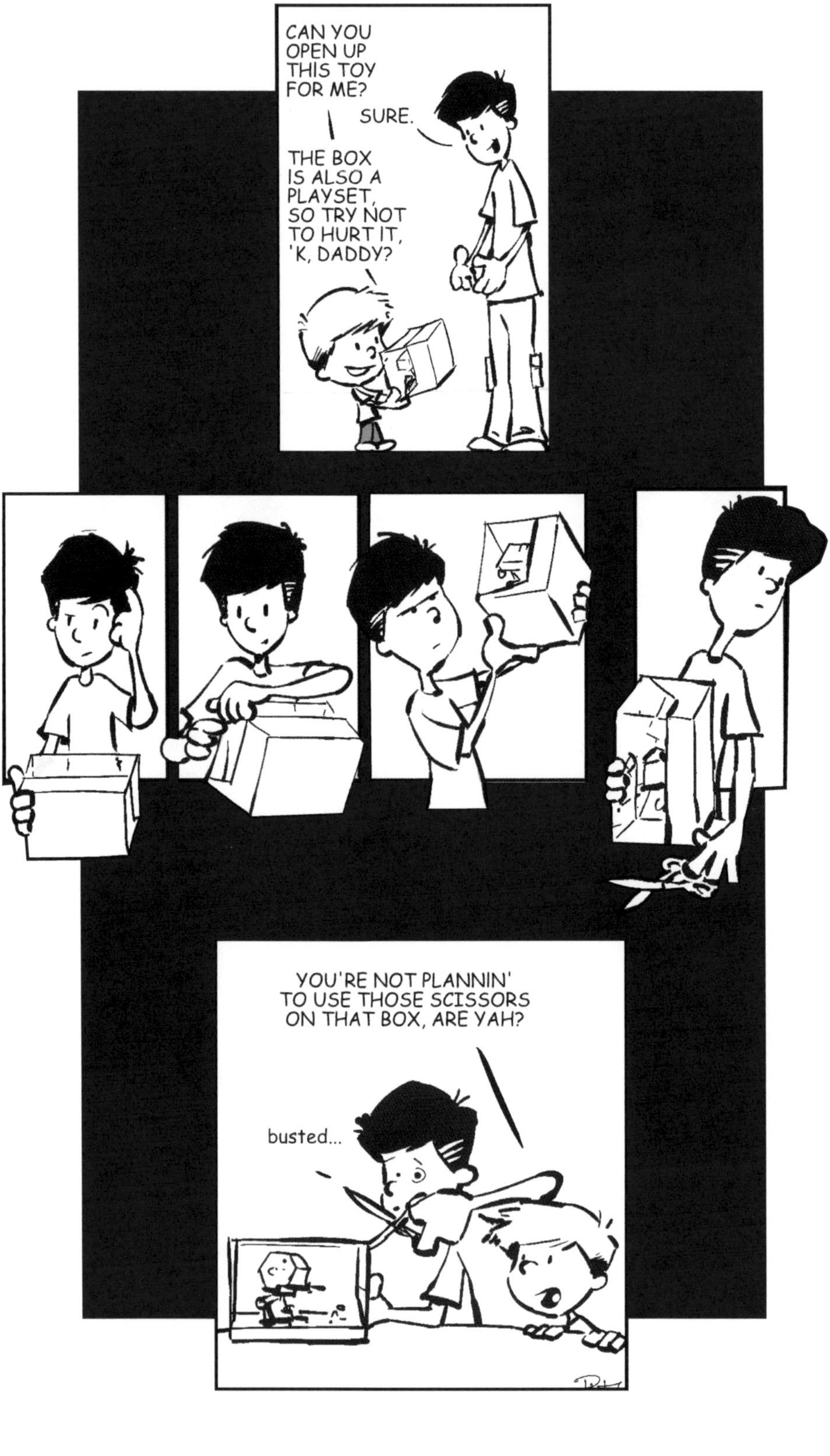
CAN YOU OPEN UP THIS TOY FOR ME?
SURE.
THE BOX IS ALSO A PLAYSET, SO TRY NOT TO HURT IT, 'K, DADDY?
YOU'RE NOT PLANNIN' TO USE THOSE SCISSORS ON THAT BOX, ARE YAH?
busted...

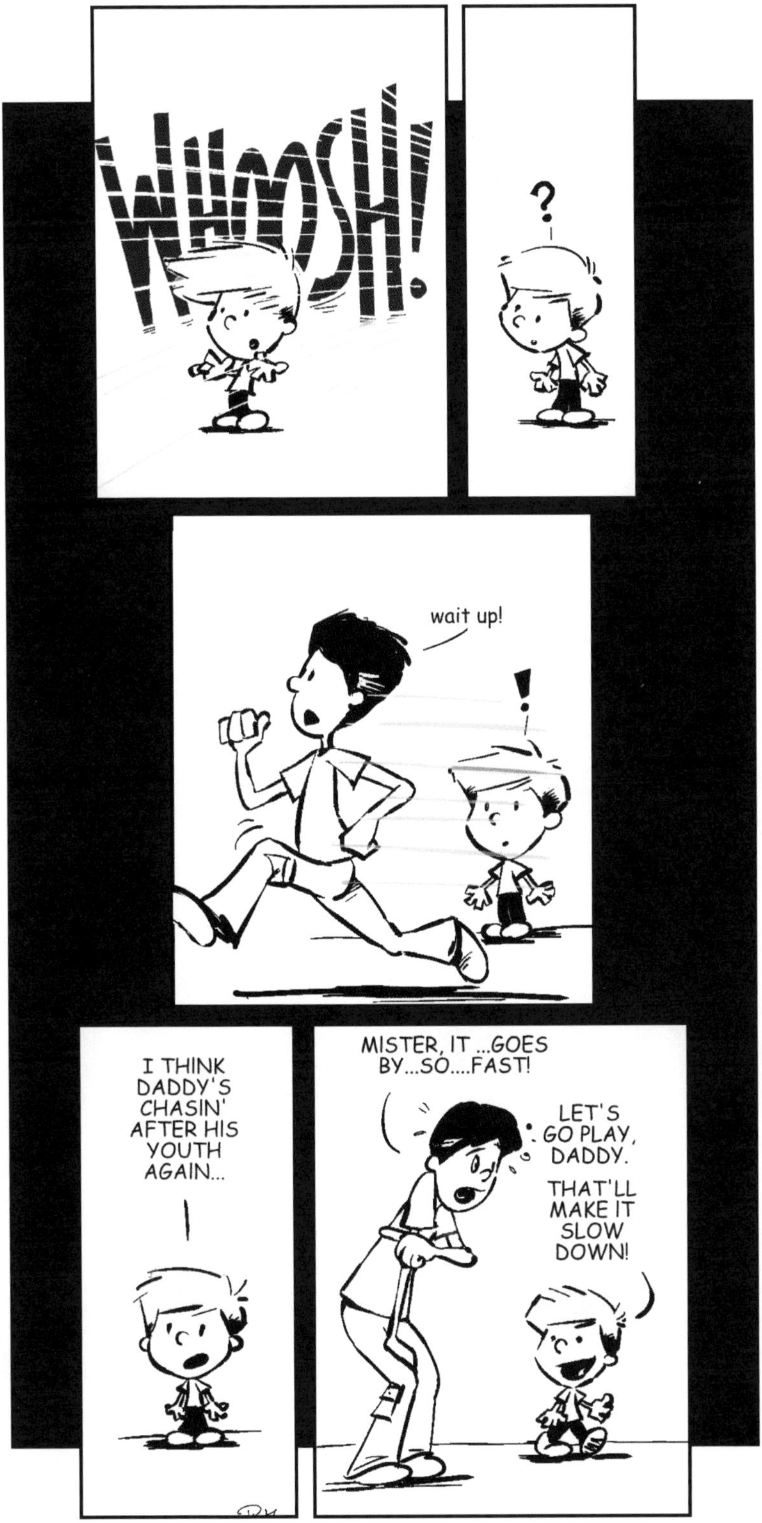
WHOOSH!
?
wait up!
!
I THINK DADDY'S CHASIN' AFTER HIS YOUTH AGAIN...
MISTER, IT ...GOES BY...SO....FAST!
LET'S GO PLAY, DADDY.
THAT'LL MAKE IT SLOW DOWN!

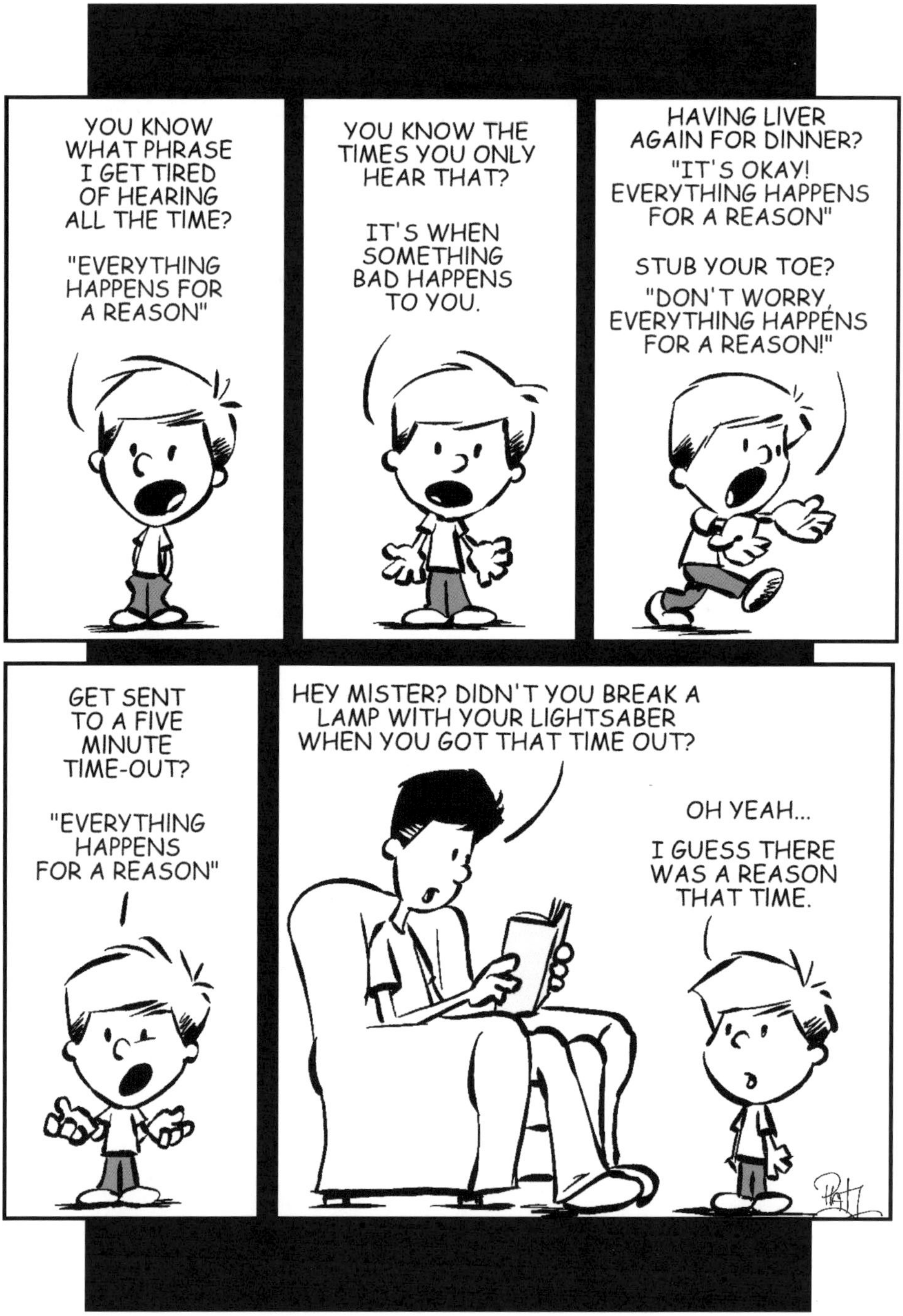
YOU KNOW WHAT PHRASE I GET TIRED OF HEARING ALL THE TIME?
"EVERYTHING HAPPENS FOR A REASON"
YOU KNOW THE TIMES YOU ONLY HEAR THAT?
IT'S WHEN SOMETHING BAD HAPPENS TO YOU.
HAVING LIVER AGAIN FOR DINNER?
"IT'S OKAY! EVERYTHING HAPPENS FOR A REASON"
STUB YOUR TOE?
"DON'T WORRY, EVERYTHING HAPPENS FOR A REASON!"
GET SENT TO A FIVE MINUTE TIME-OUT?
"EVERYTHING HAPPENS FOR A REASON"
HEY MISTER? DIDN'T YOU BREAK A LAMP WITH YOUR LIGHTSABER WHEN YOU GOT THAT TIME OUT?
OH YEAH...
I GUESS THERE WAS A REASON THAT TIME.

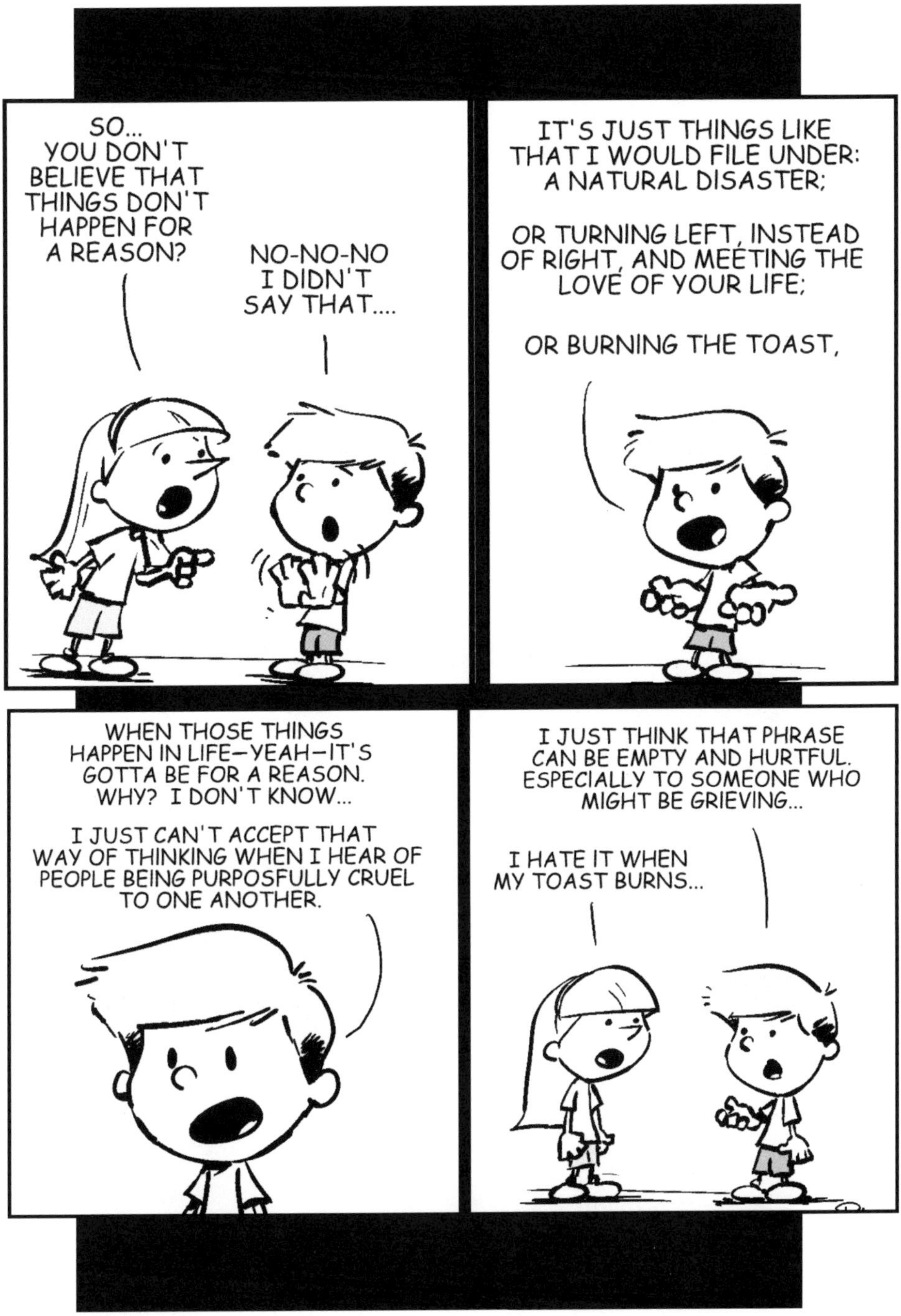
SO... YOU DON'T BELIEVE THAT THINGS DON'T HAPPEN FOR A REASON?
NO-NO-NO I DIDN'T SAY THAT....
IT'S JUST THINGS LIKE THAT I WOULD FILE UNDER: A NATURAL DISASTER;
OR TURNING LEFT, INSTEAD OF RIGHT, AND MEETING THE LOVE OF YOUR LIFE;
OR BURNING THE TOAST,
WHEN THOSE THINGS HAPPEN IN LIFE—YEAH—IT'S GOTTA BE FOR A REASON. WHY? I DON'T KNOW...
I JUST CAN'T ACCEPT THAT WAY OF THINKING WHEN I HEAR OF PEOPLE BEING PURPOSFULLY CRUEL TO ONE ANOTHER.
I JUST THINK THAT PHRASE CAN BE EMPTY AND HURTFUL. ESPECIALLY TO SOMEONE WHO MIGHT BE GRIEVING...
I HATE IT WHEN MY TOAST BURNS...

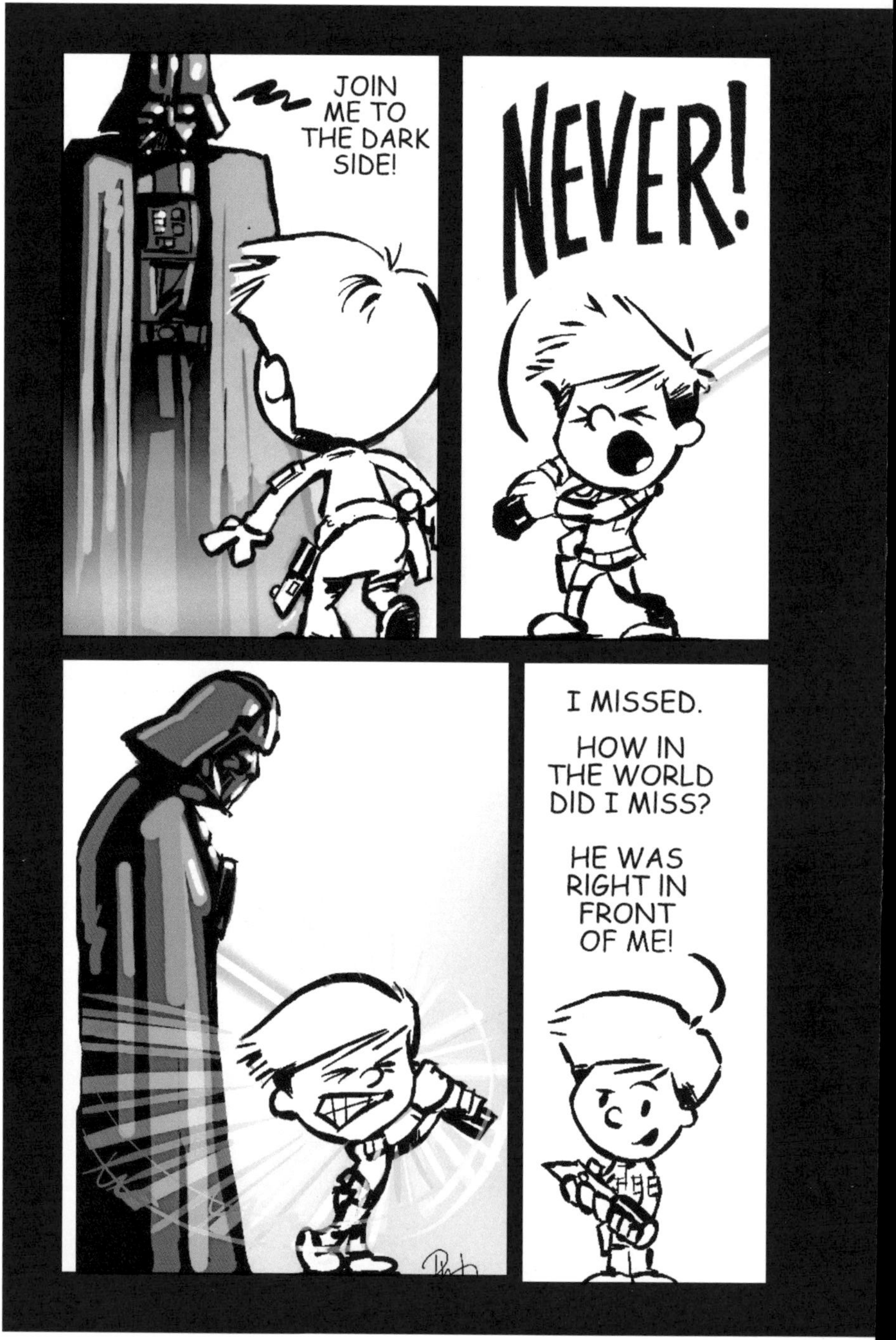
JOIN ME TO THE DARK SIDE!
NEVER!
I MISSED.
HOW IN THE WORLD DID I MISS?
HE WAS RIGHT IN FRONT OF ME!

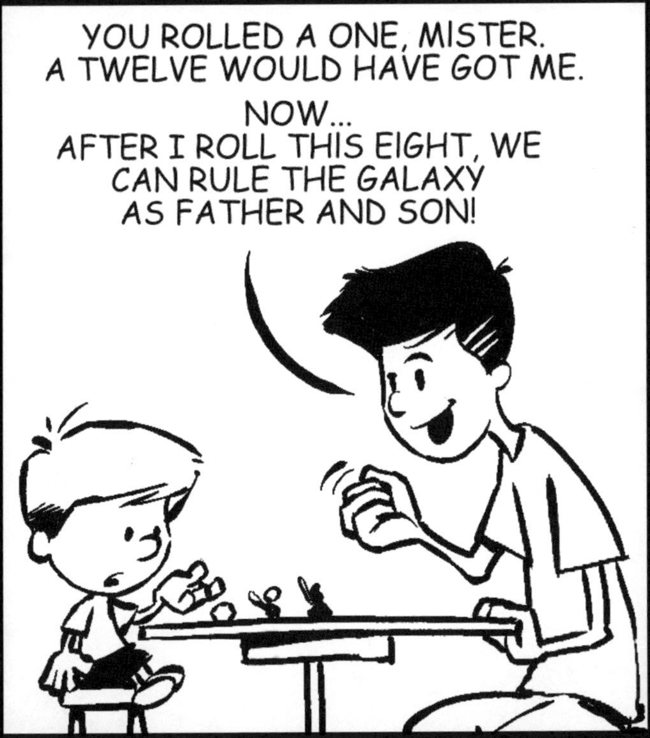
YOU ROLLED A ONE, MISTER. A TWELVE WOULD HAVE GOT ME. NOW... AFTER I ROLL THIS EIGHT, WE CAN RULE THE GALAXY AS FATHER AND SON!

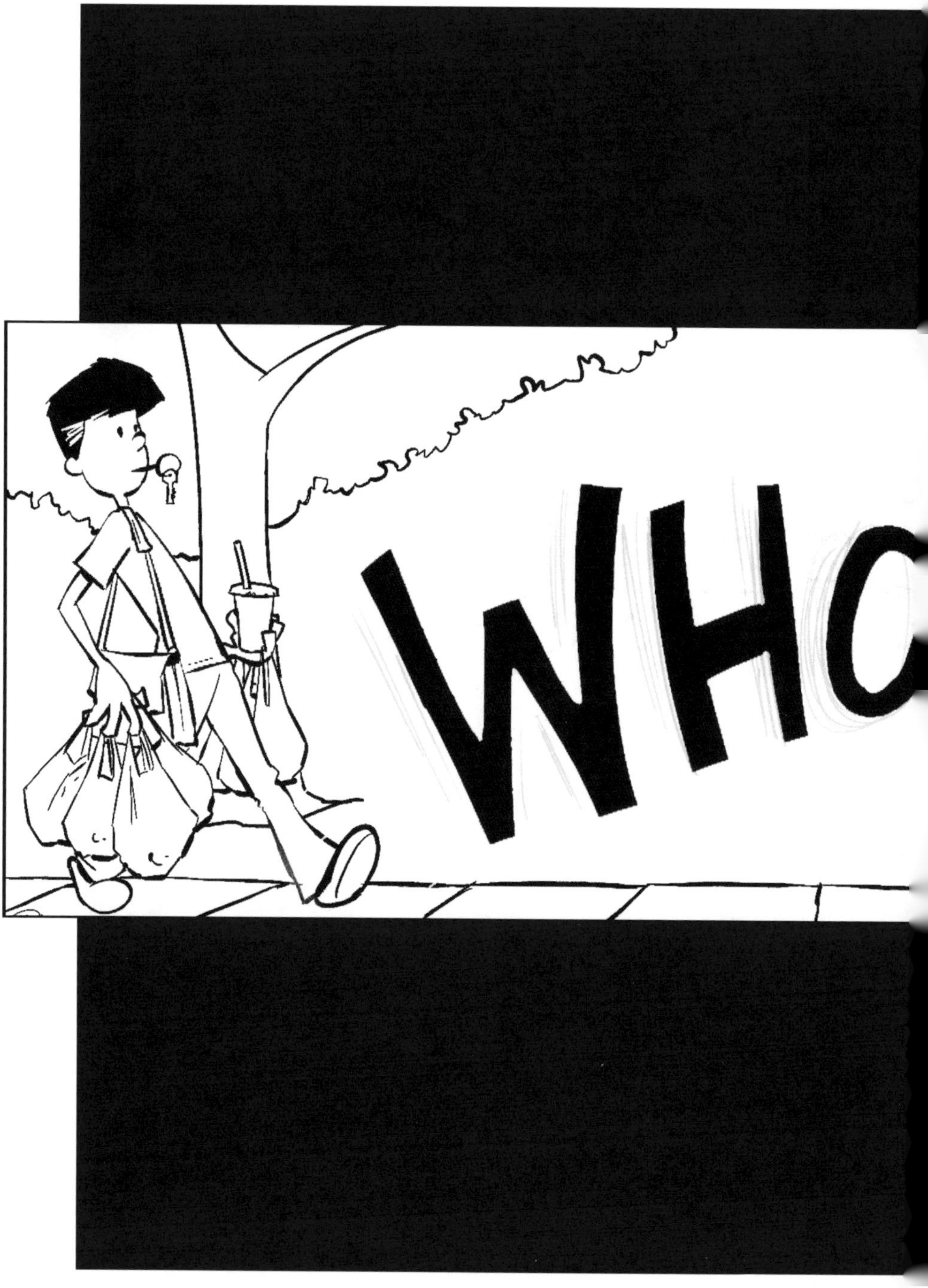
WHO

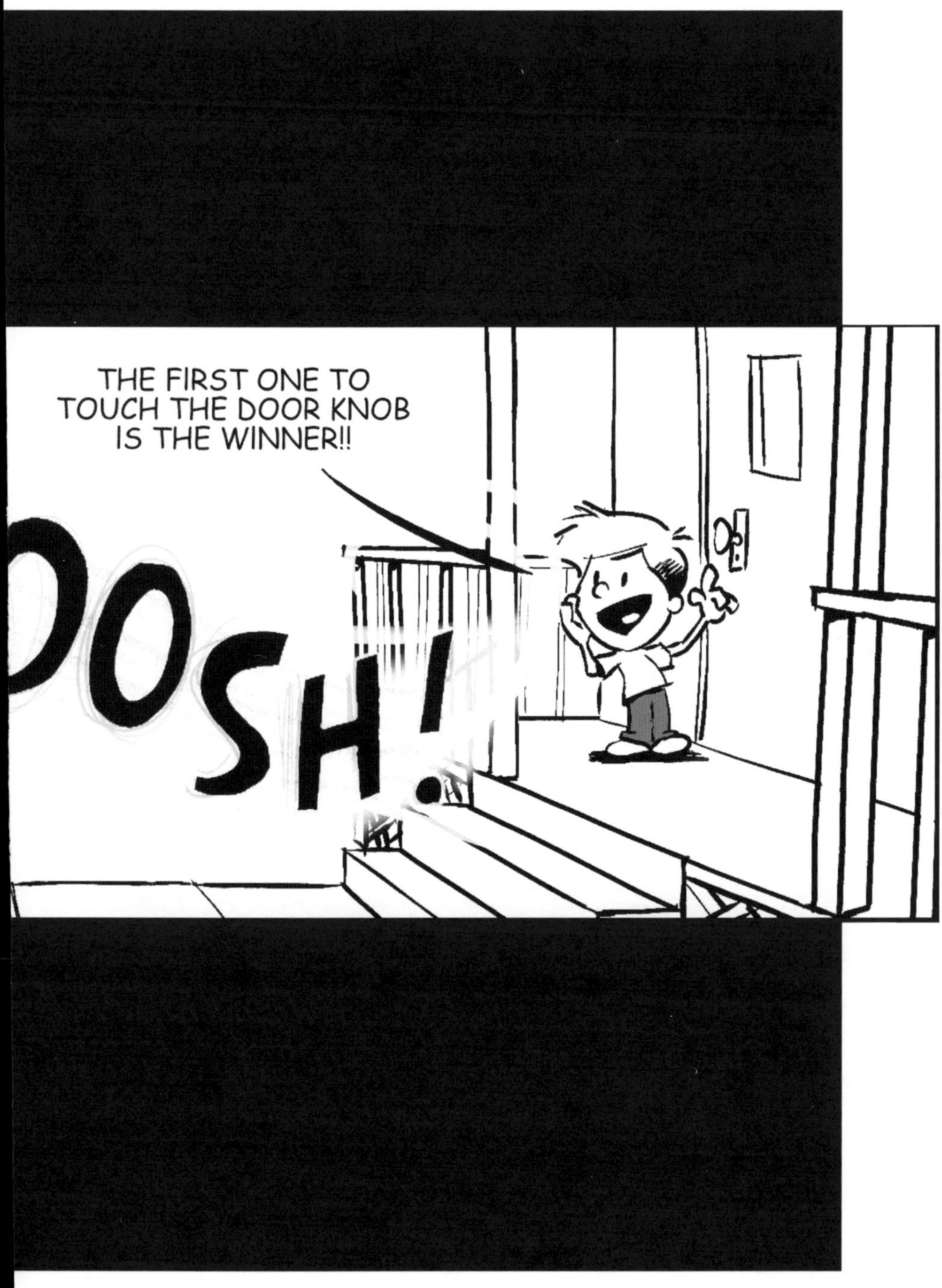
THE FIRST ONE TO TOUCH THE DOOR KNOB IS THE WINNER!!
OOSH!

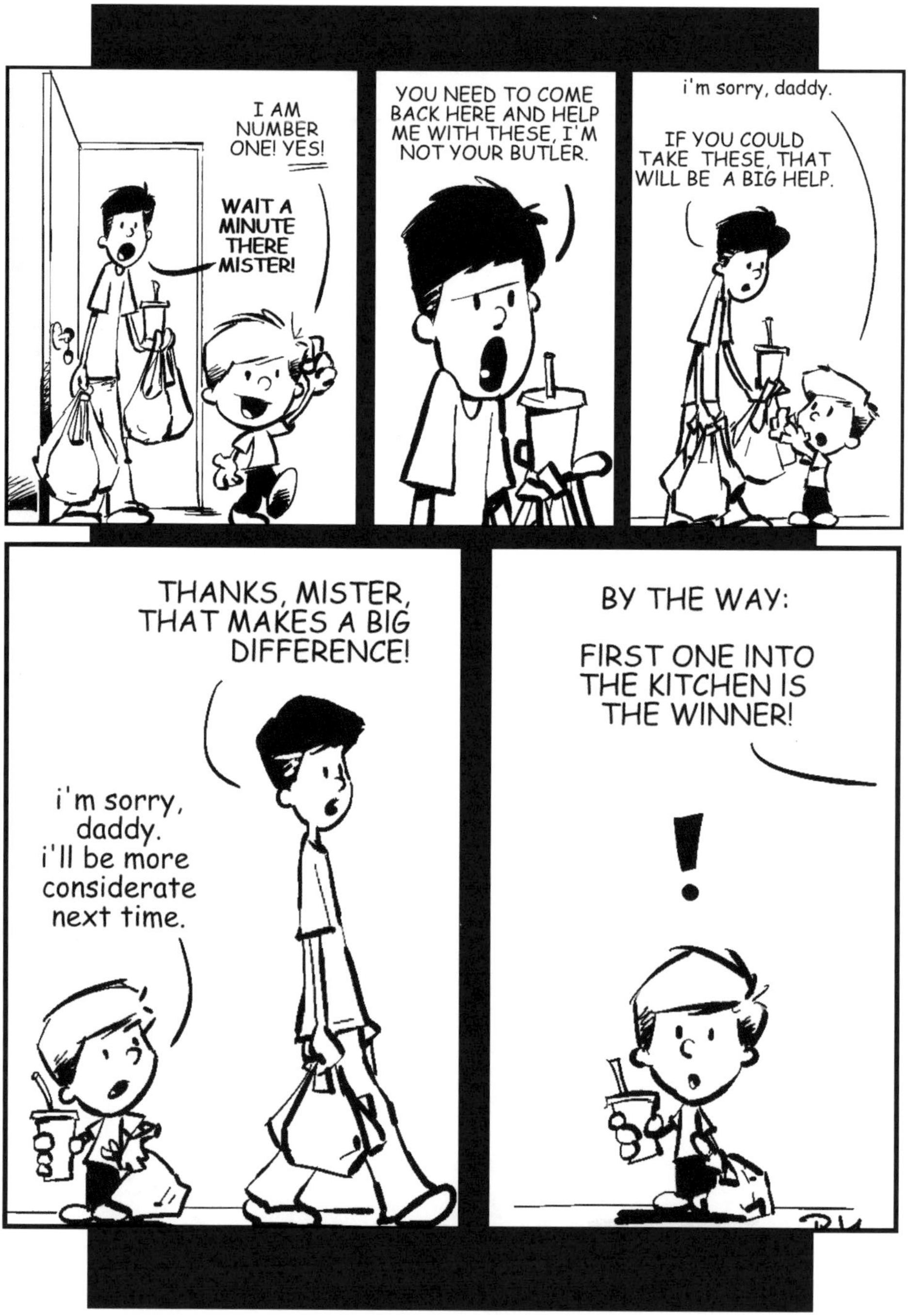
I AM NUMBER ONE! YES!
WAIT A MINUTE THERE MISTER!
YOU NEED TO COME BACK HERE AND HELP ME WITH THESE, I'M NOT YOUR BUTLER.
i'm sorry, daddy.
IF YOU COULD TAKE THESE, THAT WILL BE A BIG HELP.
THANKS, MISTER, THAT MAKES A BIG DIFFERENCE!
i'm sorry, daddy. i'll be more considerate next time.
BY THE WAY:
FIRST ONE INTO THE KITCHEN IS THE WINNER!
!

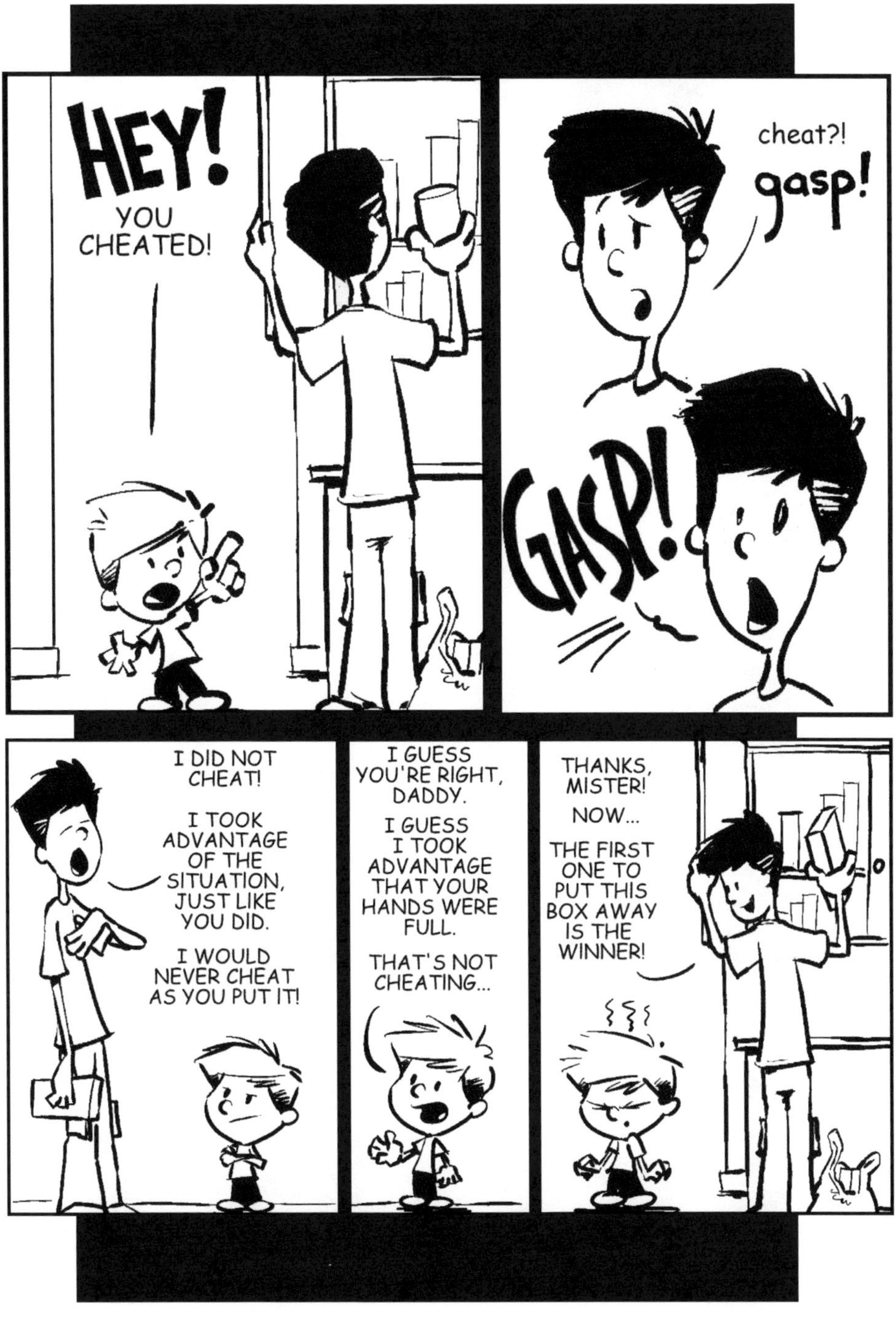
HEY!
YOU CHEATED!
cheat?!
gasp!
GASP!
I DID NOT CHEAT!
I TOOK ADVANTAGE OF THE SITUATION, JUST LIKE YOU DID.
I WOULD NEVER CHEAT AS YOU PUT IT!
I GUESS YOU'RE RIGHT, DADDY.
I GUESS I TOOK ADVANTAGE THAT YOUR HANDS WERE FULL.
THAT'S NOT CHEATING...
THANKS, MISTER!
NOW...
THE FIRST ONE TO PUT THIS BOX AWAY IS THE WINNER!

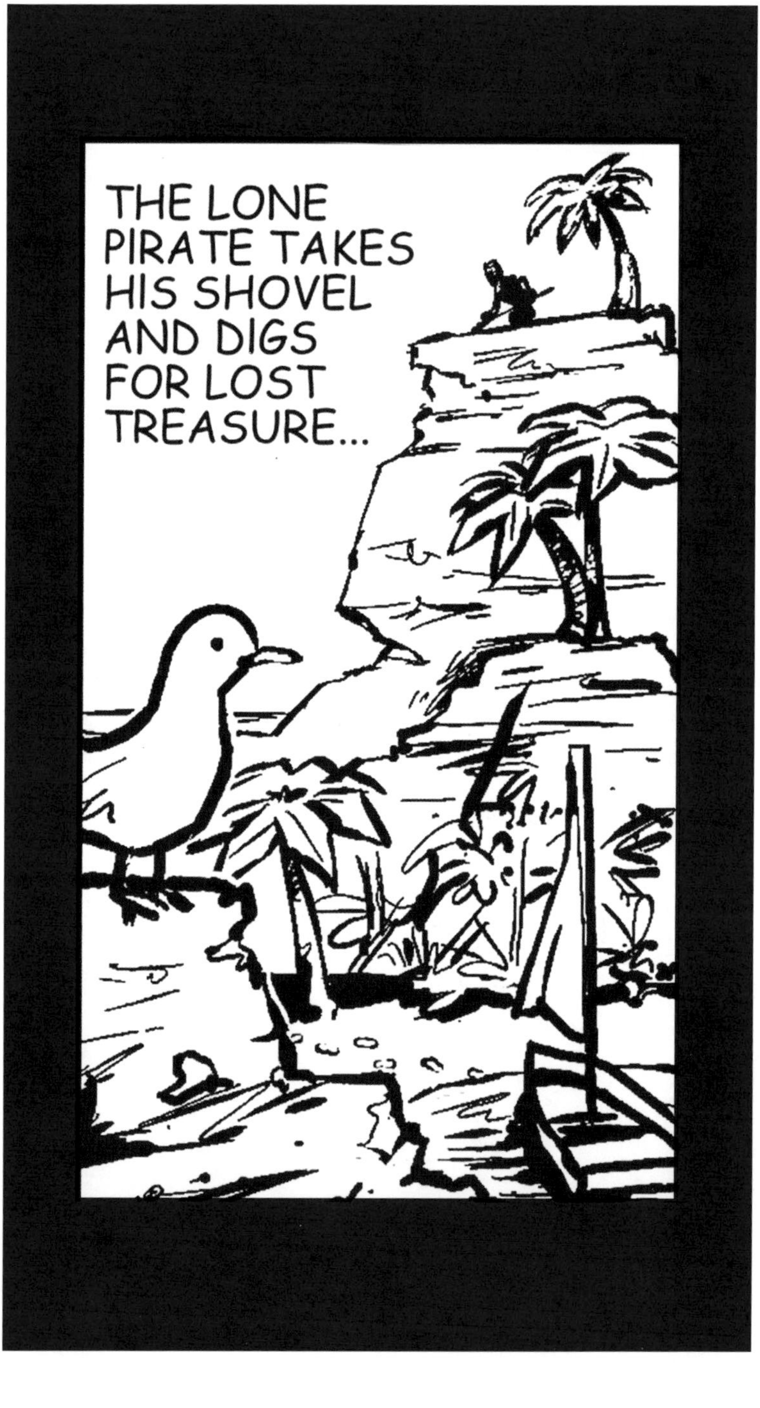
THE LONE PIRATE TAKES HIS SHOVEL AND DIGS FOR LOST TREASURE...

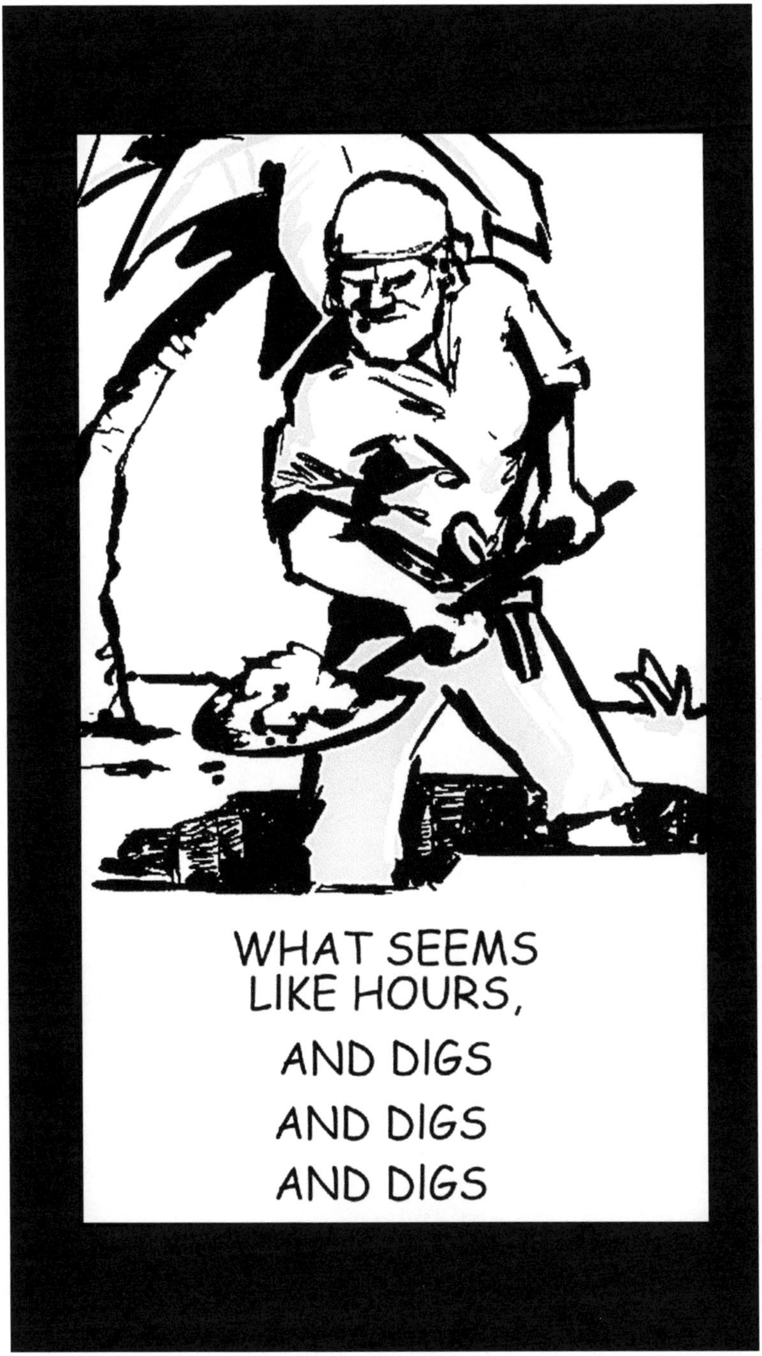
WHAT SEEMS
LIKE HOURS,
AND DIGS
AND DIGS
AND DIGS

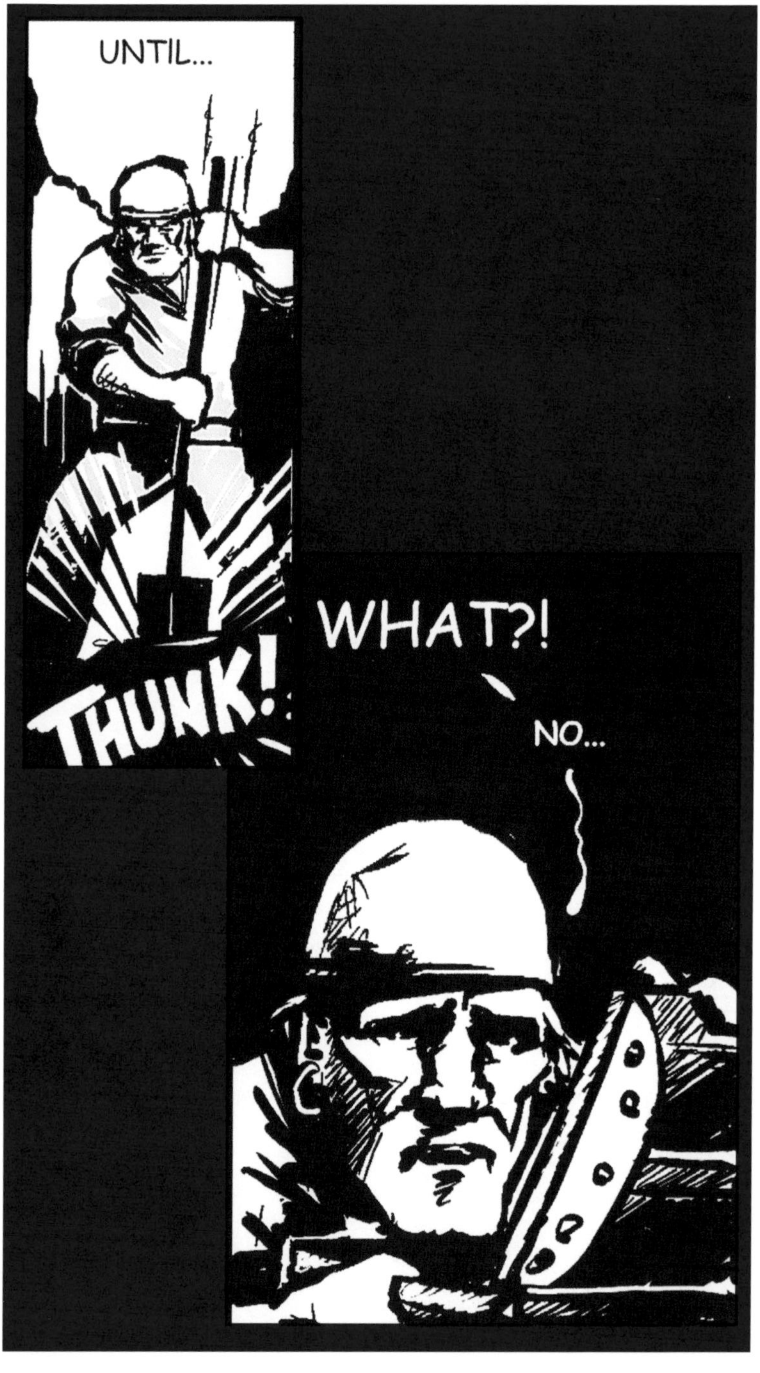
UNTIL...
THUNK!
WHAT?!
NO...

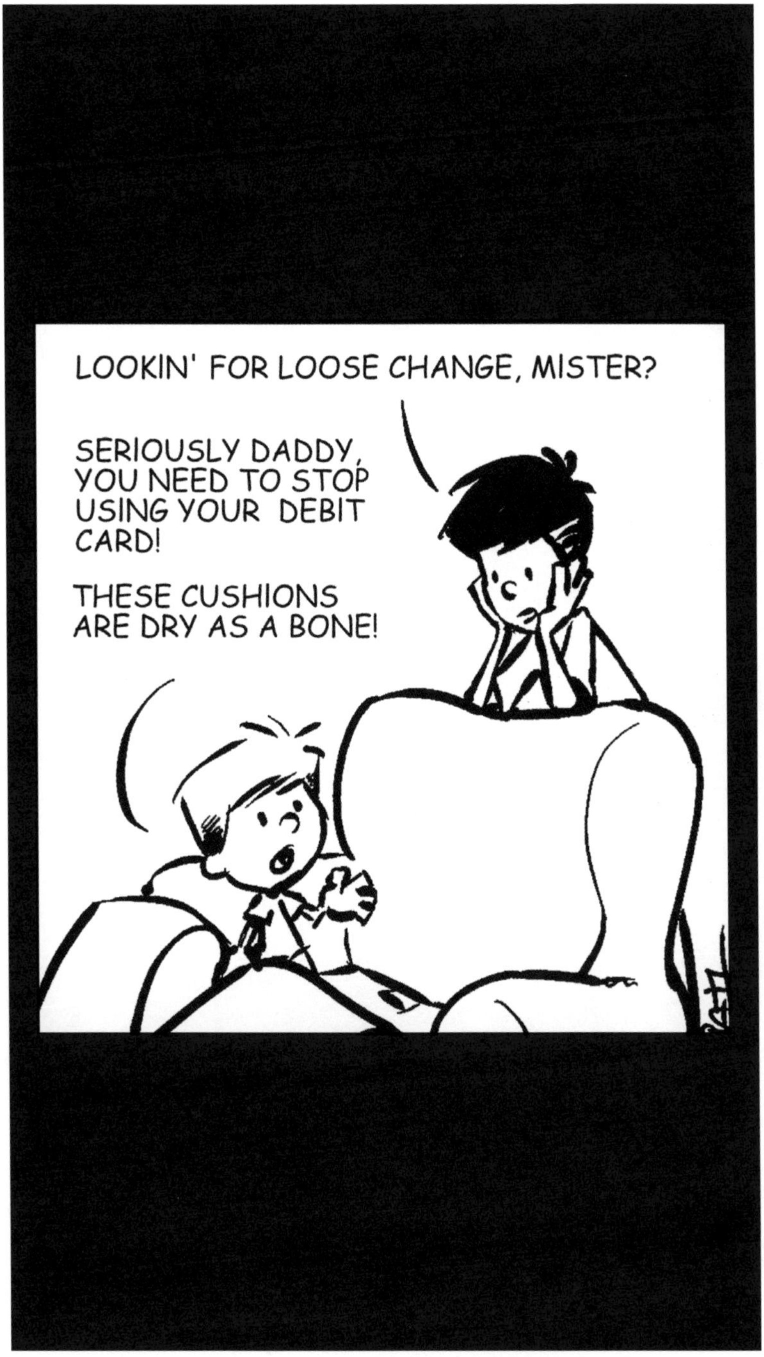
LOOKIN' FOR LOOSE CHANGE, MISTER?
SERIOUSLY DADDY, YOU NEED TO STOP USING YOUR DEBIT CARD!
THESE CUSHIONS ARE DRY AS A BONE!

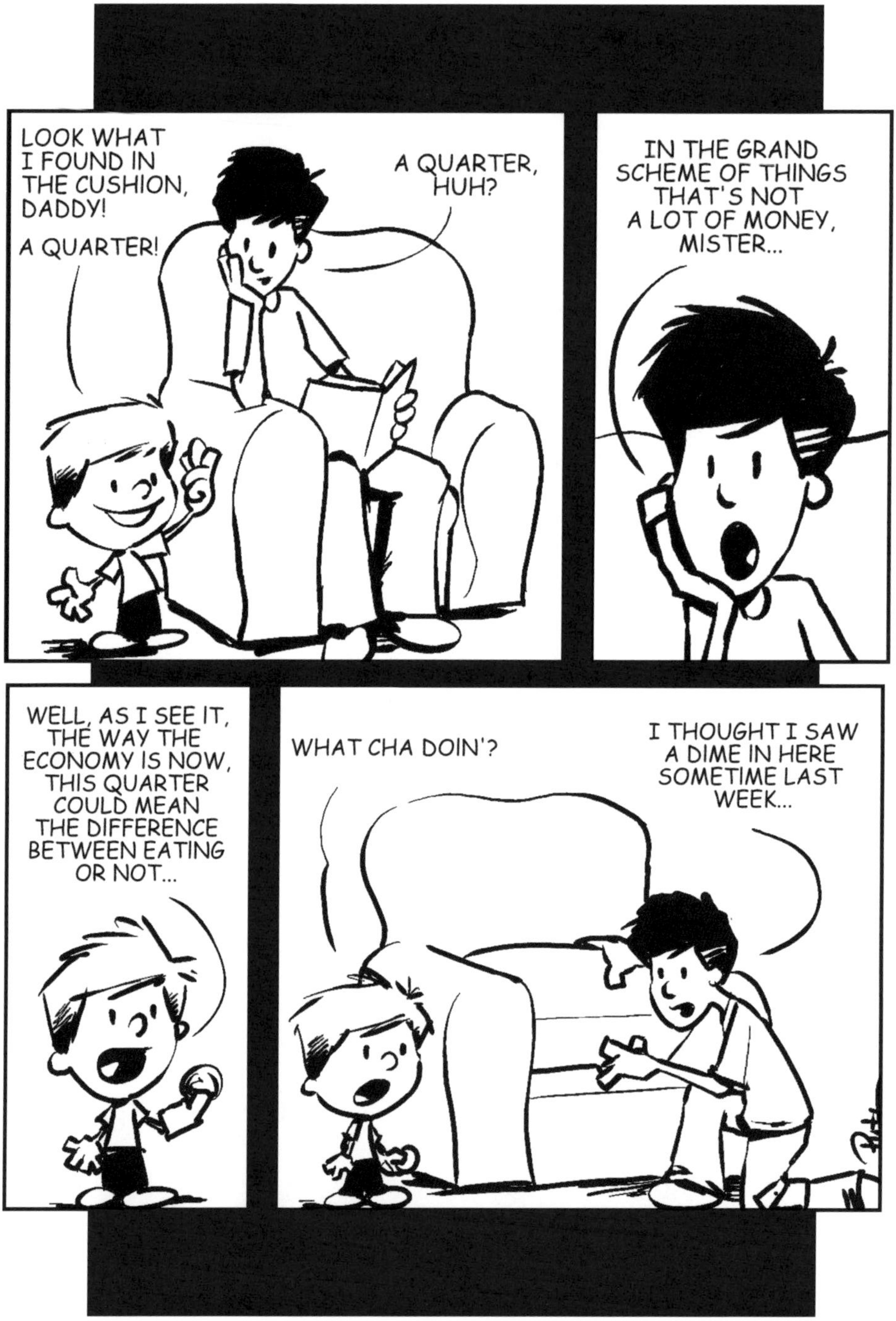
LOOK WHAT I FOUND IN THE CUSHION, DADDY!
A QUARTER!
A QUARTER, HUH?
IN THE GRAND SCHEME OF THINGS THAT'S NOT A LOT OF MONEY, MISTER...
WELL, AS I SEE IT, THE WAY THE ECONOMY IS NOW, THIS QUARTER COULD MEAN THE DIFFERENCE BETWEEN EATING OR NOT...
WHAT CHA DOIN'?
I THOUGHT I SAW A DIME IN HERE SOMETIME LAST WEEK...

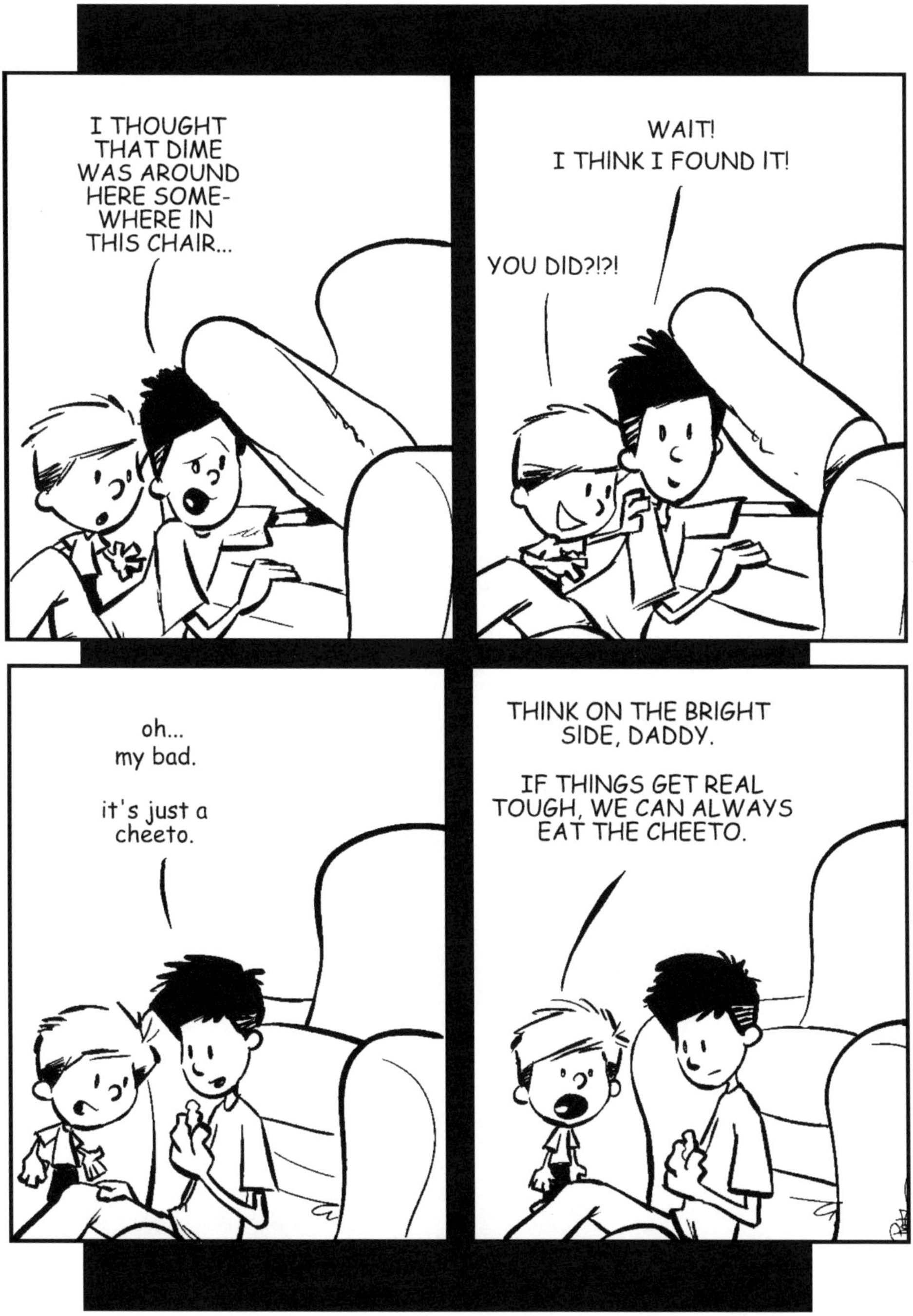
I THOUGHT THAT DIME WAS AROUND HERE SOME-WHERE IN THIS CHAIR...
WAIT! I THINK I FOUND IT!
YOU DID?!?!
oh... my bad.
it's just a cheeto.
THINK ON THE BRIGHT SIDE, DADDY.
IF THINGS GET REAL TOUGH, WE CAN ALWAYS EAT THE CHEETO.

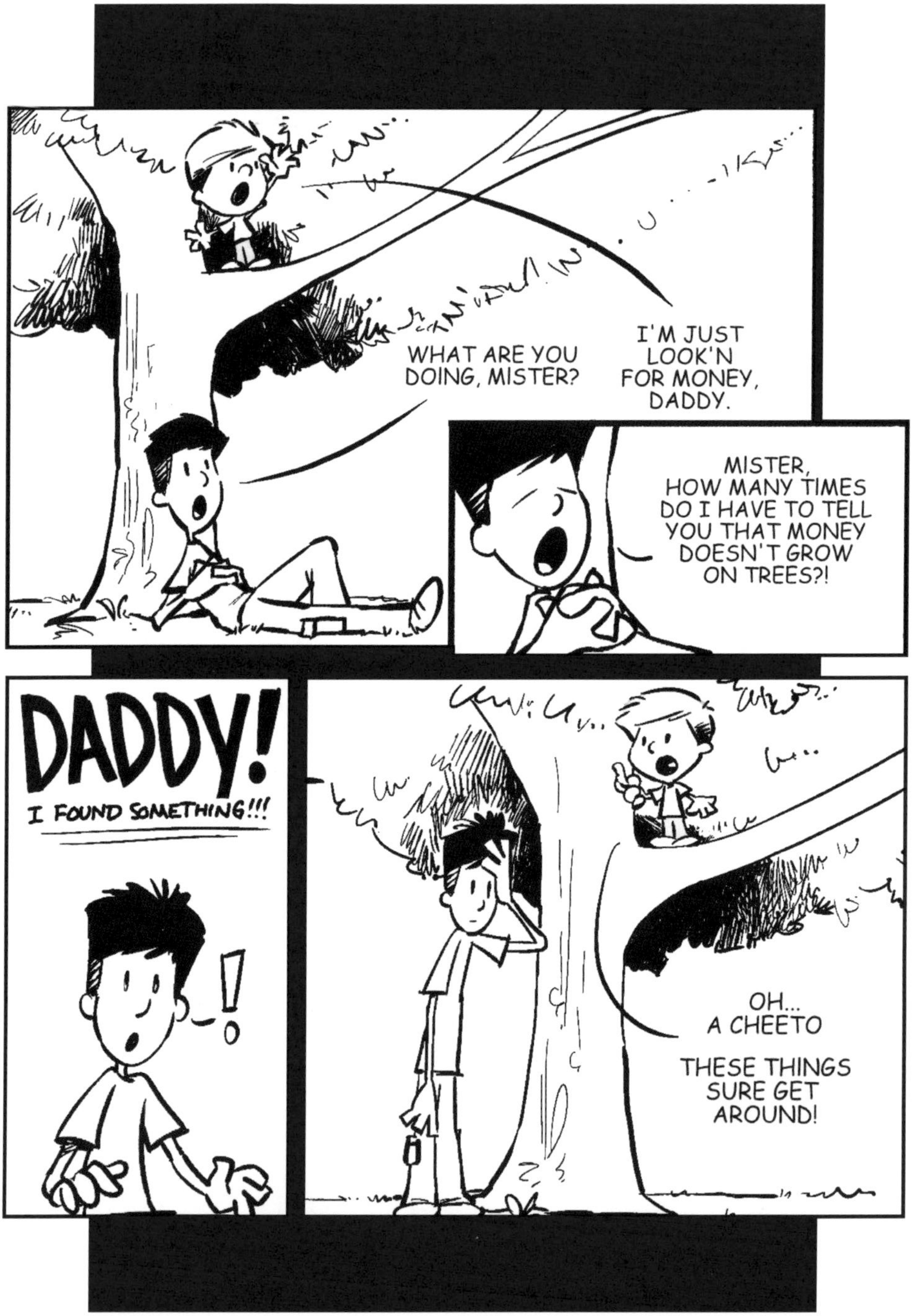
WHAT ARE YOU DOING, MISTER?
I'M JUST LOOK'N FOR MONEY, DADDY.
MISTER, HOW MANY TIMES DO I HAVE TO TELL YOU THAT MONEY DOESN'T GROW ON TREES?!
DADDY! I FOUND SOMETHING!!!
OH... A CHEETO
THESE THINGS SURE GET AROUND!

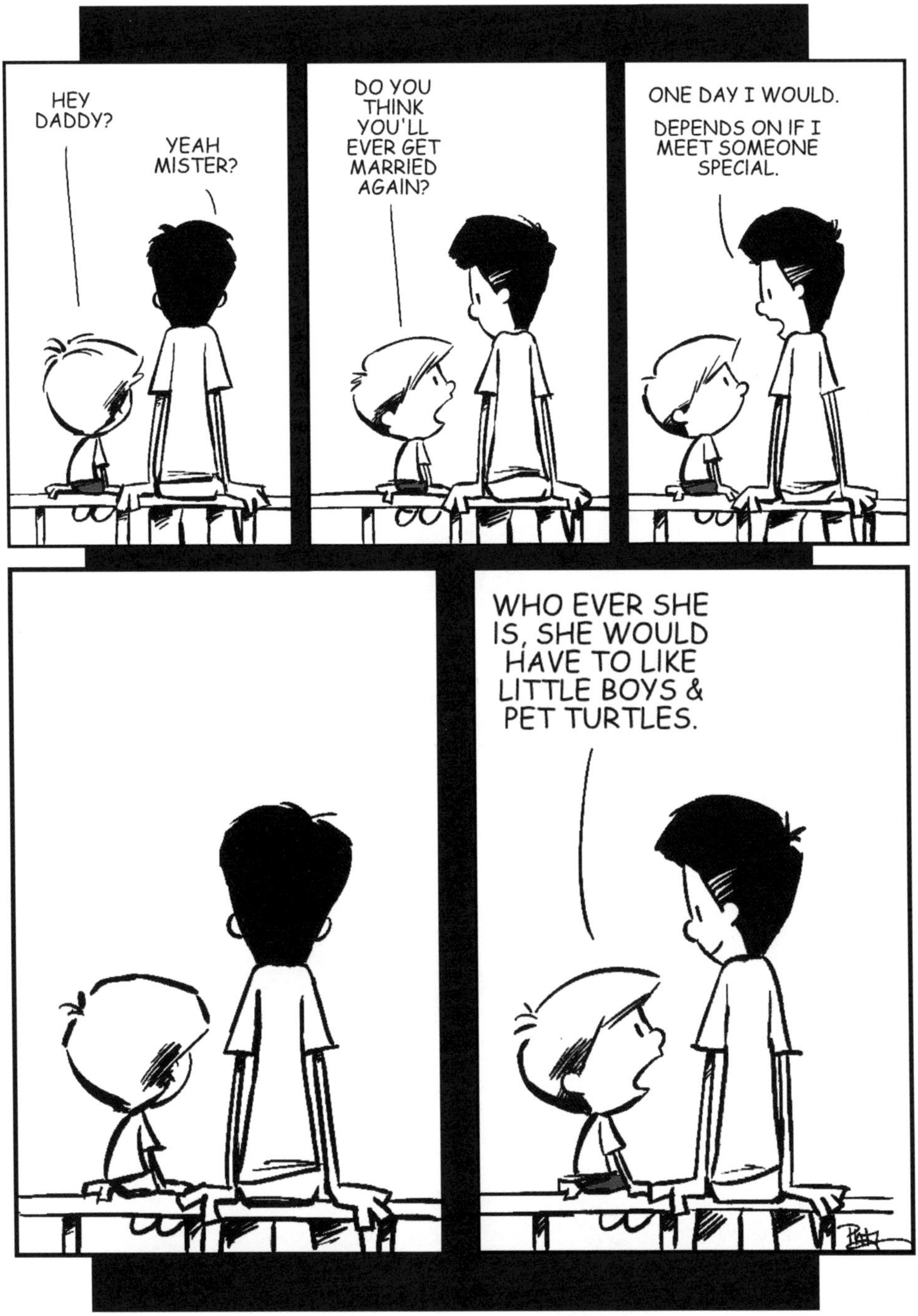
HEY DADDY?
YEAH MISTER?
DO YOU THINK YOU'LL EVER GET MARRIED AGAIN?
ONE DAY I WOULD.
DEPENDS ON IF I MEET SOMEONE SPECIAL.
WHO EVER SHE IS, SHE WOULD HAVE TO LIKE LITTLE BOYS & PET TURTLES.

?..
HMM HMM HMM

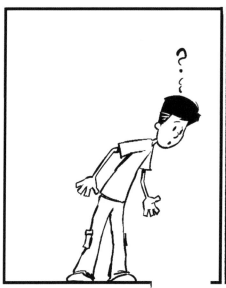

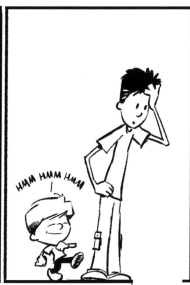

*pant*pant* WHY WOULD SOMEONE HAVE A HOLE THERE?! I COULDA DIED! *pant*pant*
IT'S CALLED LAZY CARTOONING, MISTER.
CARTOONISTS LOSE MORE CHARACTERS THAT WAY.

WHAT CHA DOIN', DADDY?.
I'M GONNA SEE WHAT'S DOWN THERE MISTER...
NO! NO! DON'T GO DOWN THERE DADDY! I'M TOO YOUNG TO BE AN ORPHAN! PLEEEEZE!!

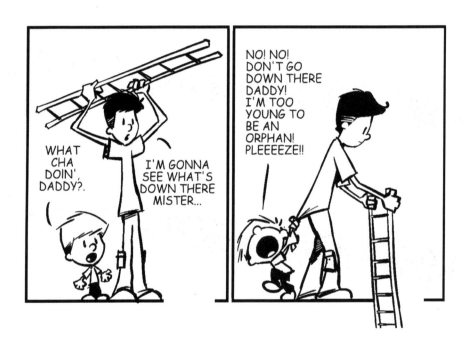

IT'LL BE OKAY, MISTER.
SOMETIMES DADDY'S JUST GOT TO DO DADDY TYPE THINGS.
and what's that?
SOMETHING REALLY STUPID...

BE CAREFUL DADDY!
DON'T WORRY, MISTER. I'LL BE OKAY.
HEY, WHAT'S THAT?
WHAT'S WHAT?!
IT'S SOME SORT OF CRAWL SPACE UNDER THE PANELS.
WHAT'S A CRAWL SPACE DOING THERE?
I DUNNO. I'M CHECKING IT OUT.

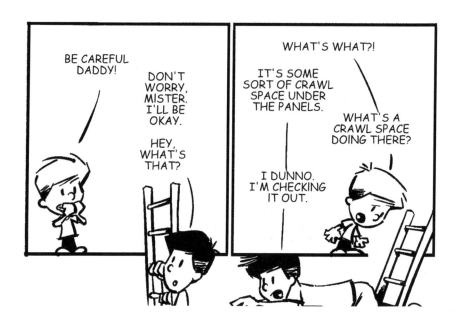

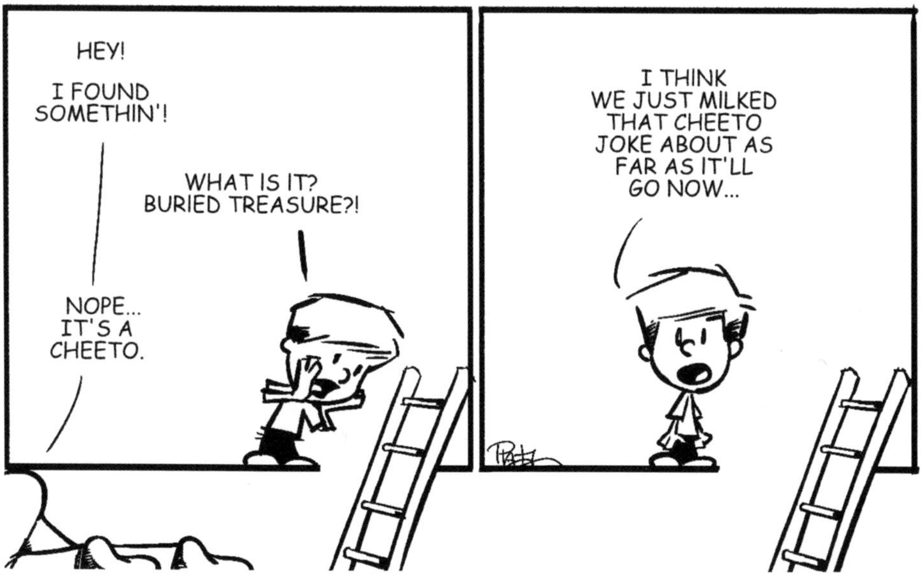
HEY!
I FOUND SOMETHIN'!
WHAT IS IT? BURIED TREASURE?!
NOPE... IT'S A CHEETO.
I THINK WE JUST MILKED THAT CHEETO JOKE ABOUT AS FAR AS IT'LL GO NOW...

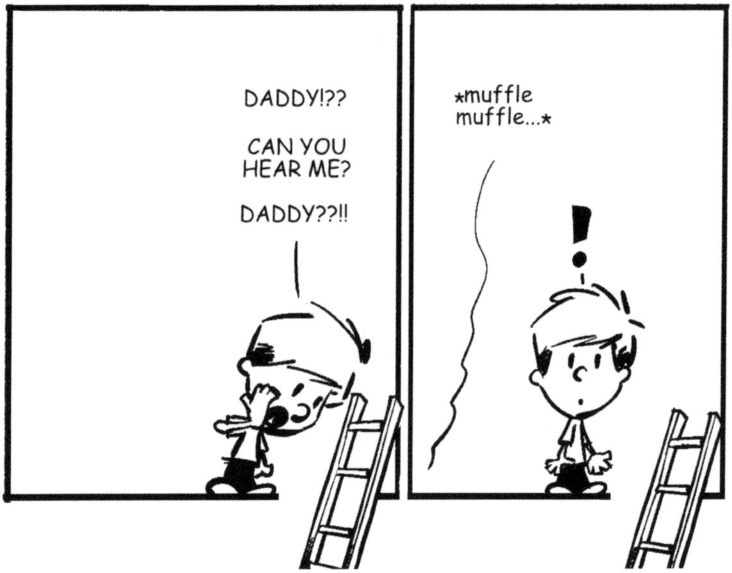
DADDY!??
CAN YOU HEAR ME?
DADDY??!!
muffle muffle...
!

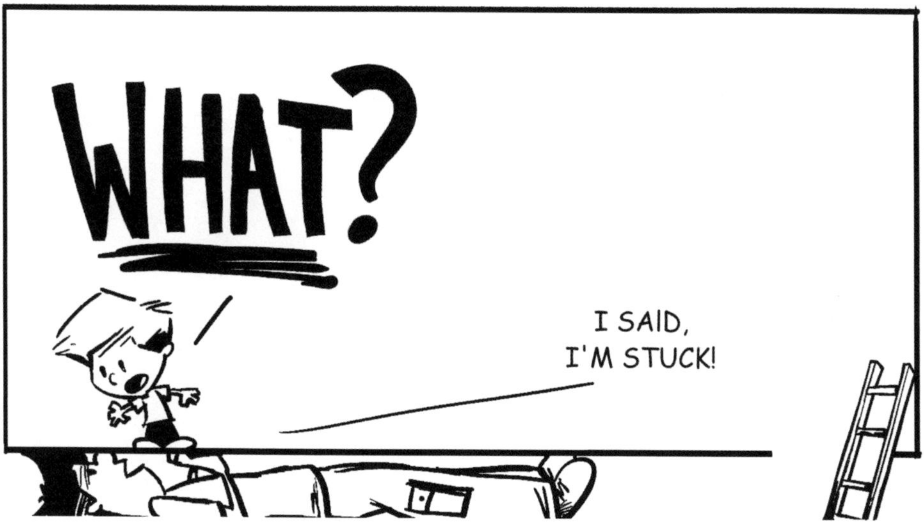
WHAT?
I SAID,
I'M STUCK!

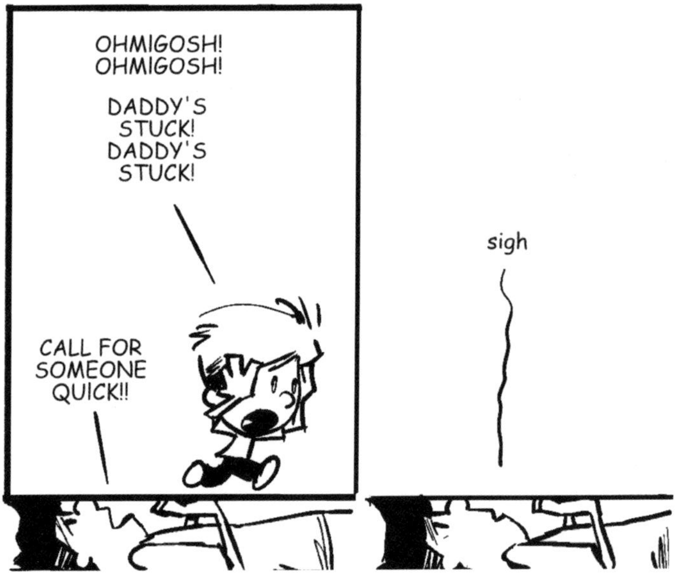
OHMIGOSH!
OHMIGOSH!
DADDY'S
STUCK!
DADDY'S
STUCK!
CALL FOR
SOMEONE
QUICK!!
sigh

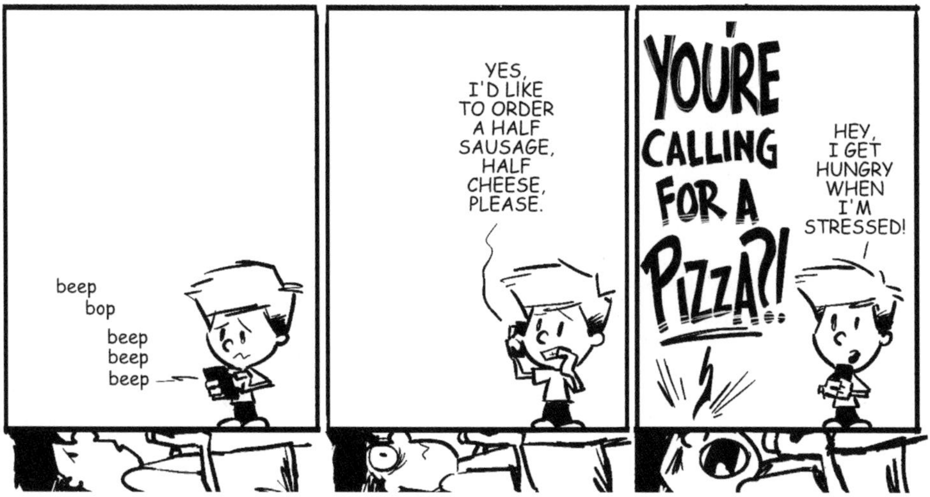
beep
bop
beep
beep
beep
YES, I'D LIKE TO ORDER A HALF SAUSAGE, HALF CHEESE, PLEASE.
YOU'RE CALLING FOR A PIZZA?!
HEY, I GET HUNGRY WHEN I'M STRESSED!

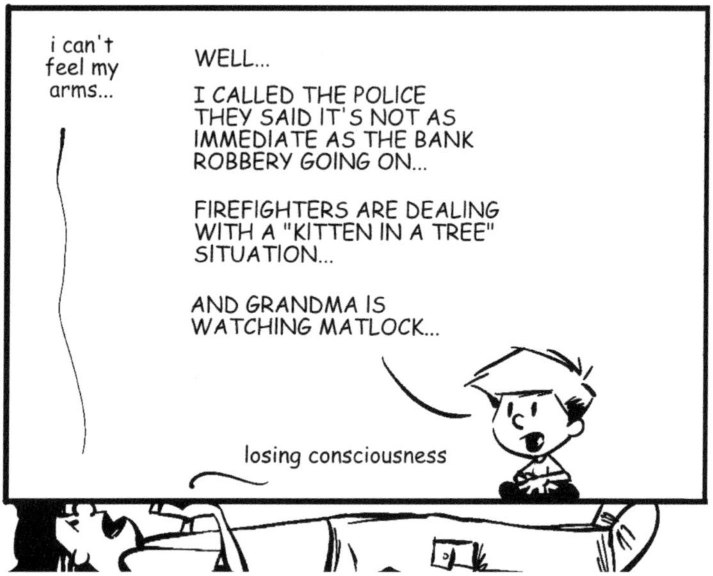
i can't feel my arms...
WELL...
I CALLED THE POLICE THEY SAID IT'S NOT AS IMMEDIATE AS THE BANK ROBBERY GOING ON...
FIREFIGHTERS ARE DEALING WITH A "KITTEN IN A TREE" SITUATION...
AND GRANDMA IS WATCHING MATLOCK...
losing consciousness

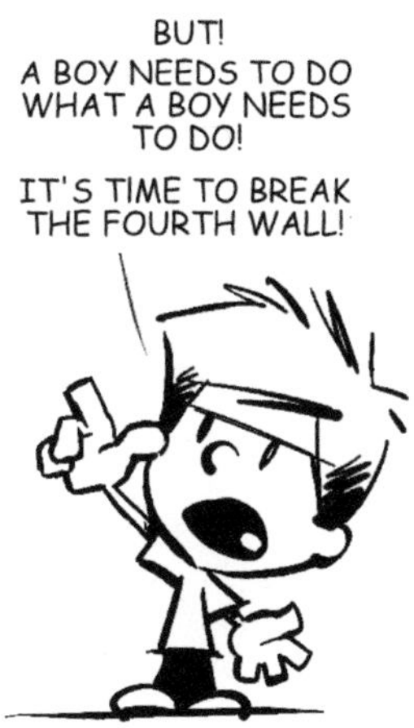
BUT!
A BOY NEEDS TO DO WHAT A BOY NEEDS TO DO!
IT'S TIME TO BREAK THE FOURTH WALL!

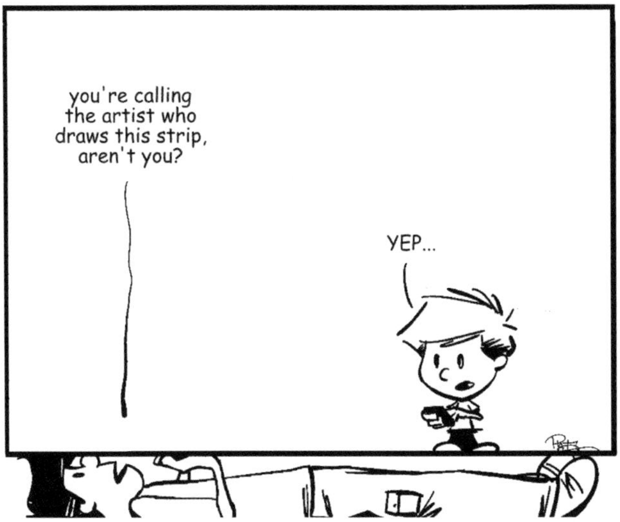
you're calling the artist who draws this strip, aren't you?
YEP...

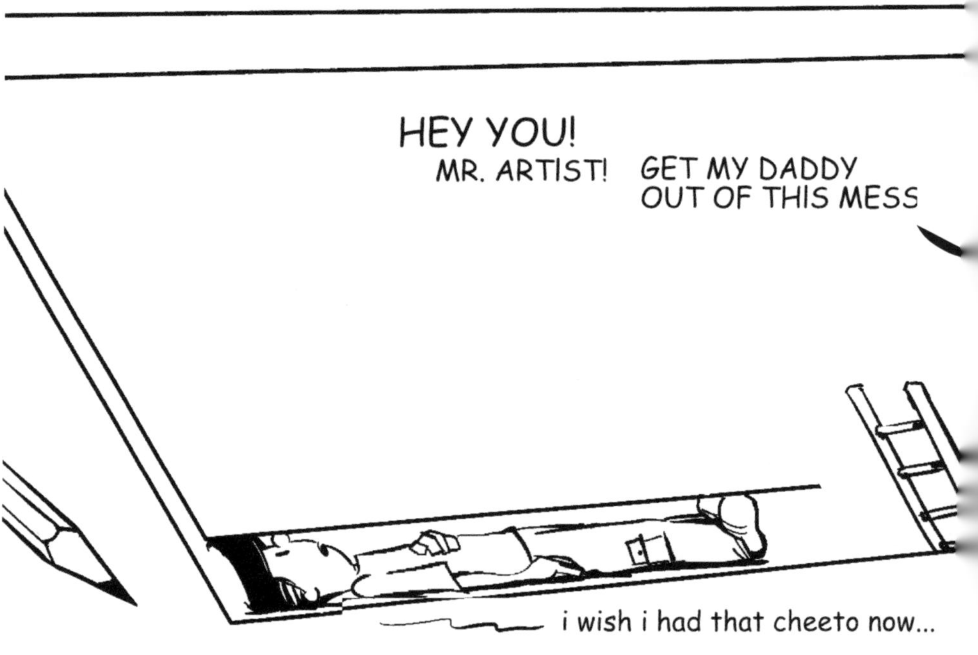
HEY YOU!
MR. ARTIST!
GET MY DADDY
OUT OF THIS MESS
i wish i had that cheeto now...

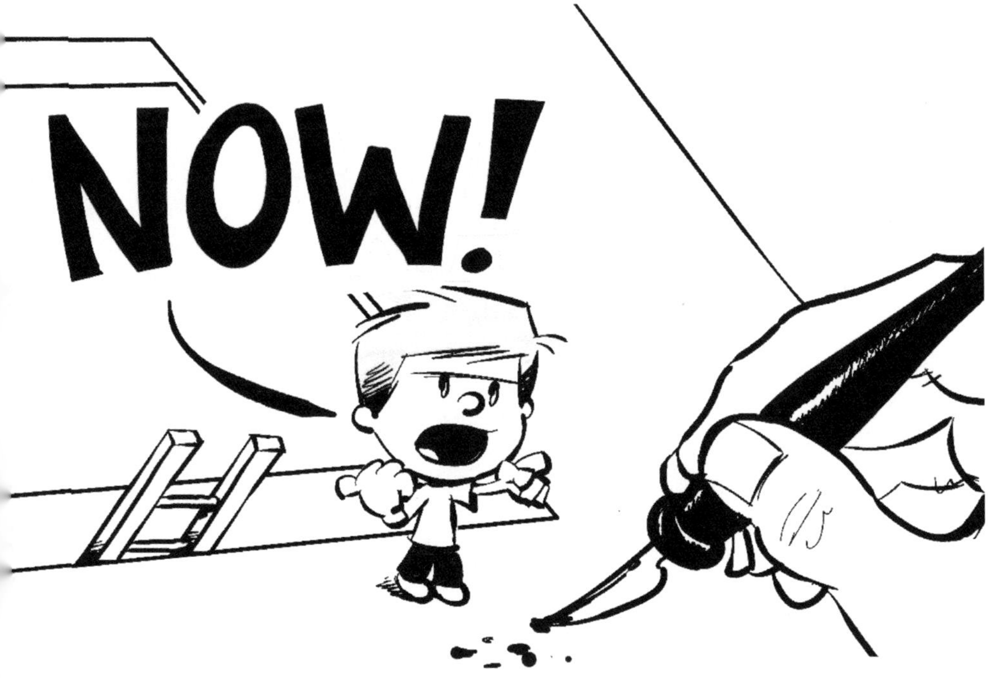
NOW!

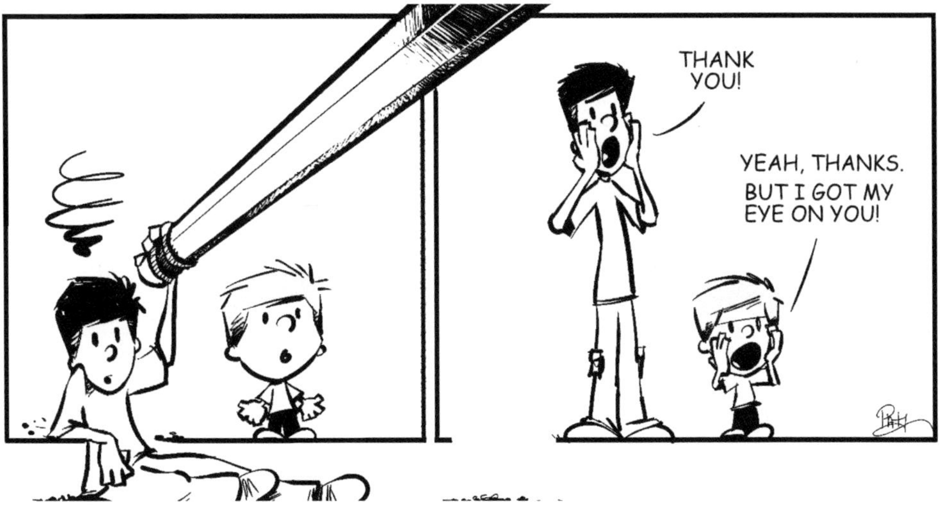
THANK YOU!
YEAH, THANKS.
BUT I GOT MY EYE ON YOU!

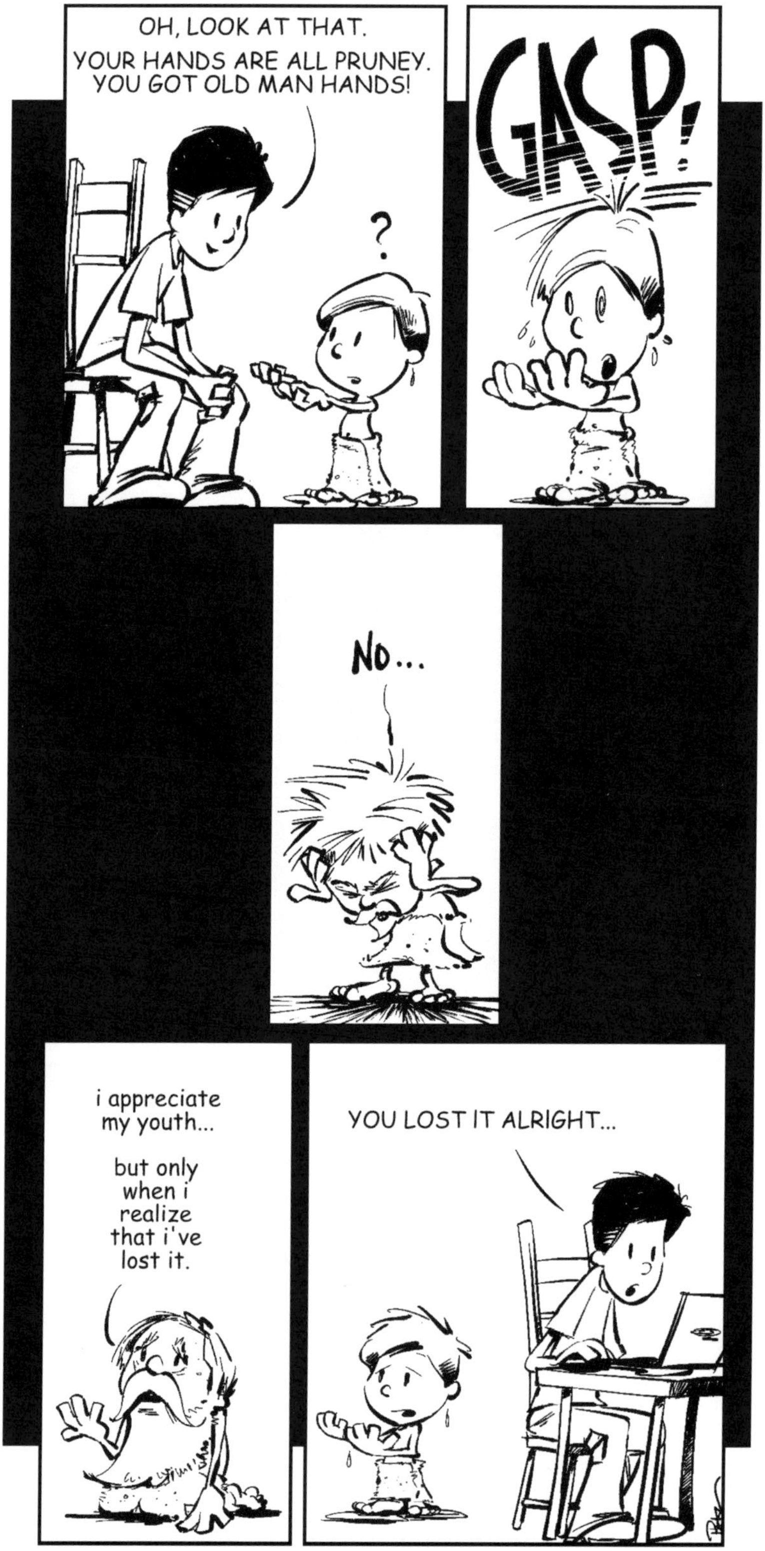
OH, LOOK AT THAT.
YOUR HANDS ARE ALL PRUNEY. YOU GOT OLD MAN HANDS!
?
GASP!
NO...
i appreciate my youth...
but only when i realize that i've lost it.
YOU LOST IT ALRIGHT...

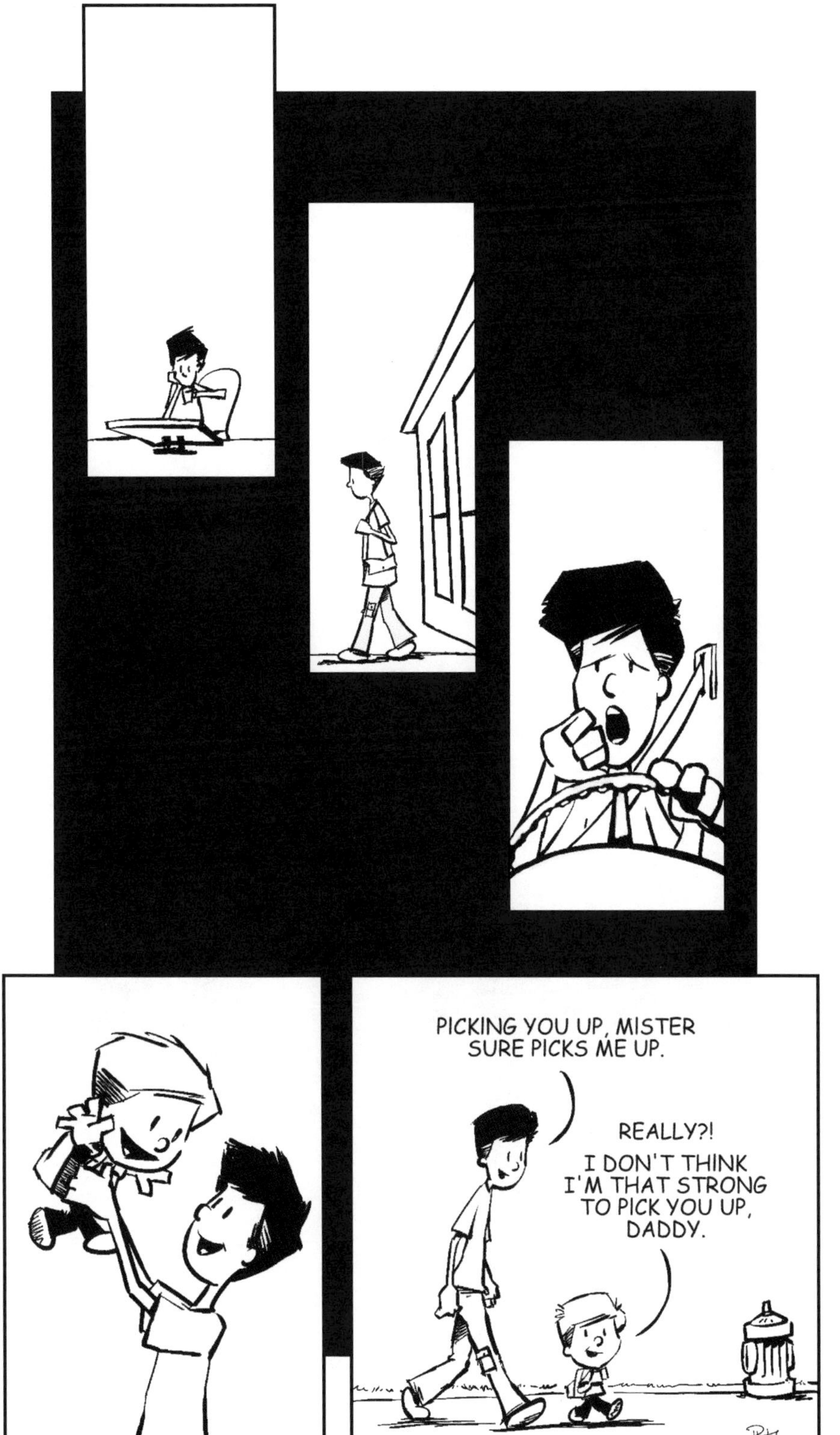
PICKING YOU UP, MISTER
SURE PICKS ME UP.
REALLY?!
I DON'T THINK
I'M THAT STRONG
TO PICK YOU UP,
DADDY.

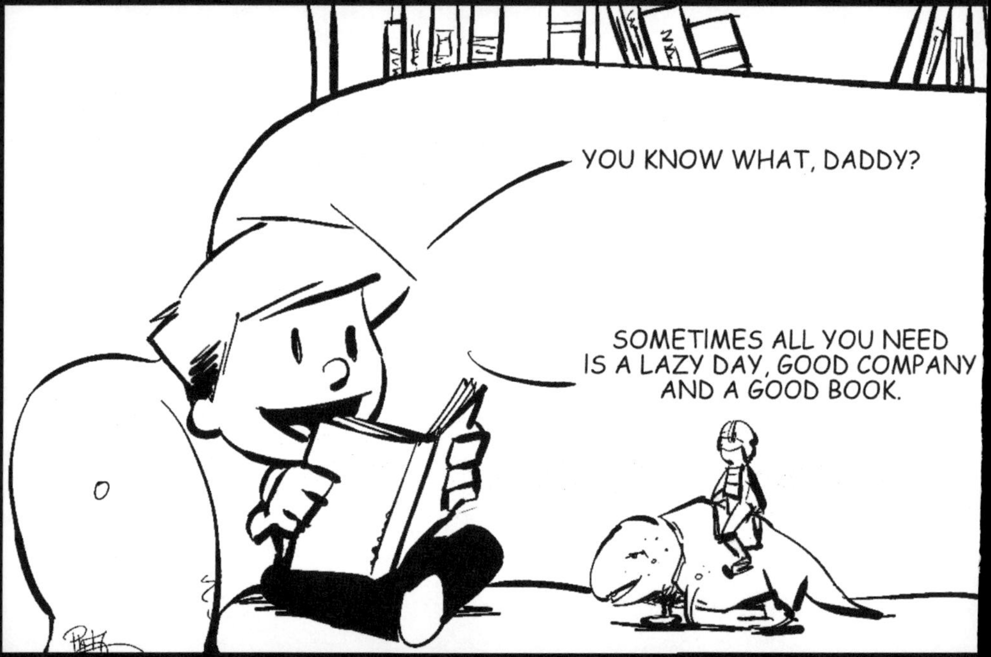
YOU KNOW WHAT, DADDY?
SOMETIMES ALL YOU NEED IS A LAZY DAY, GOOD COMPANY AND A GOOD BOOK.

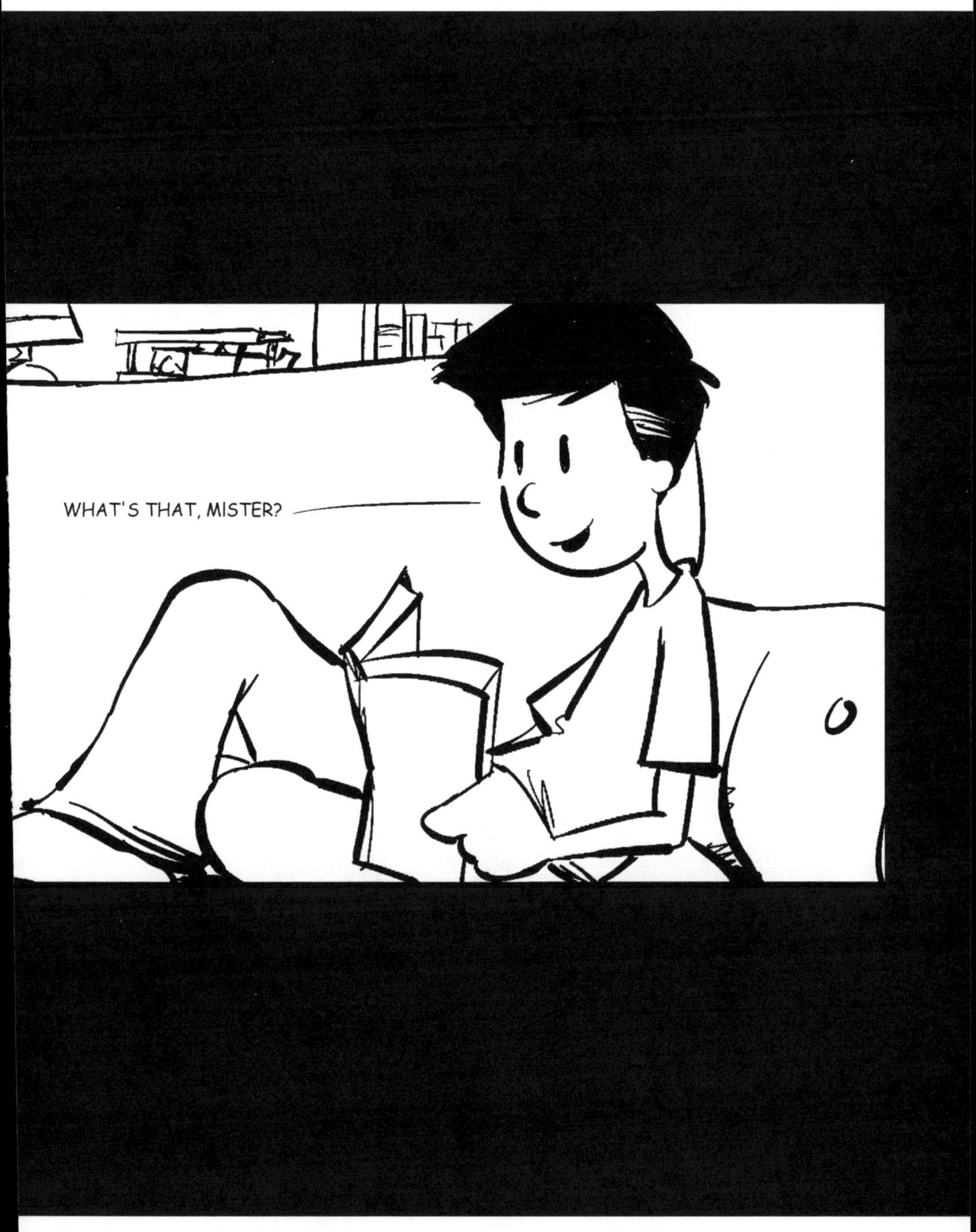
WHAT'S THAT, MISTER?

ACHOO!
'scuse me...

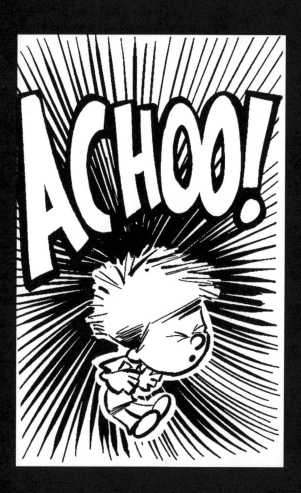

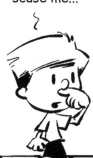

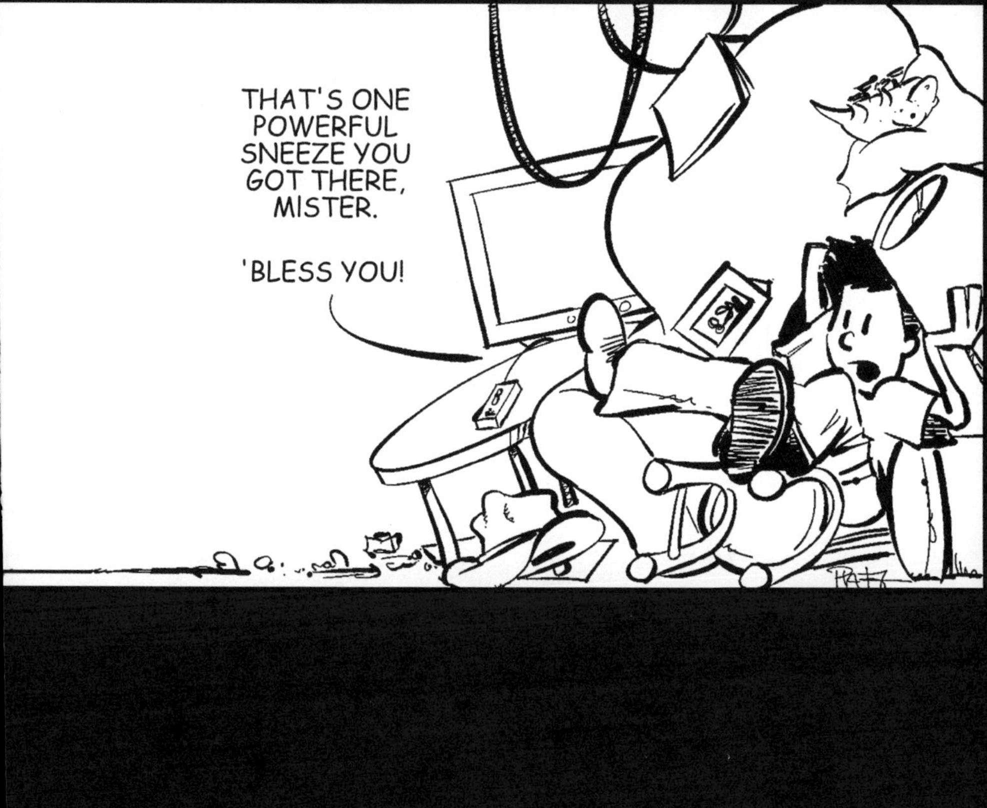
THAT'S ONE POWERFUL SNEEZE YOU GOT THERE, MISTER.
'BLESS YOU!

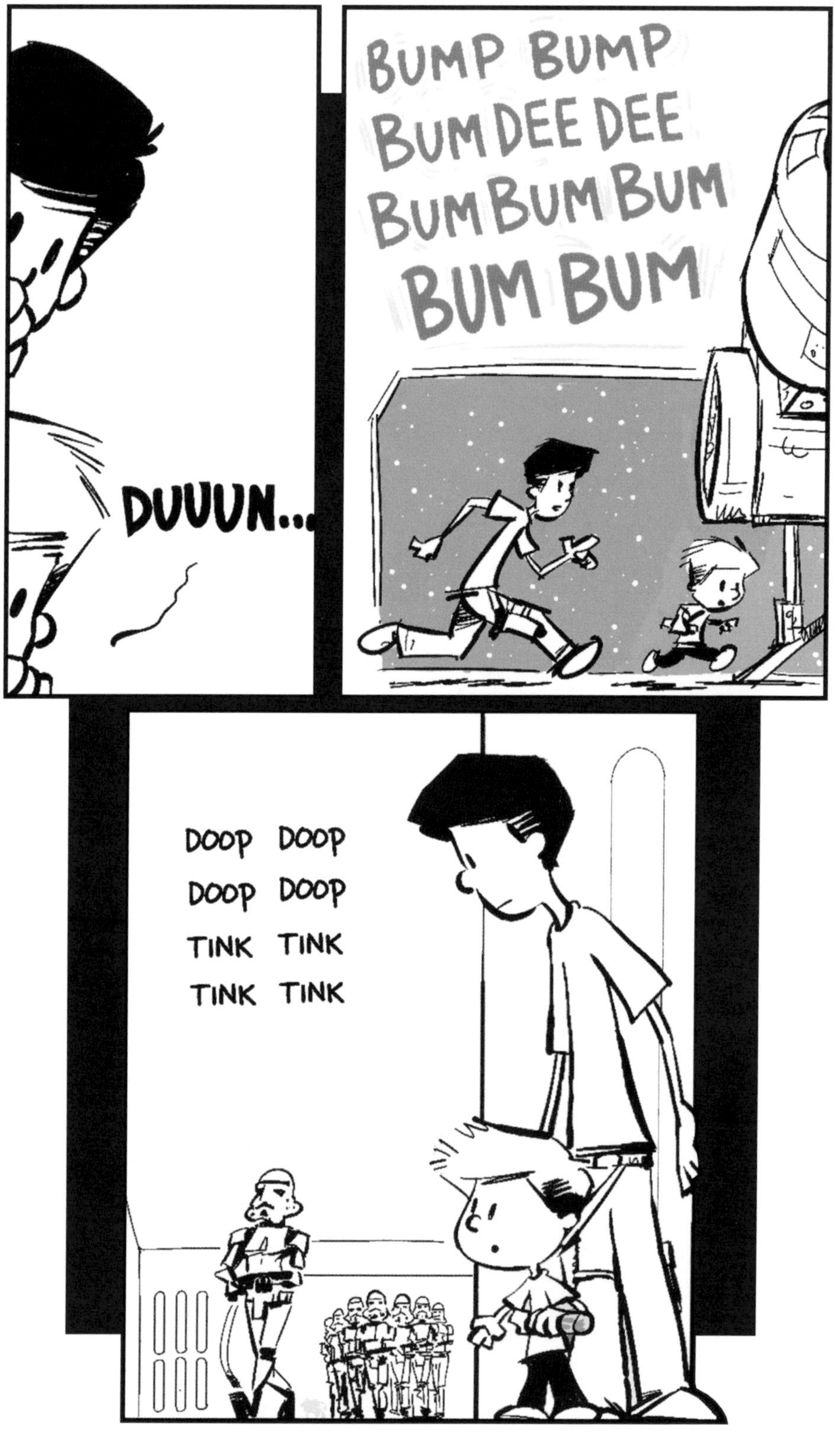
DUUUN...
BUMP BUMP
BUM DEE DEE
BUM BUM BUM
BUM BUM
DOOP DOOP
DOOP DOOP
TINK TINK
TINK TINK

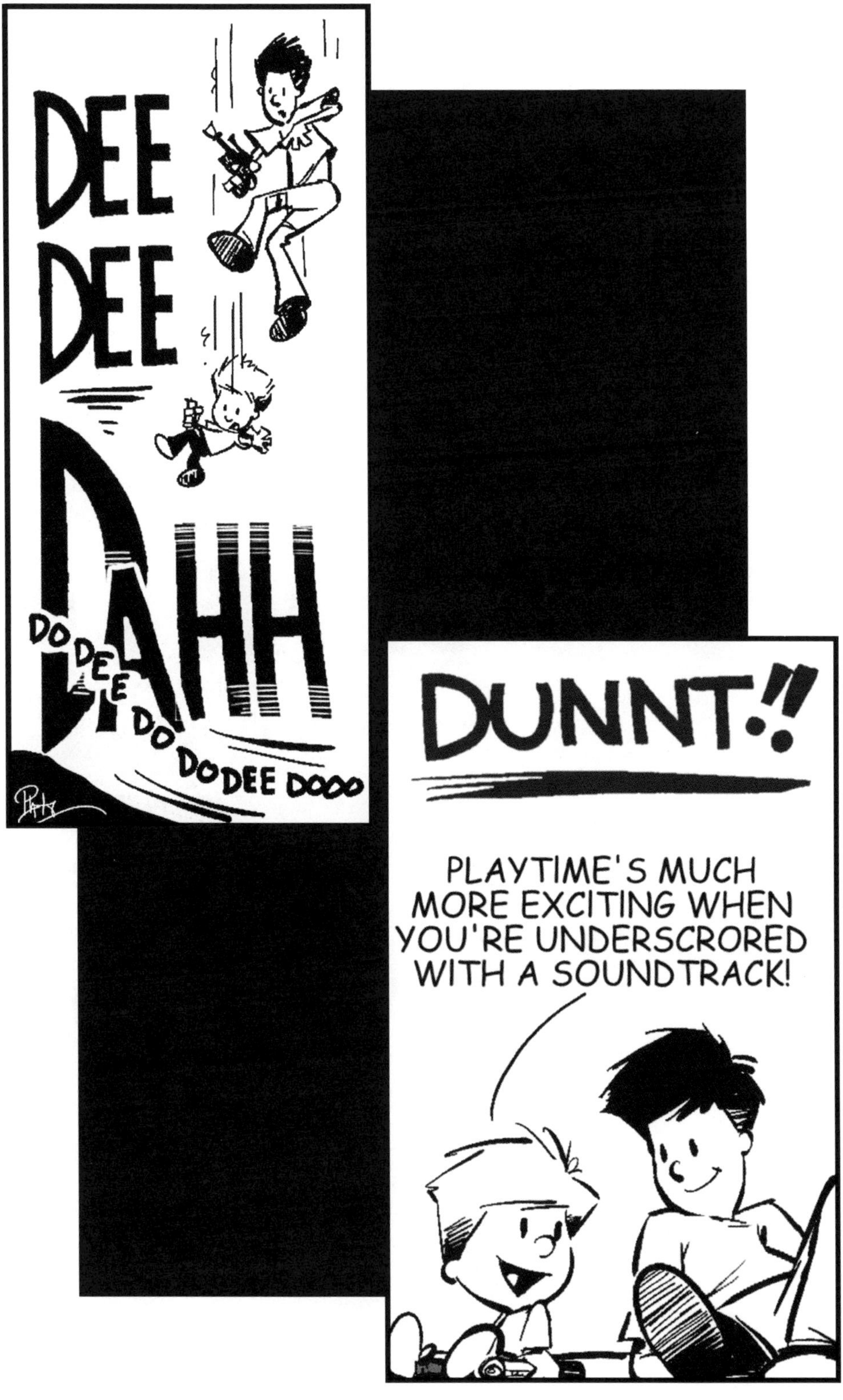
DEE
DEE
DAHH
DO DEE DO DO DODEE DOOO
DUNNT!!
PLAYTIME'S MUCH MORE EXCITING WHEN YOU'RE UNDERSCRORED WITH A SOUNDTRACK!

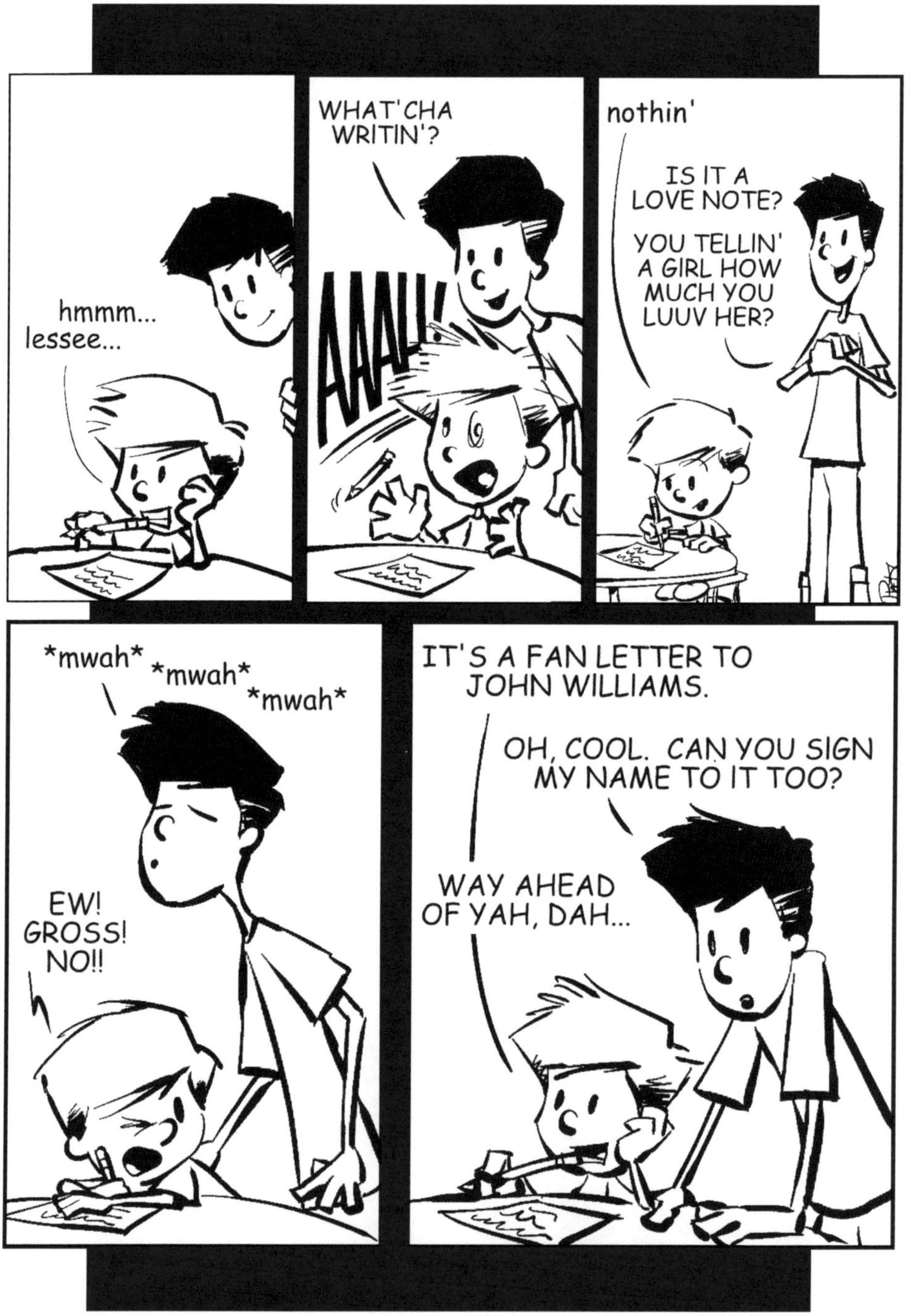
hmmm... lessee...
WHAT'CHA WRITIN'?
AAAH!
nothin'
IS IT A LOVE NOTE?
YOU TELLIN' A GIRL HOW MUCH YOU LUUV HER?
mwah *mwah* *mwah*
EW! GROSS! NO!!
IT'S A FAN LETTER TO JOHN WILLIAMS.
OH, COOL. CAN YOU SIGN MY NAME TO IT TOO?
WAY AHEAD OF YAH, DAH...

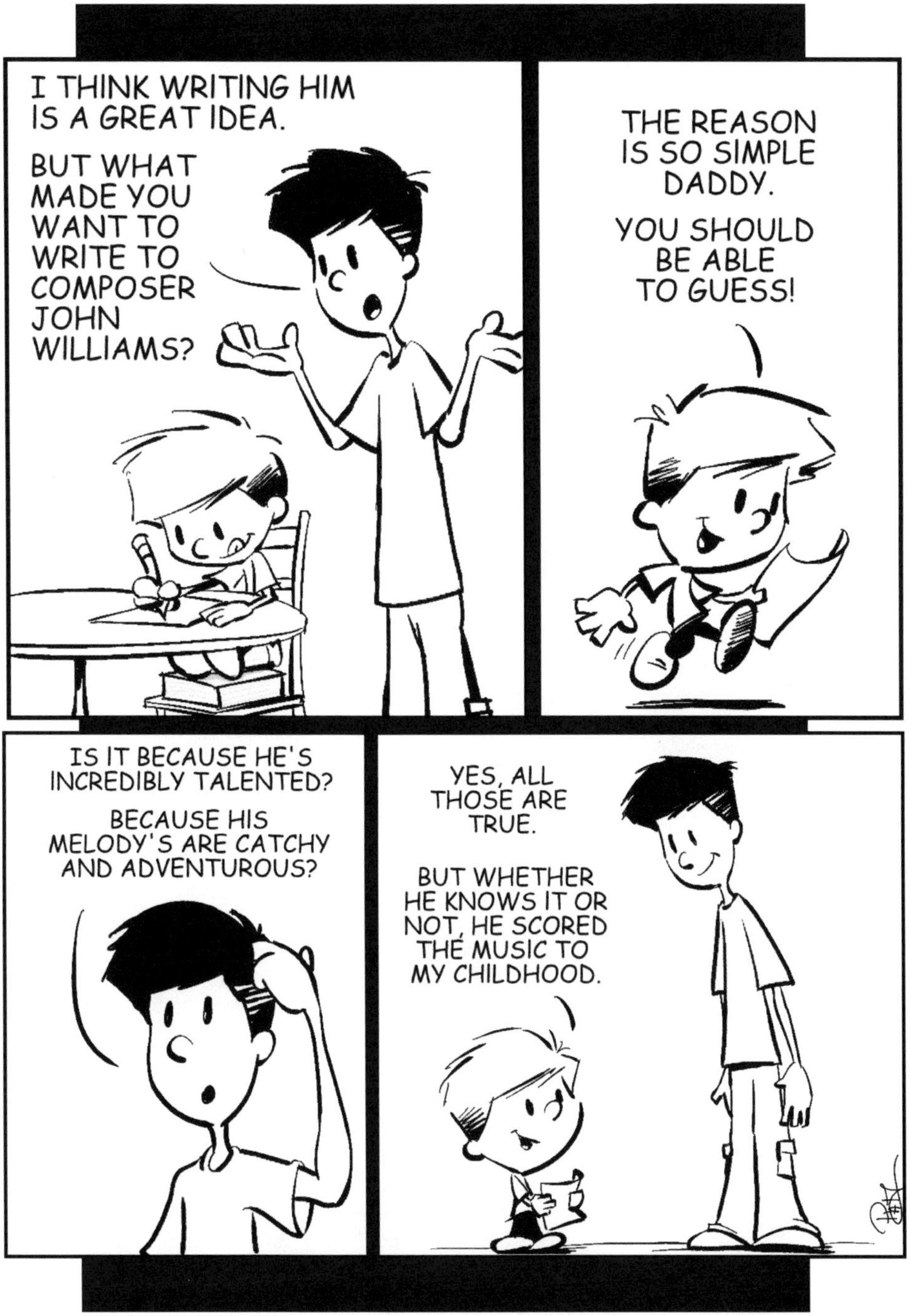
I THINK WRITING HIM IS A GREAT IDEA.
BUT WHAT MADE YOU WANT TO WRITE TO COMPOSER JOHN WILLIAMS?
THE REASON IS SO SIMPLE DADDY.
YOU SHOULD BE ABLE TO GUESS!
IS IT BECAUSE HE'S INCREDIBLY TALENTED?
BECAUSE HIS MELODY'S ARE CATCHY AND ADVENTUROUS?
YES, ALL THOSE ARE TRUE.
BUT WHETHER HE KNOWS IT OR NOT, HE SCORED THE MUSIC TO MY CHILDHOOD.

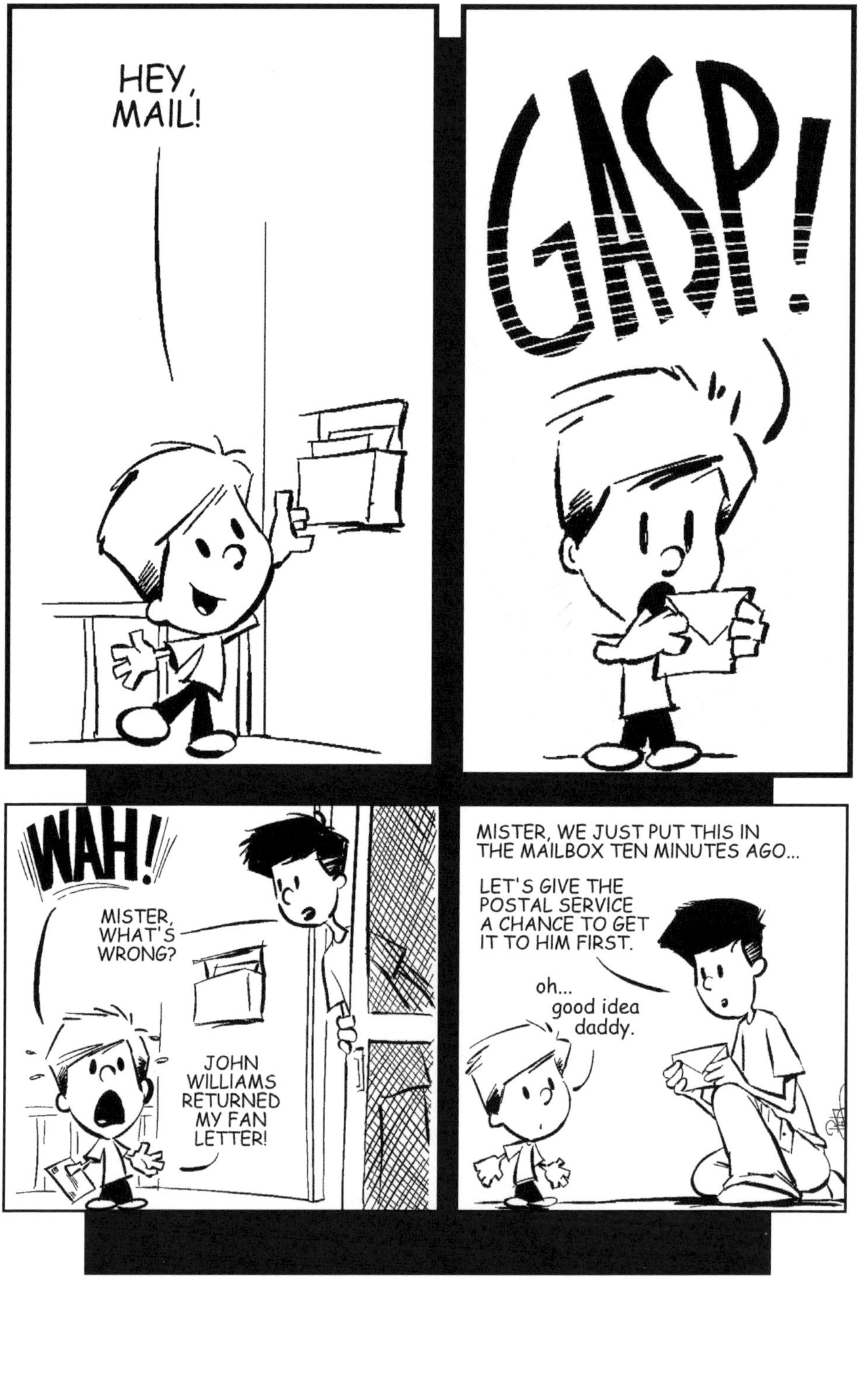
HEY, MAIL!
GASP!
WAH!
MISTER, WHAT'S WRONG?
JOHN WILLIAMS RETURNED MY FAN LETTER!
MISTER, WE JUST PUT THIS IN THE MAILBOX TEN MINUTES AGO...
LET'S GIVE THE POSTAL SERVICE A CHANCE TO GET IT TO HIM FIRST.
oh... good idea daddy.

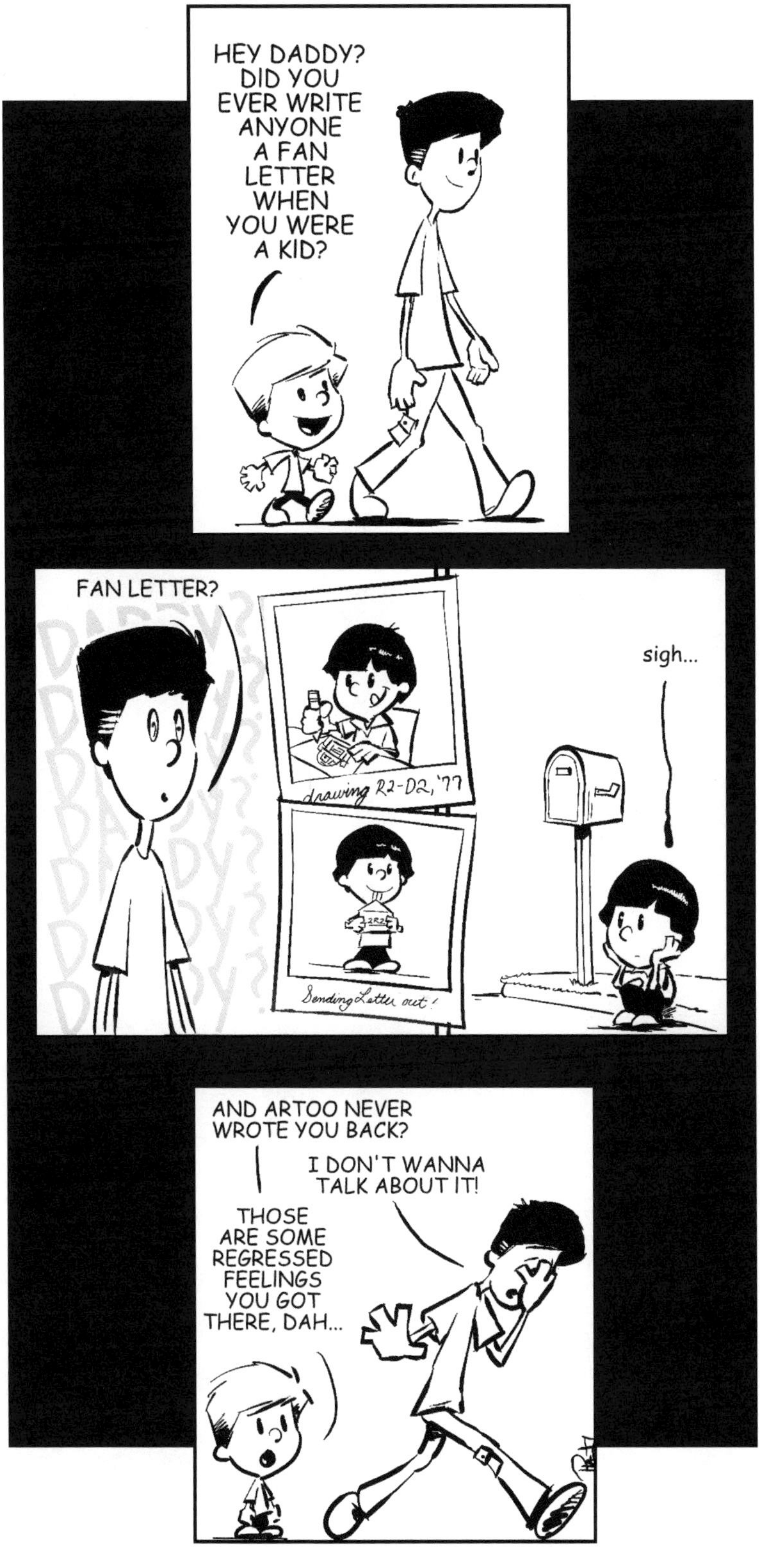
HEY DADDY? DID YOU EVER WRITE ANYONE A FAN LETTER WHEN YOU WERE A KID?
FAN LETTER?
DADDY? DADDY? DADDY? DADDY? DADDY? DADDY?
drawing R2-D2, '77
Sending Letter out!
sigh...
AND ARTOO NEVER WROTE YOU BACK?
I DON'T WANNA TALK ABOUT IT!
THOSE ARE SOME REGRESSED FEELINGS YOU GOT THERE, DAH...

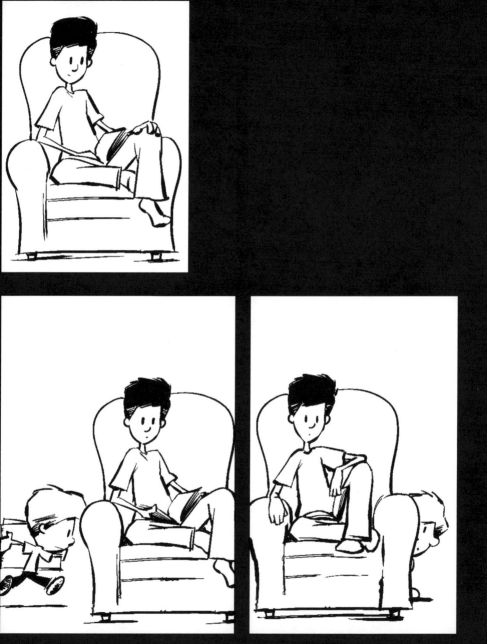

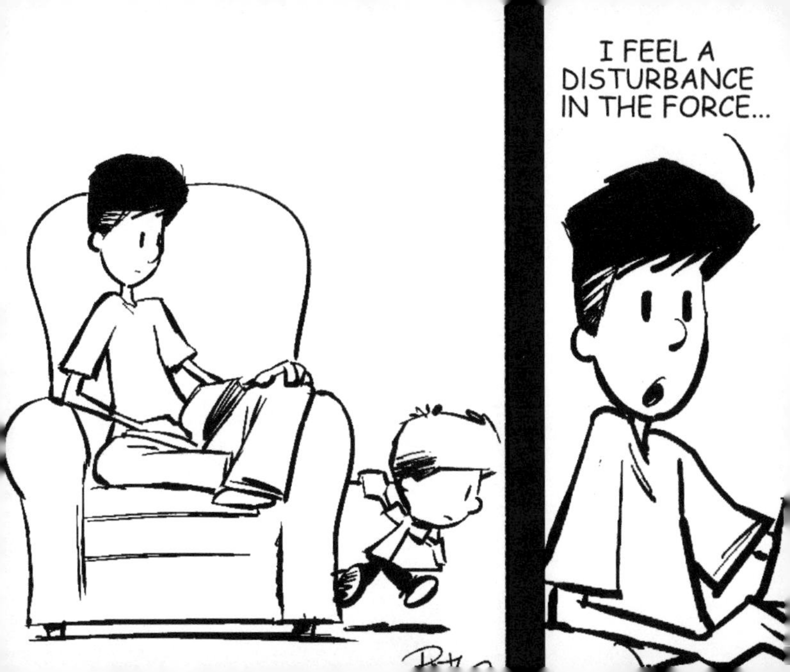
I FEEL A DISTURBANCE IN THE FORCE...

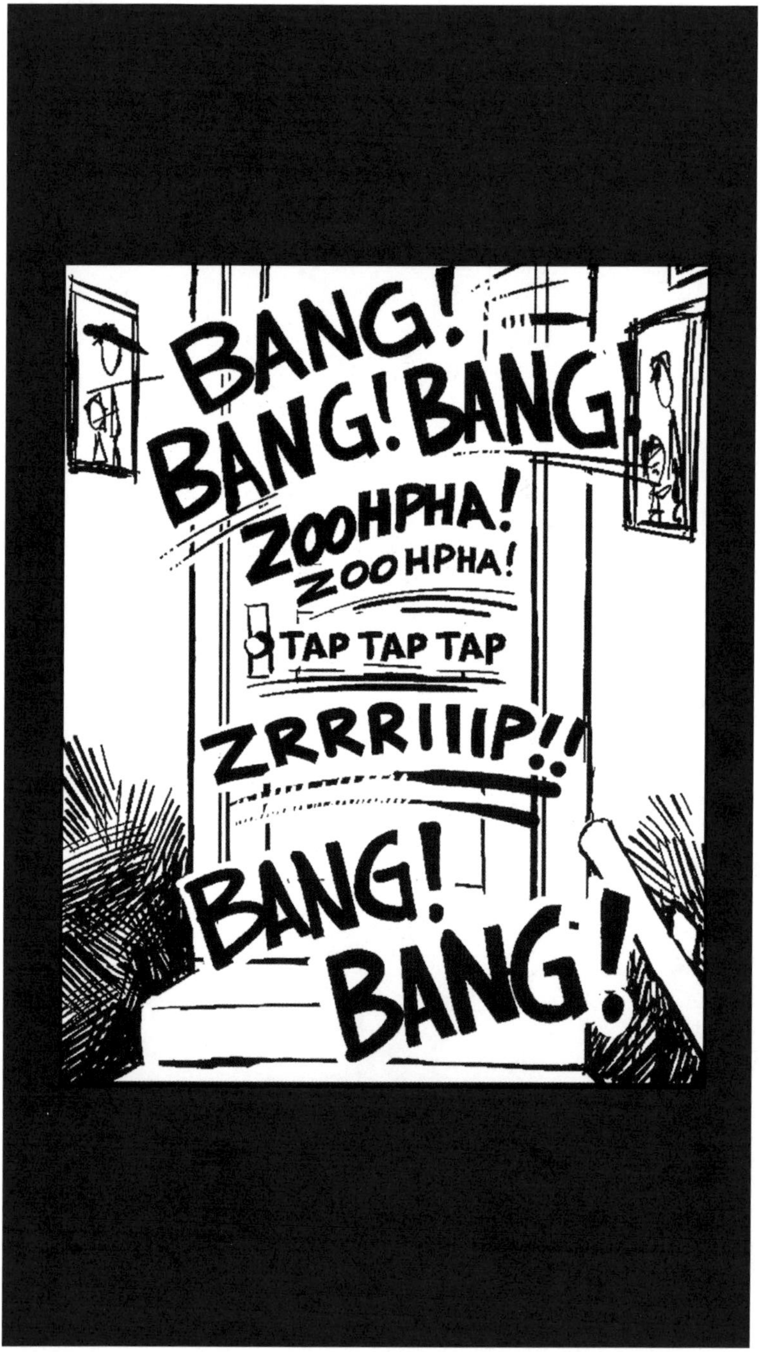
BANG!
BANG! BANG!
ZOOHPHA!
ZOOHPHA!
TAP TAP TAP
ZRRRIIIP!!
BANG!
BANG!

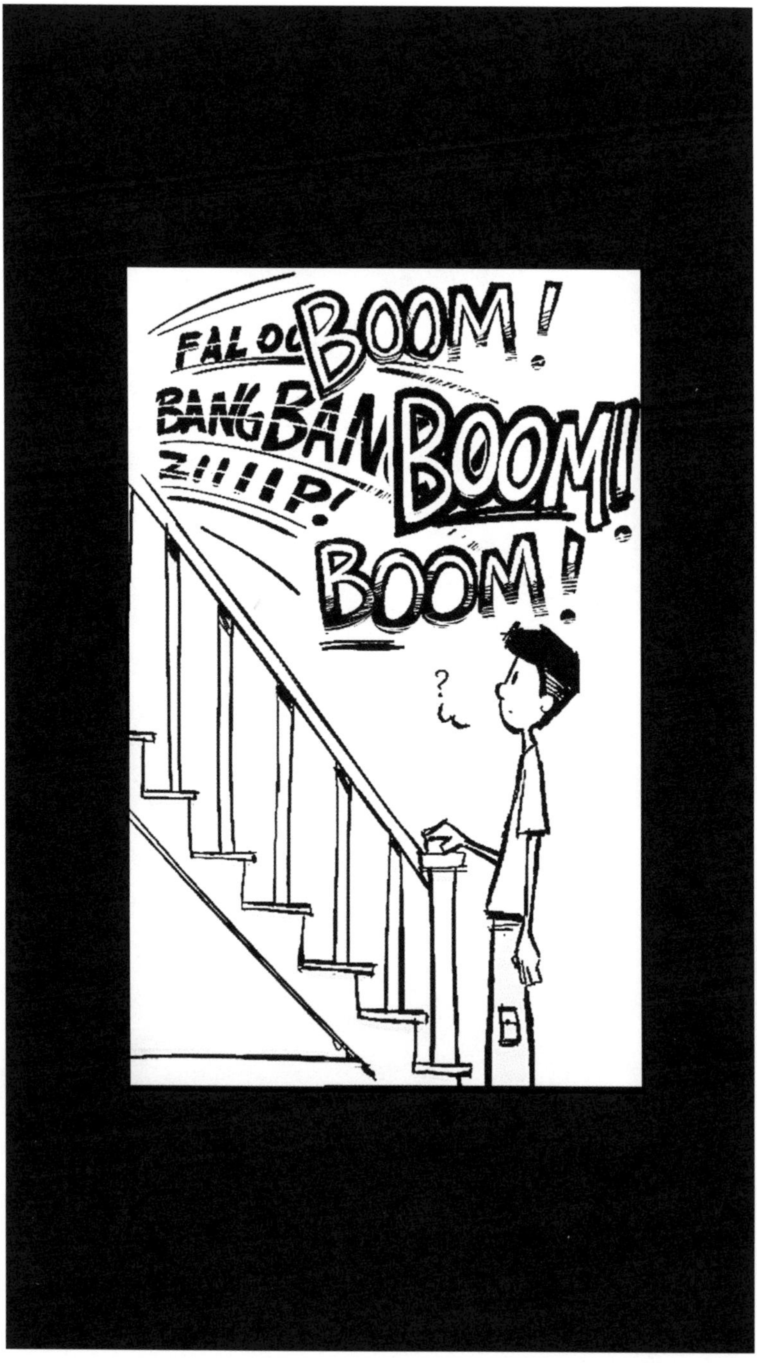
FAL OO
BOOM!
BANG BAM
BOOM!
ZIIIIP!
BOOM!
?

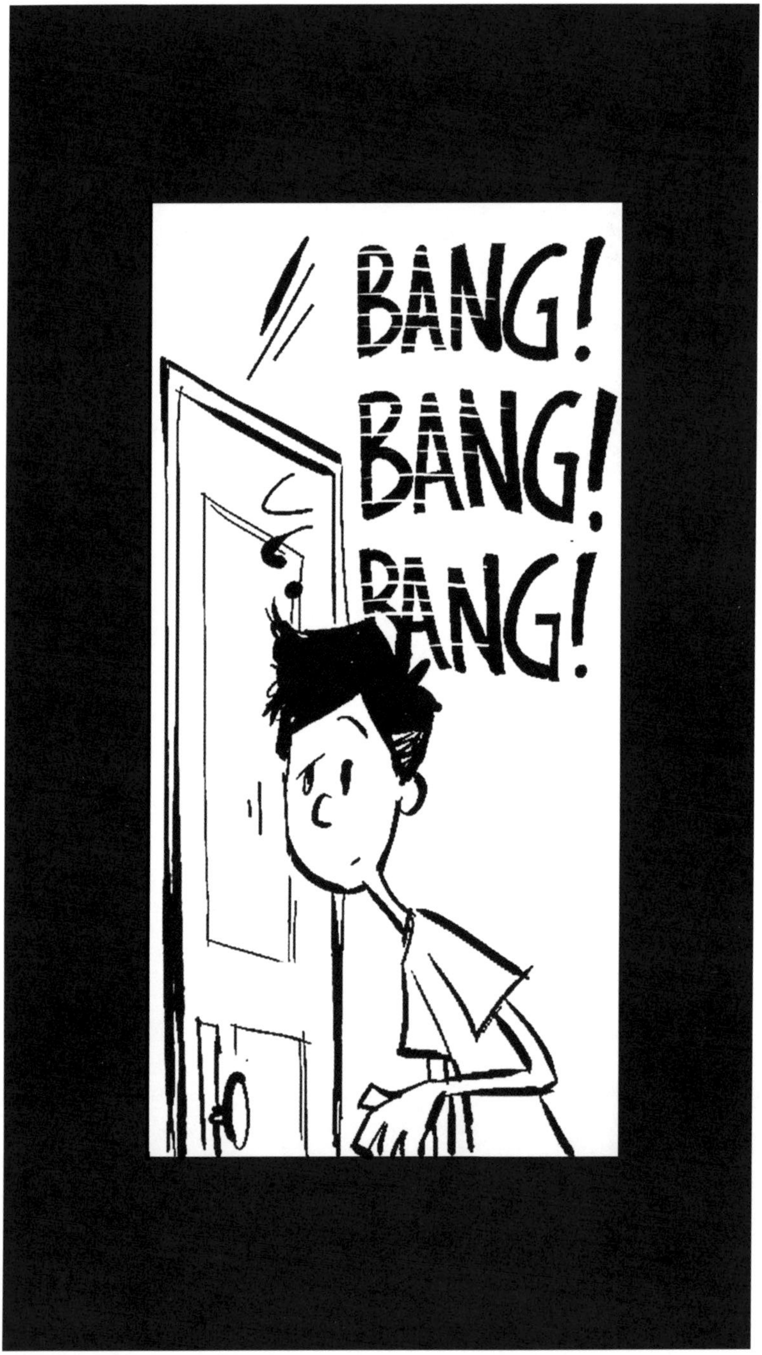
BANG!
BANG!
BANG!

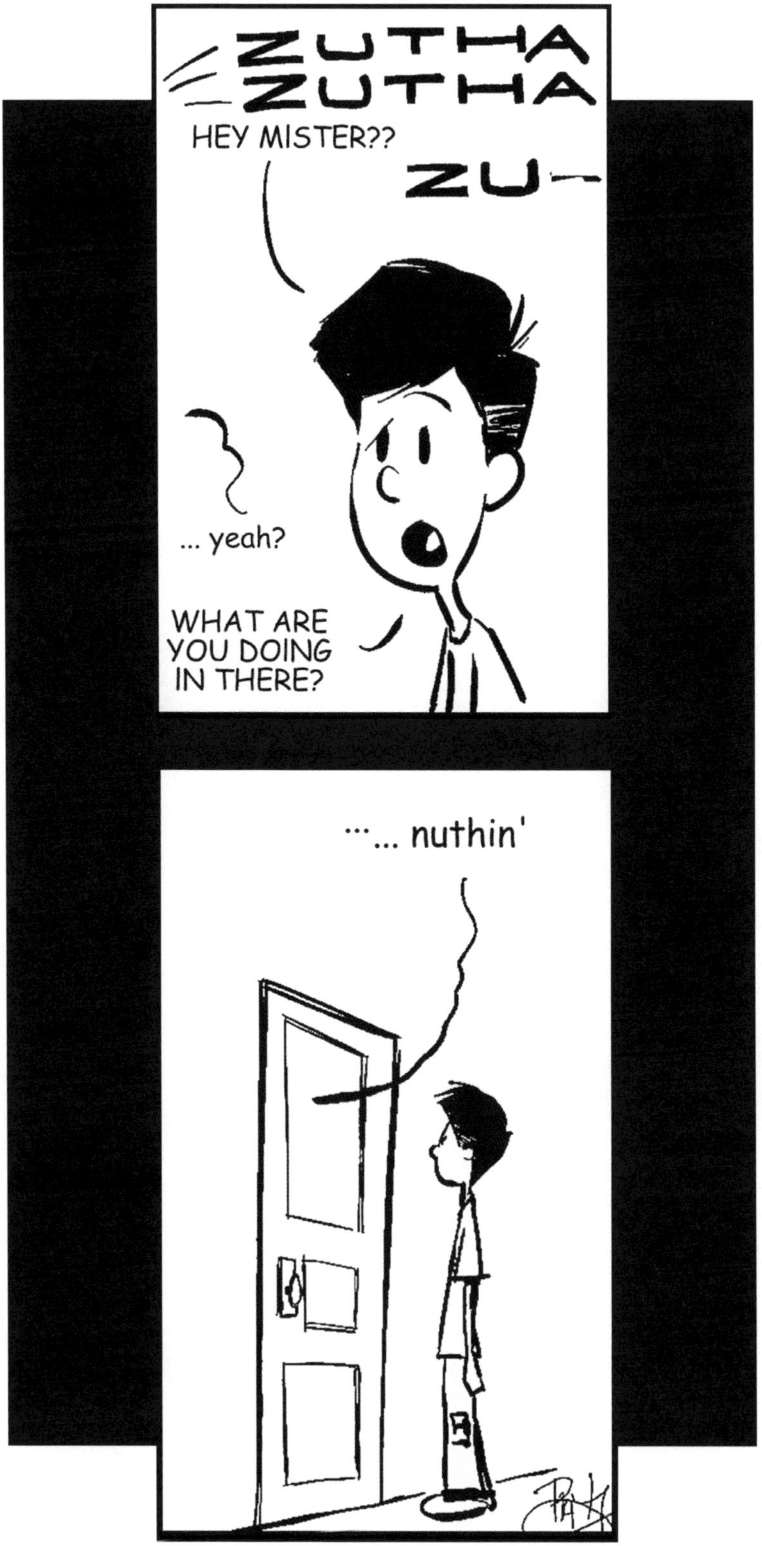
ZUTHA ZUTHA
HEY MISTER??
ZU—
... yeah?
WHAT ARE YOU DOING IN THERE?
...... nuthin'

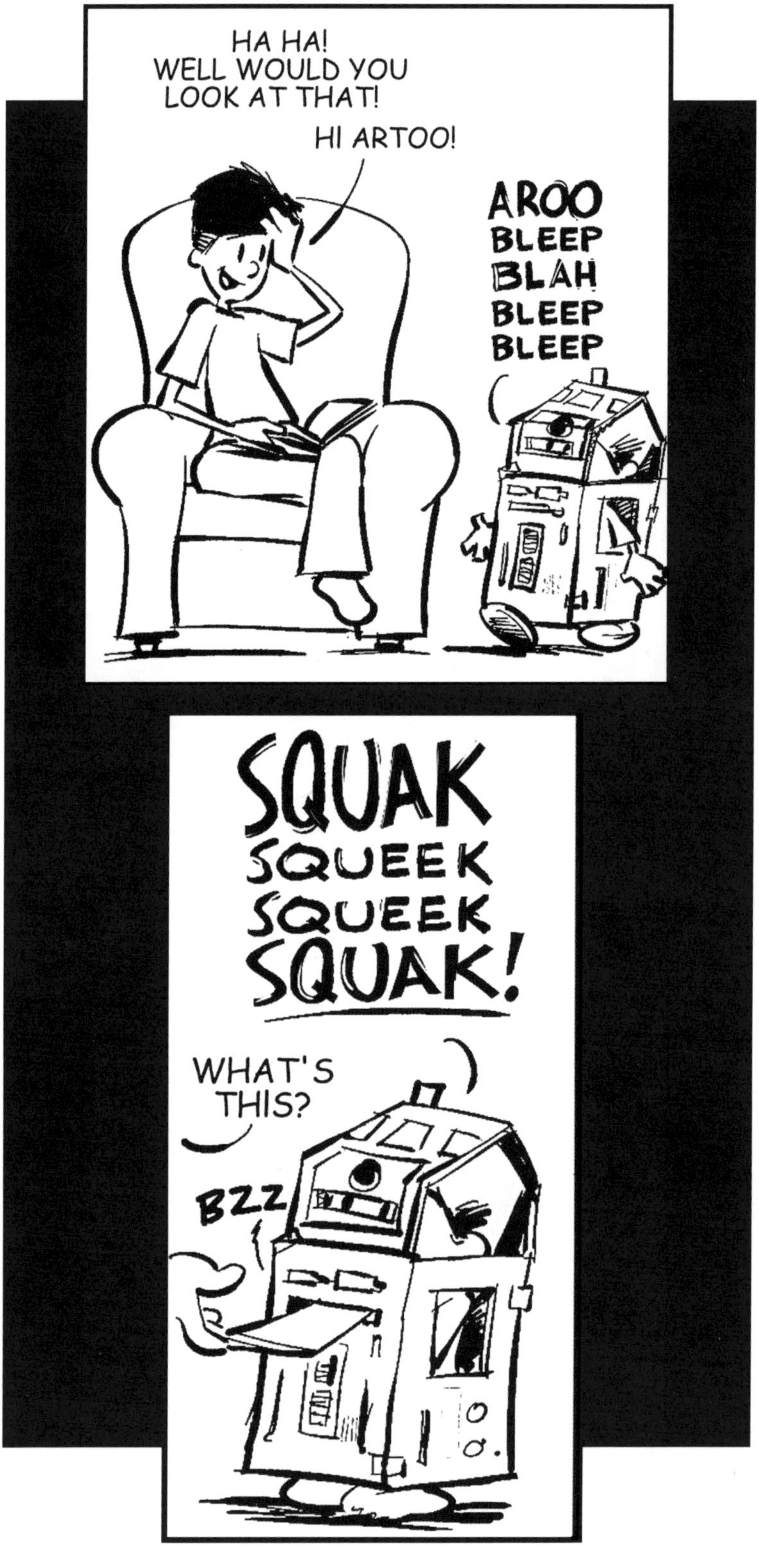
HA HA!
WELL WOULD YOU
LOOK AT THAT!
HI ARTOO!
AROO
BLEEP
BLAH
BLEEP
BLEEP
SQUAK
SQUEEK
SQUEEK
SQUAK!
WHAT'S
THIS?
BZZ

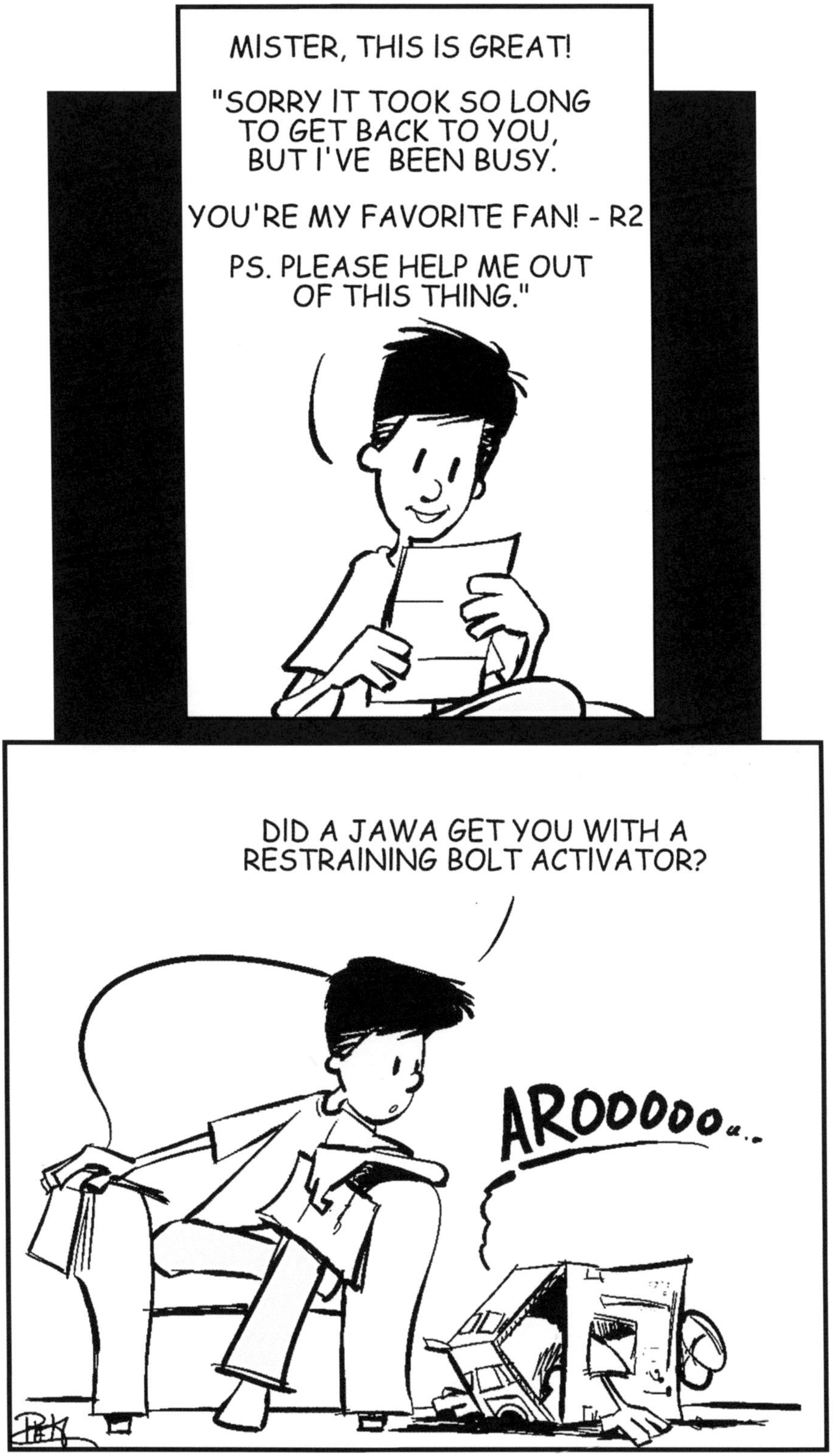
MISTER, THIS IS GREAT!
"SORRY IT TOOK SO LONG TO GET BACK TO YOU, BUT I'VE BEEN BUSY.
YOU'RE MY FAVORITE FAN! - R2
PS. PLEASE HELP ME OUT OF THIS THING."
DID A JAWA GET YOU WITH A RESTRAINING BOLT ACTIVATOR?
AROOOOOu..

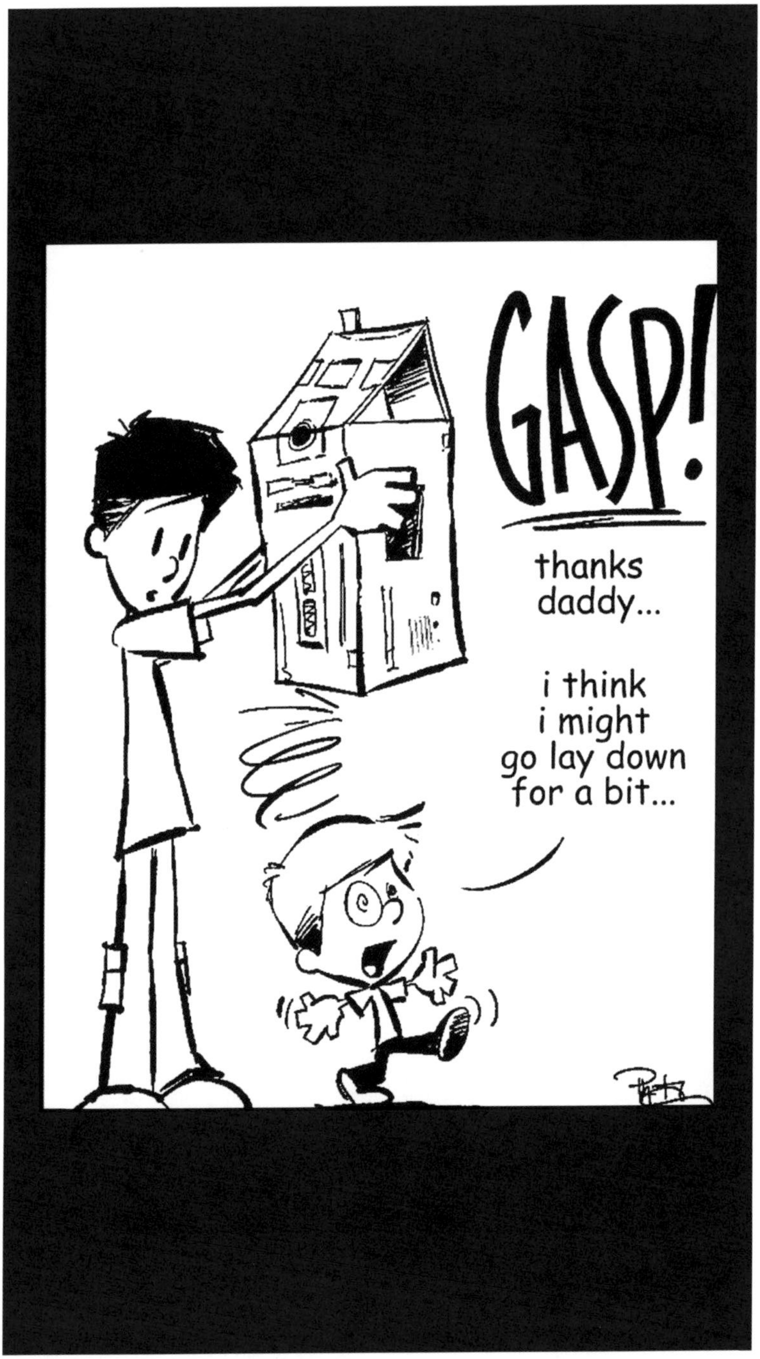
GASP!
thanks daddy...
i think i might go lay down for a bit...

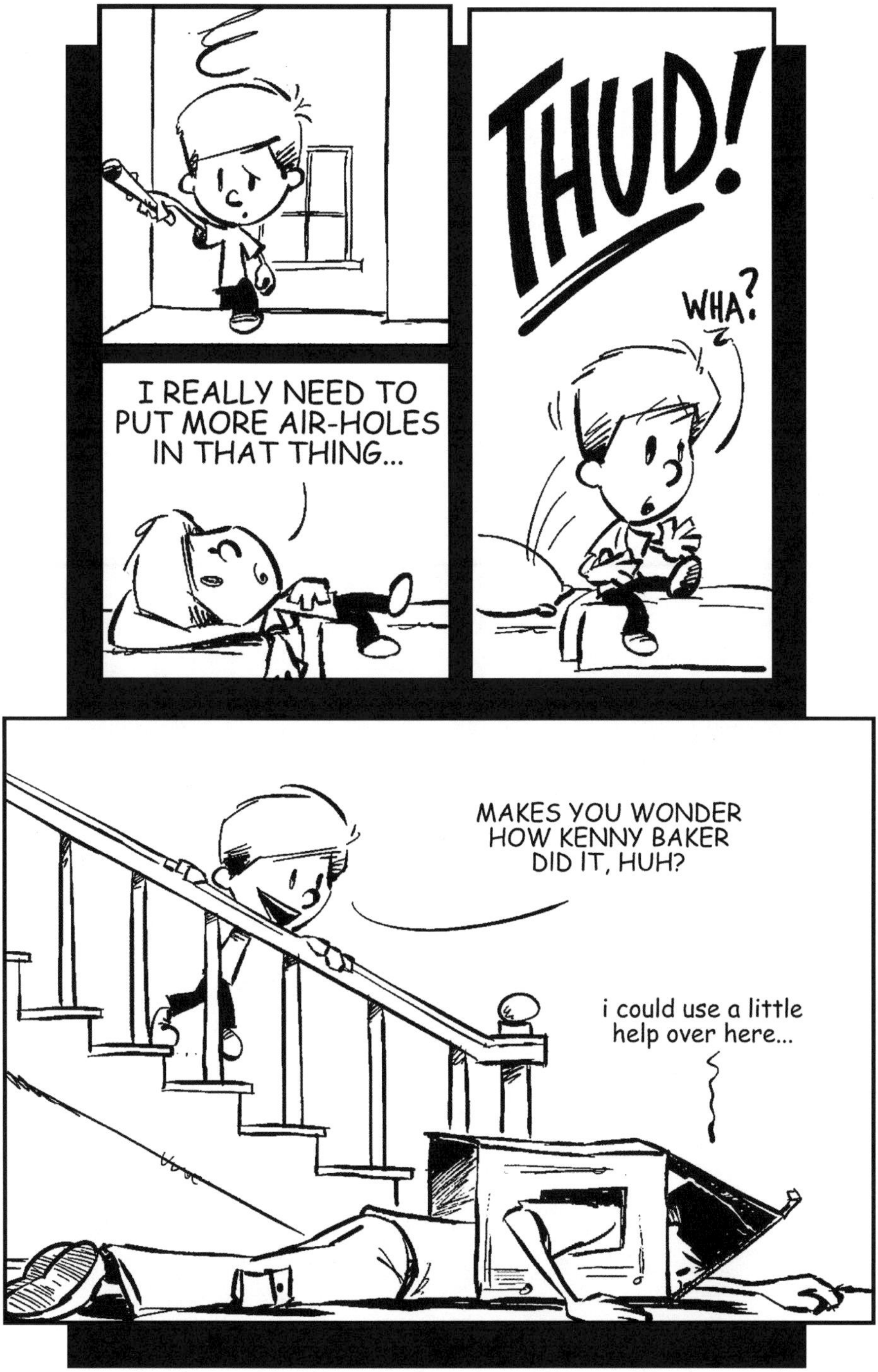
THUD!
WHA?
I REALLY NEED TO PUT MORE AIR-HOLES IN THAT THING...
MAKES YOU WONDER HOW KENNY BAKER DID IT, HUH?
i could use a little help over here...

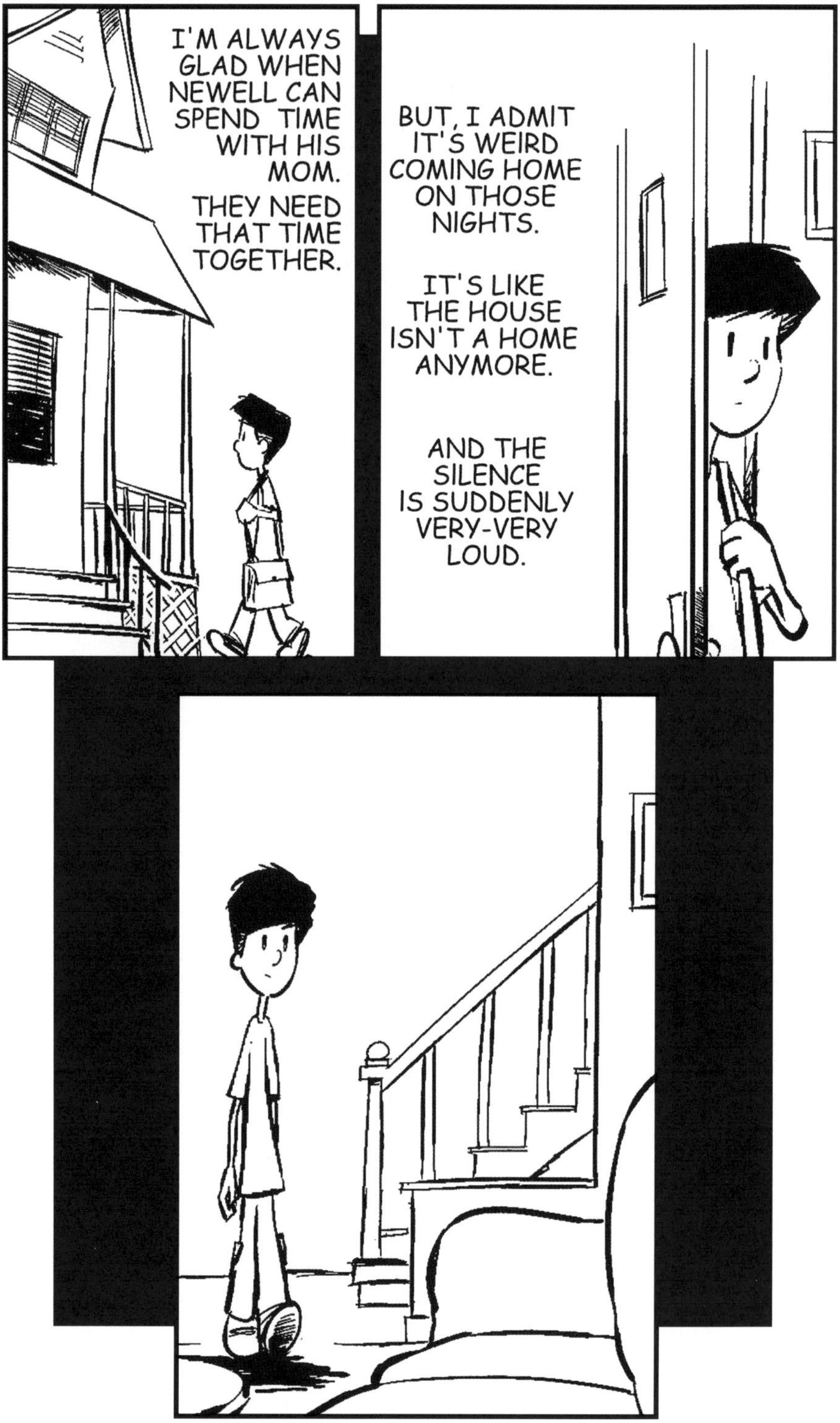
I'M ALWAYS GLAD WHEN NEWELL CAN SPEND TIME WITH HIS MOM.
THEY NEED THAT TIME TOGETHER.
BUT, I ADMIT IT'S WEIRD COMING HOME ON THOSE NIGHTS.
IT'S LIKE THE HOUSE ISN'T A HOME ANYMORE.
AND THE SILENCE IS SUDDENLY VERY-VERY LOUD.

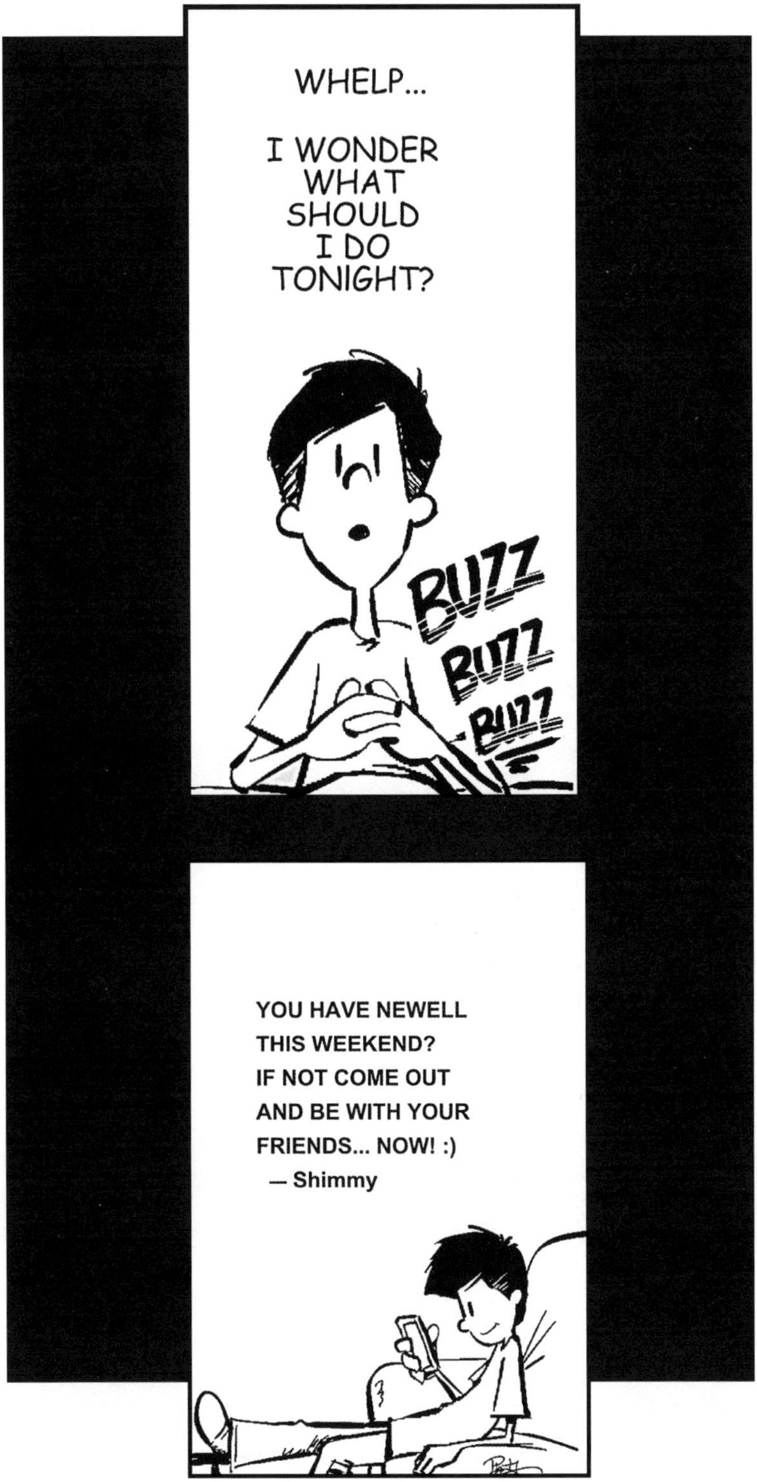
WHELP...
I WONDER WHAT SHOULD I DO TONIGHT?
BUZZ
BUZZ
BUZZ
YOU HAVE NEWELL THIS WEEKEND? IF NOT COME OUT AND BE WITH YOUR FRIENDS... NOW! :)
— Shimmy

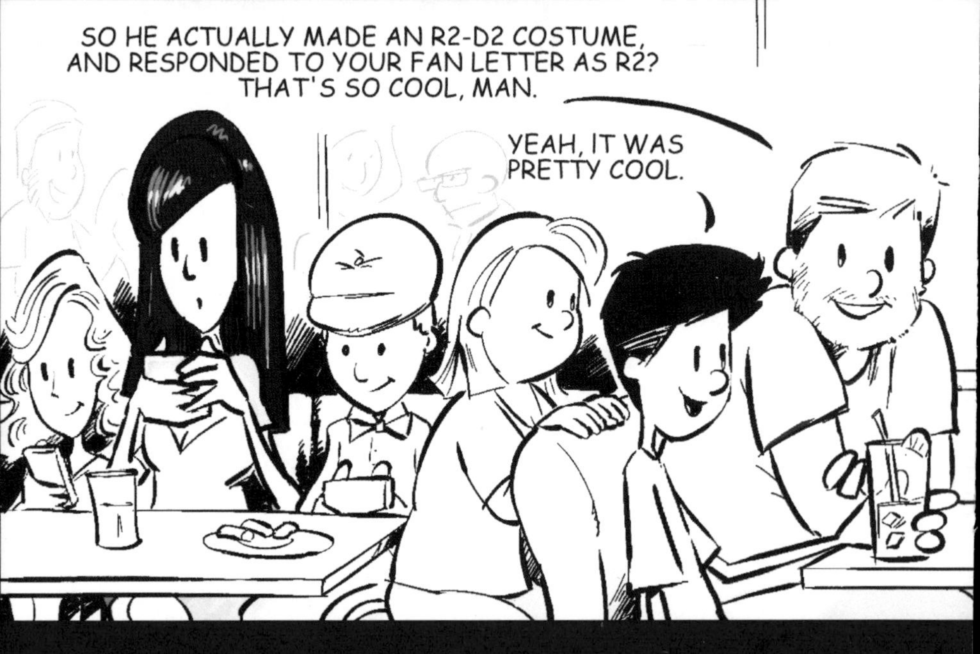
SO HE ACTUALLY MADE AN R2-D2 COSTUME, AND RESPONDED TO YOUR FAN LETTER AS R2? THAT'S SO COOL, MAN.
YEAH, IT WAS PRETTY COOL.

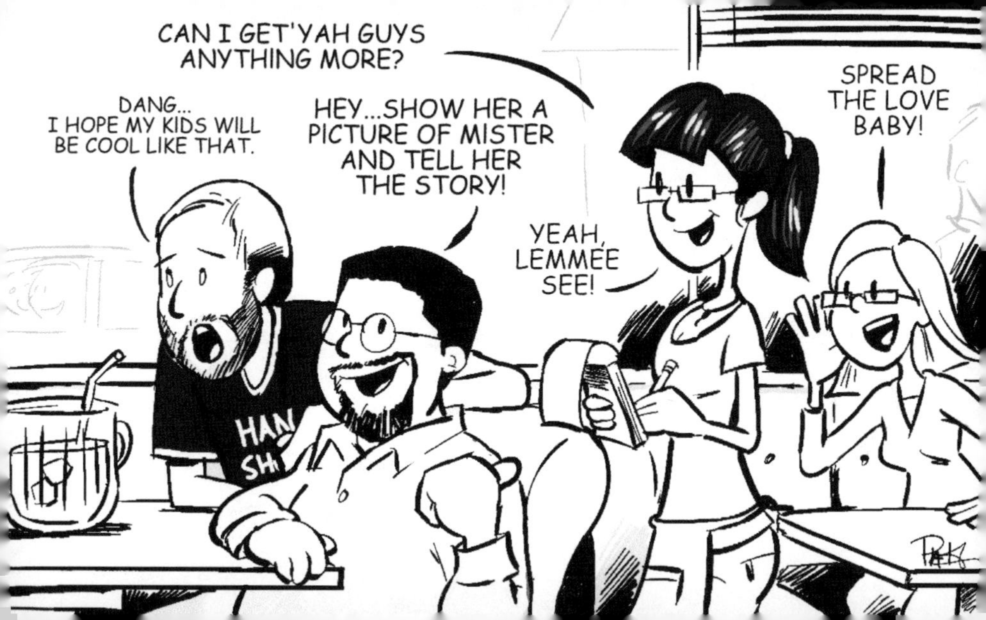
DANG...
I HOPE MY KIDS WILL BE COOL LIKE THAT.
HEY...SHOW HER A PICTURE OF MISTER AND TELL HER THE STORY!
CAN I GET'YAH GUYS ANYTHING MORE?
YEAH, LEMMEE SEE!
SPREAD THE LOVE BABY!

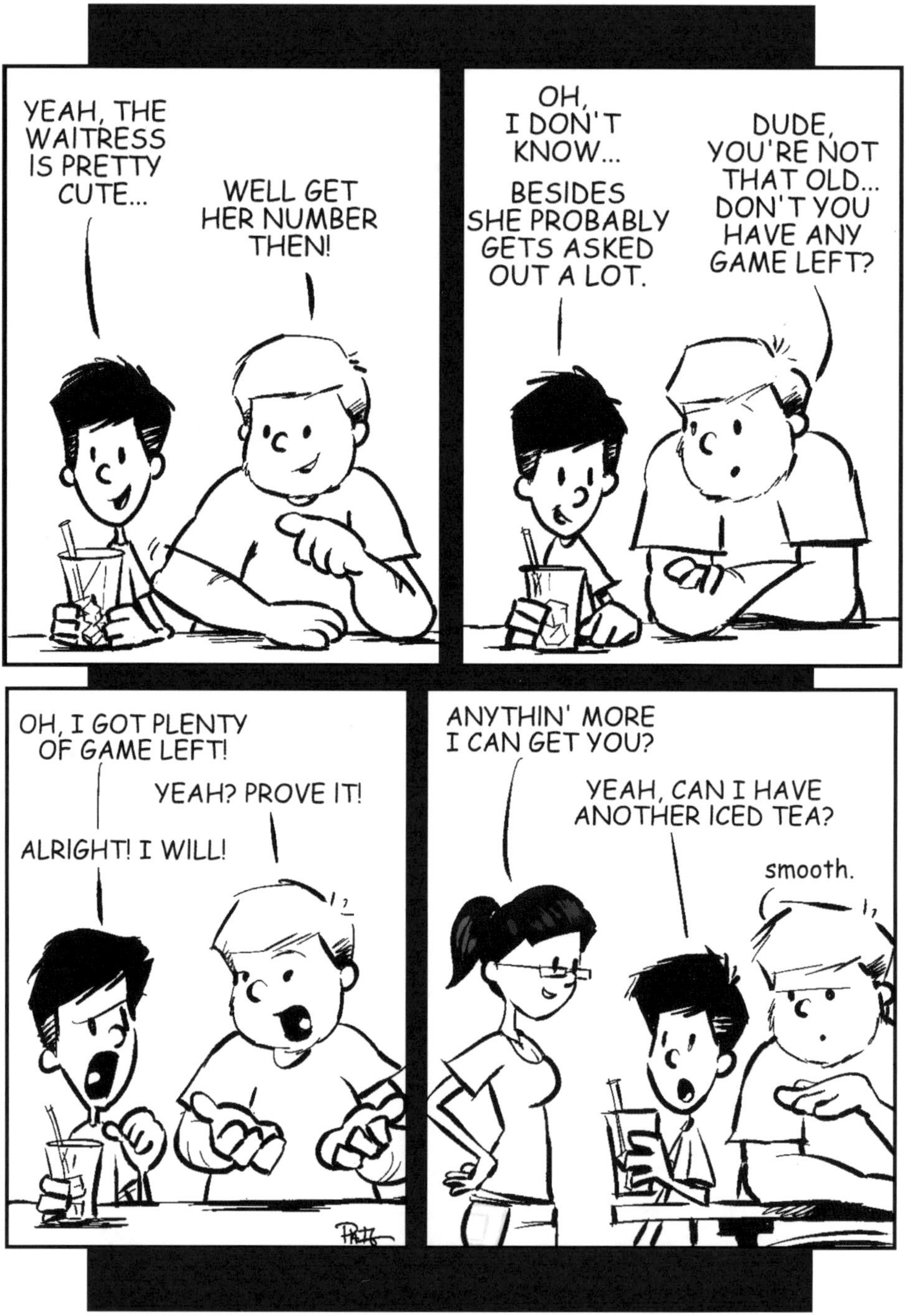

YEAH, THE WAITRESS IS PRETTY CUTE...
WELL GET HER NUMBER THEN!
OH, I DON'T KNOW...
BESIDES SHE PROBABLY GETS ASKED OUT A LOT.
DUDE, YOU'RE NOT THAT OLD... DON'T YOU HAVE ANY GAME LEFT?
OH, I GOT PLENTY OF GAME LEFT!
YEAH? PROVE IT!
ALRIGHT! I WILL!
ANYTHIN' MORE I CAN GET YOU?
YEAH, CAN I HAVE ANOTHER ICED TEA?
smooth.

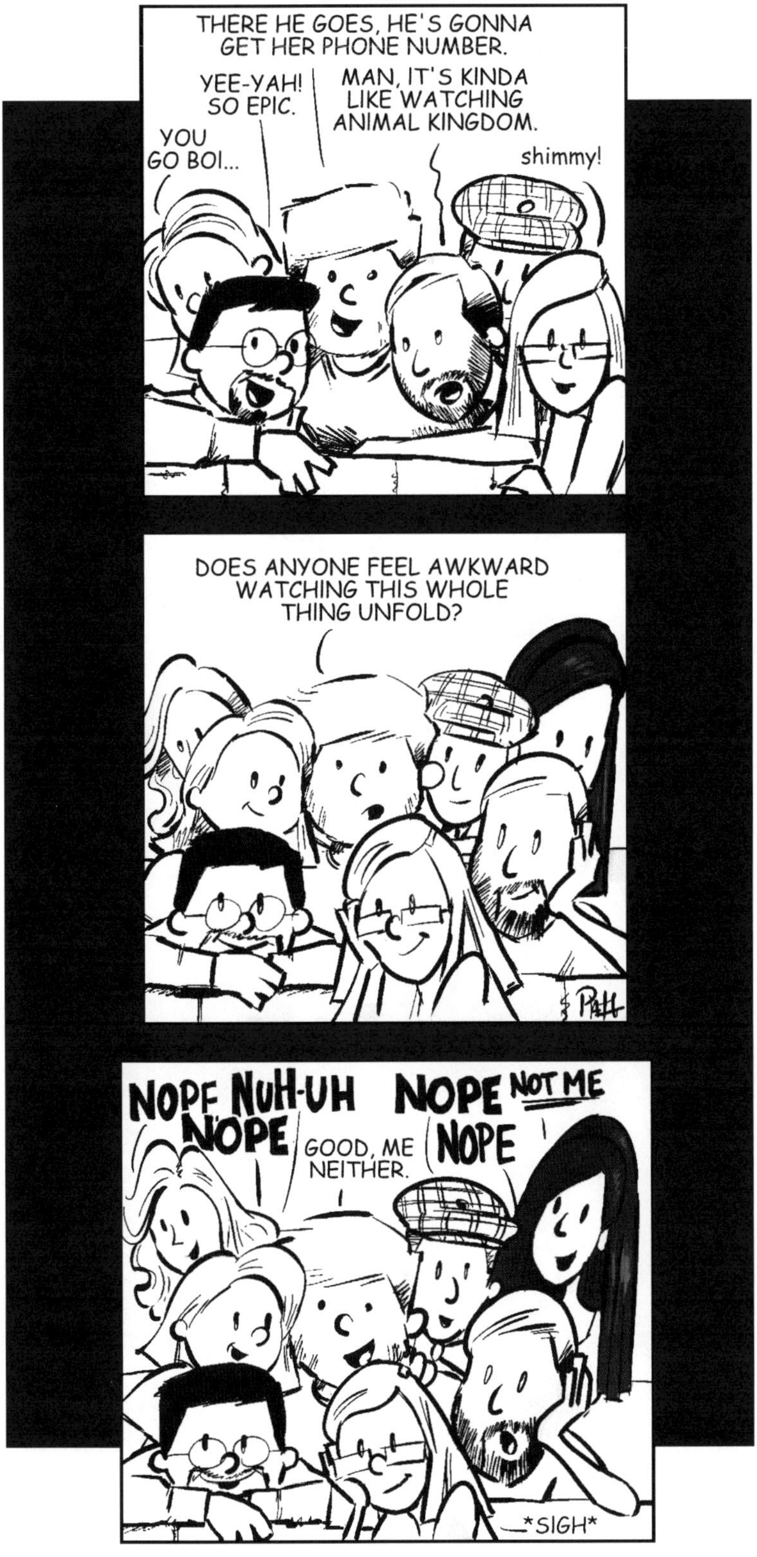
THERE HE GOES, HE'S GONNA GET HER PHONE NUMBER.
YEE-YAH! SO EPIC.
MAN, IT'S KINDA LIKE WATCHING ANIMAL KINGDOM.
YOU GO BOI...
shimmy!
DOES ANYONE FEEL AWKWARD WATCHING THIS WHOLE THING UNFOLD?
NOPE
NUH-UH
NOPE
NOPE
NOT ME
NOPE
GOOD, ME NEITHER.
SIGH

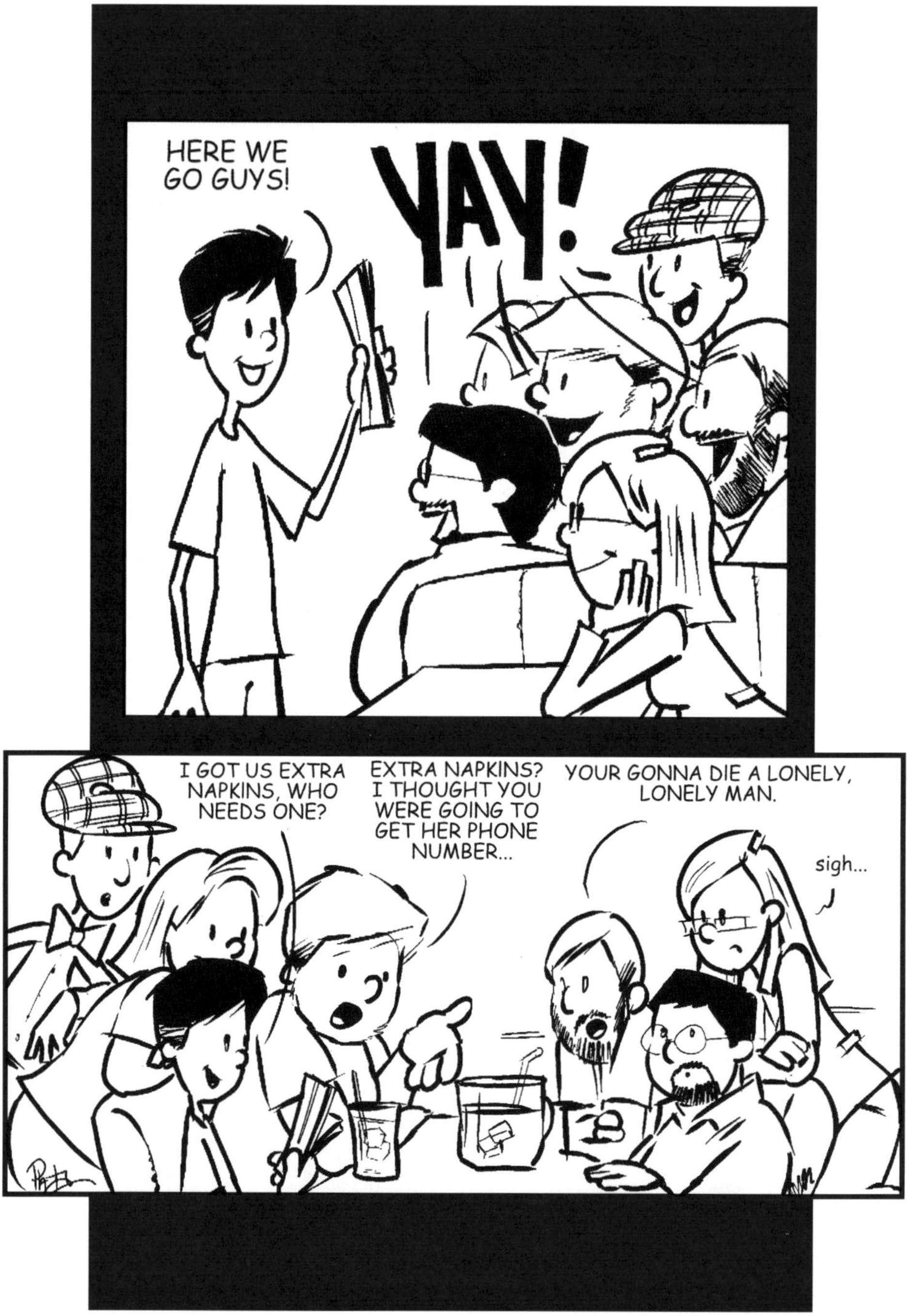
HERE WE GO GUYS!
YAY!
I GOT US EXTRA NAPKINS, WHO NEEDS ONE?
EXTRA NAPKINS? I THOUGHT YOU WERE GOING TO GET HER PHONE NUMBER...
YOUR GONNA DIE A LONELY, LONELY MAN.
sigh...

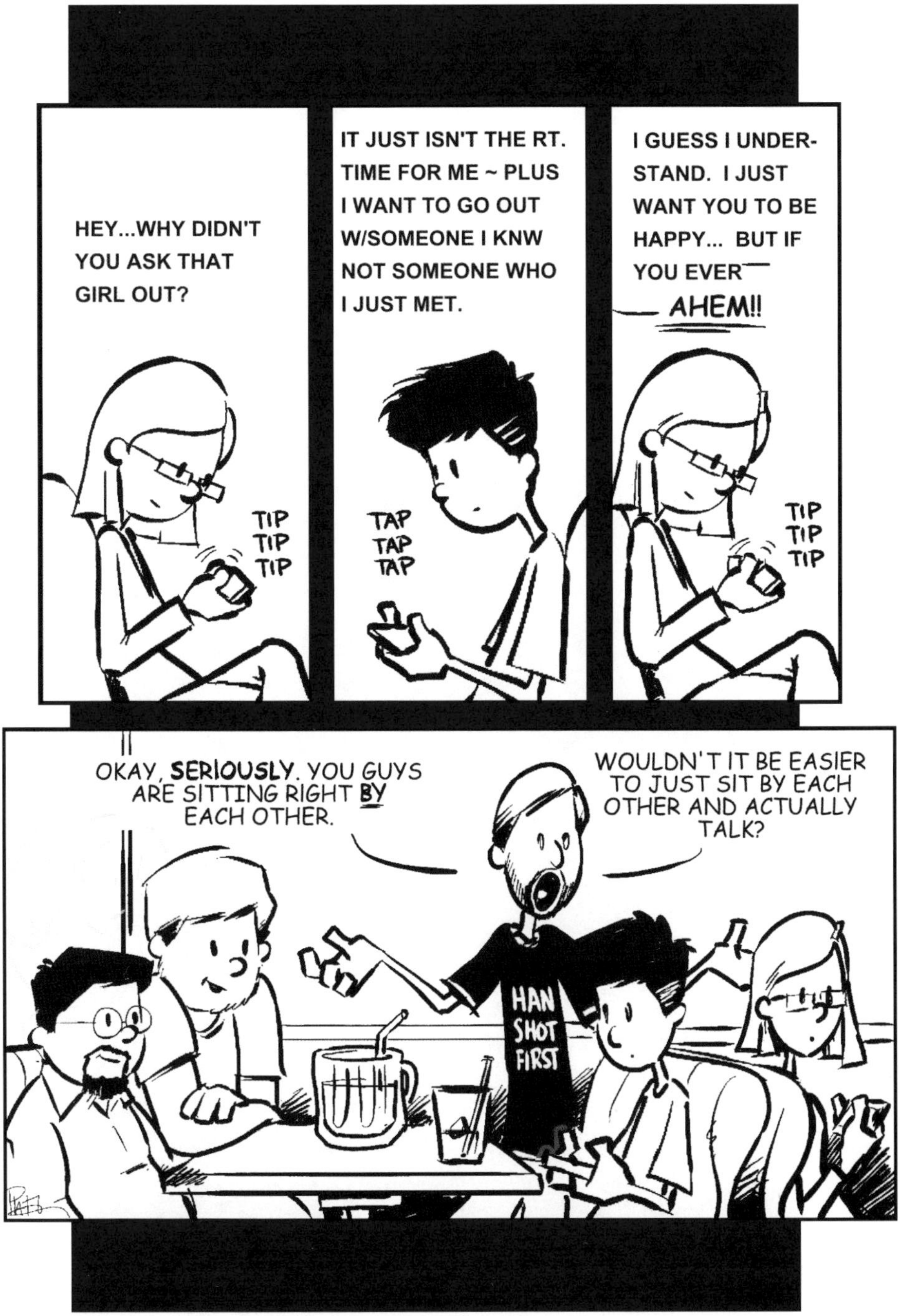
HEY...WHY DIDN'T YOU ASK THAT GIRL OUT?
TIP TIP TIP
IT JUST ISN'T THE RT. TIME FOR ME ~ PLUS I WANT TO GO OUT W/SOMEONE I KNW NOT SOMEONE WHO I JUST MET.
TAP TAP TAP
I GUESS I UNDER-STAND. I JUST WANT YOU TO BE HAPPY... BUT IF YOU EVER—
—AHEM!!
TIP TIP TIP
OKAY, SERIOUSLY. YOU GUYS ARE SITTING RIGHT BY EACH OTHER.
WOULDN'T IT BE EASIER TO JUST SIT BY EACH OTHER AND ACTUALLY TALK?
HAN SHOT FIRST

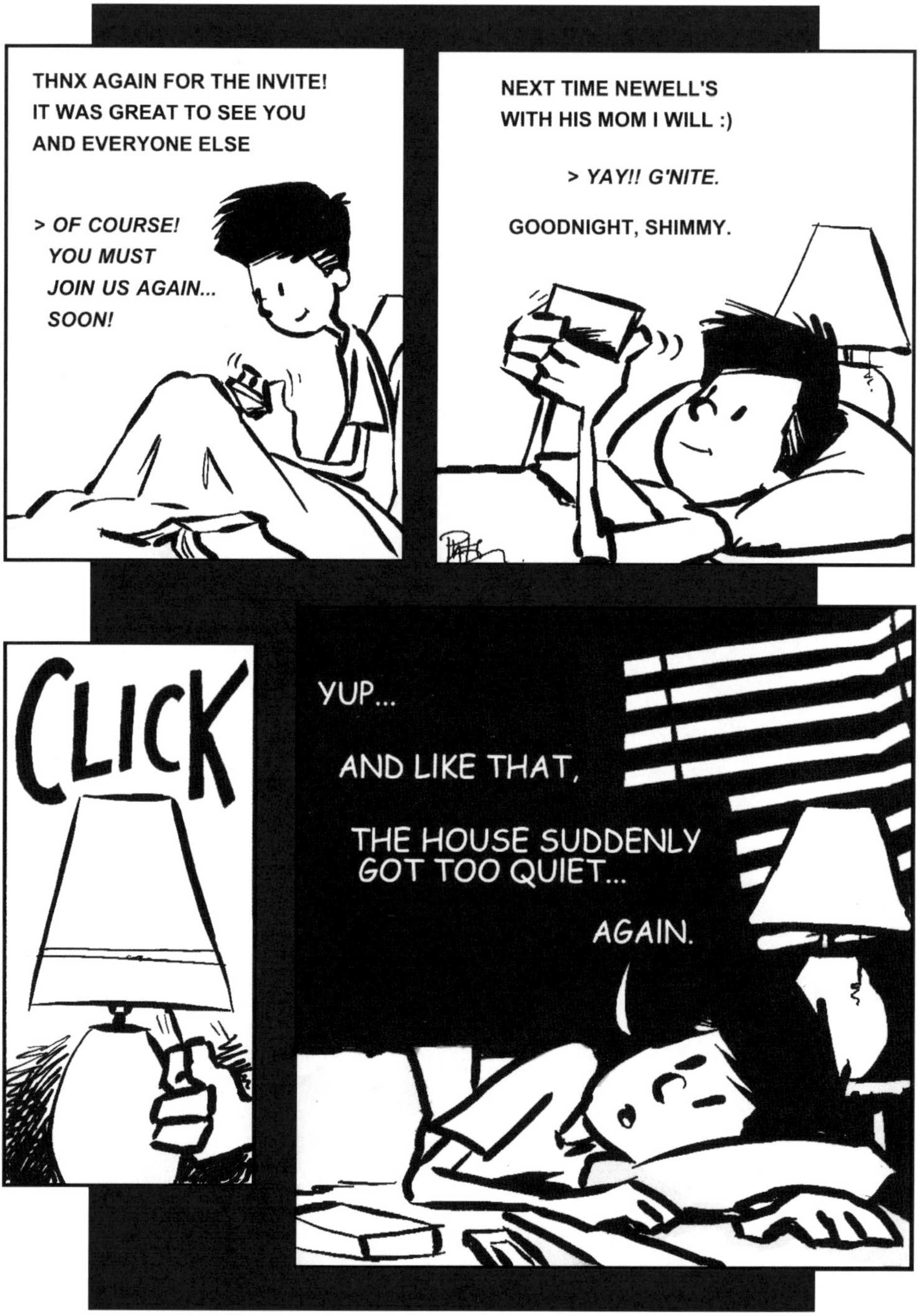
THNX AGAIN FOR THE INVITE! IT WAS GREAT TO SEE YOU AND EVERYONE ELSE
> OF COURSE! YOU MUST JOIN US AGAIN... SOON!
NEXT TIME NEWELL'S WITH HIS MOM I WILL :)
> YAY!! G'NITE.
GOODNIGHT, SHIMMY.
CLICK
YUP...
AND LIKE THAT,
THE HOUSE SUDDENLY GOT TOO QUIET...
AGAIN.

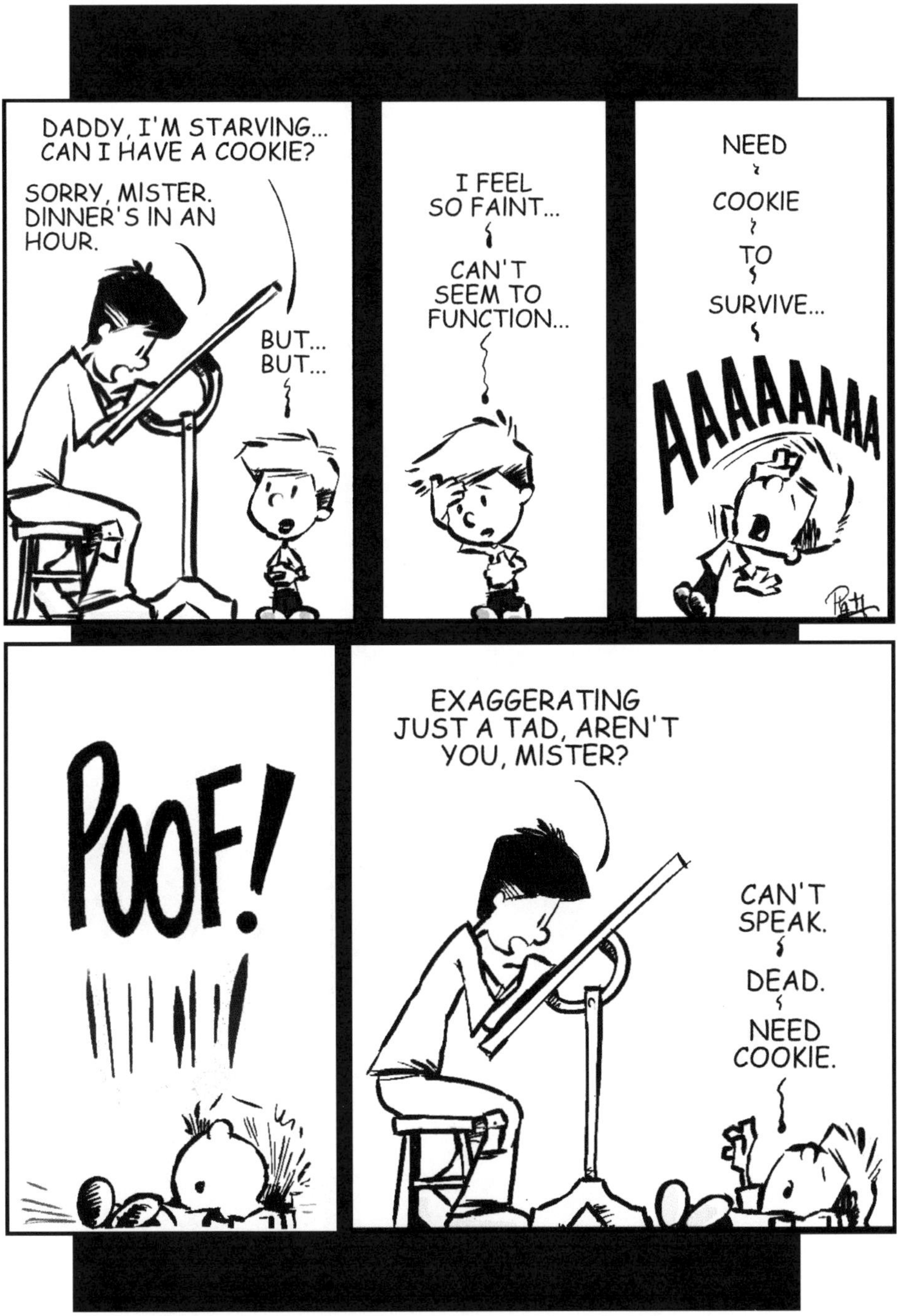
DADDY, I'M STARVING... CAN I HAVE A COOKIE?
SORRY, MISTER. DINNER'S IN AN HOUR.
BUT... BUT...
I FEEL SO FAINT...
CAN'T SEEM TO FUNCTION...
NEED
COOKIE
TO
SURVIVE...
AAAAAAA
POOF!
EXAGGERATING JUST A TAD, AREN'T YOU, MISTER?
CAN'T SPEAK.
DEAD.
NEED COOKIE.

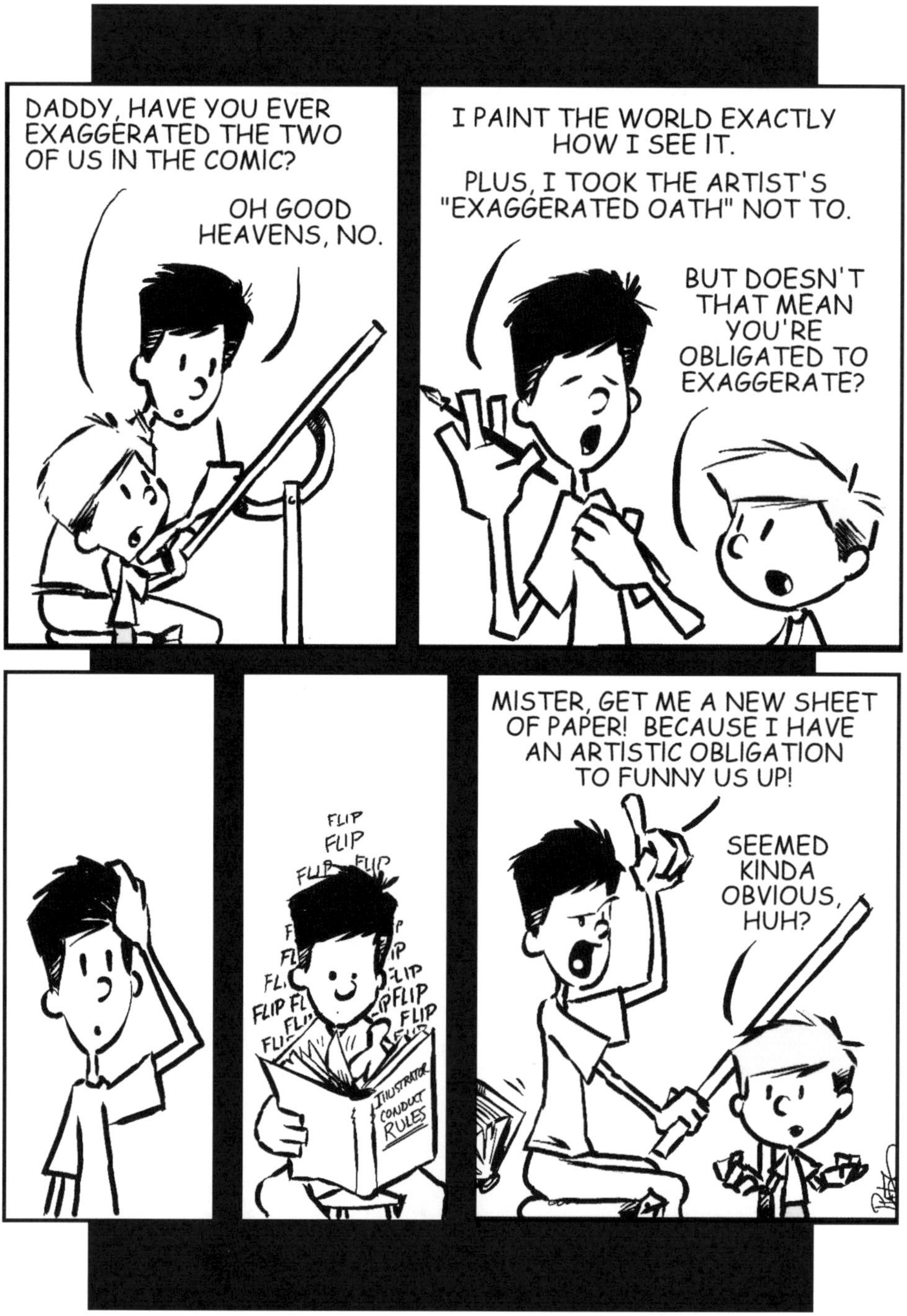
DADDY, HAVE YOU EVER EXAGGERATED THE TWO OF US IN THE COMIC?
OH GOOD HEAVENS, NO.
I PAINT THE WORLD EXACTLY HOW I SEE IT.
PLUS, I TOOK THE ARTIST'S "EXAGGERATED OATH" NOT TO.
BUT DOESN'T THAT MEAN YOU'RE OBLIGATED TO EXAGGERATE?
FLIP
FLIP
FLIP
FLIP
ILLUSTRATOR CONDUCT RULES
MISTER, GET ME A NEW SHEET OF PAPER! BECAUSE I HAVE AN ARTISTIC OBLIGATION TO FUNNY US UP!
SEEMED KINDA OBVIOUS, HUH?

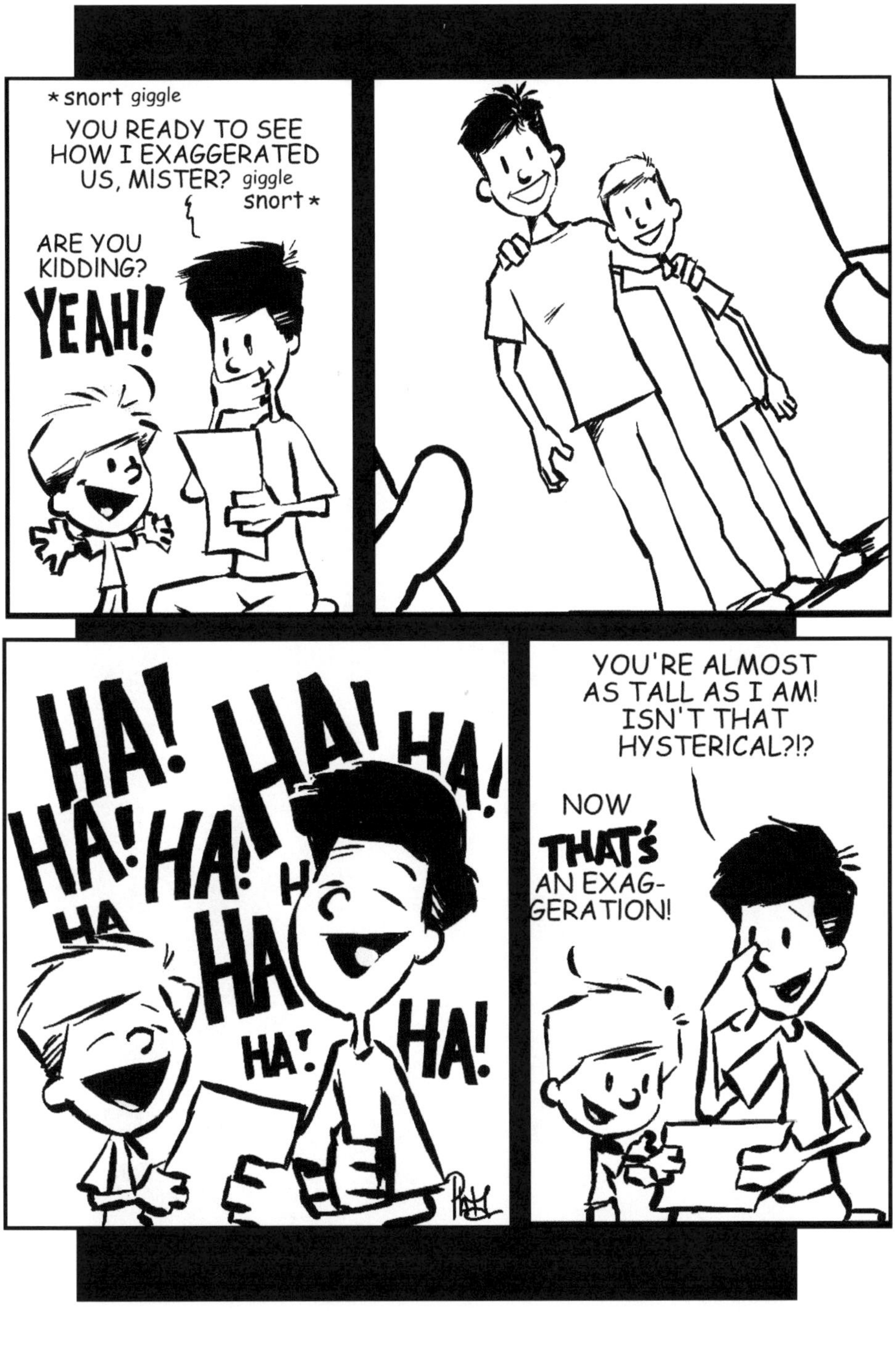
*snort giggle
YOU READY TO SEE HOW I EXAGGERATED US, MISTER? giggle snort*
ARE YOU KIDDING? YEAH!
HA! HA! HA! HA! HA! HA! H HA HA HA! HA!
YOU'RE ALMOST AS TALL AS I AM! ISN'T THAT HYSTERICAL?!?
NOW THAT'S AN EXAG-GERATION!

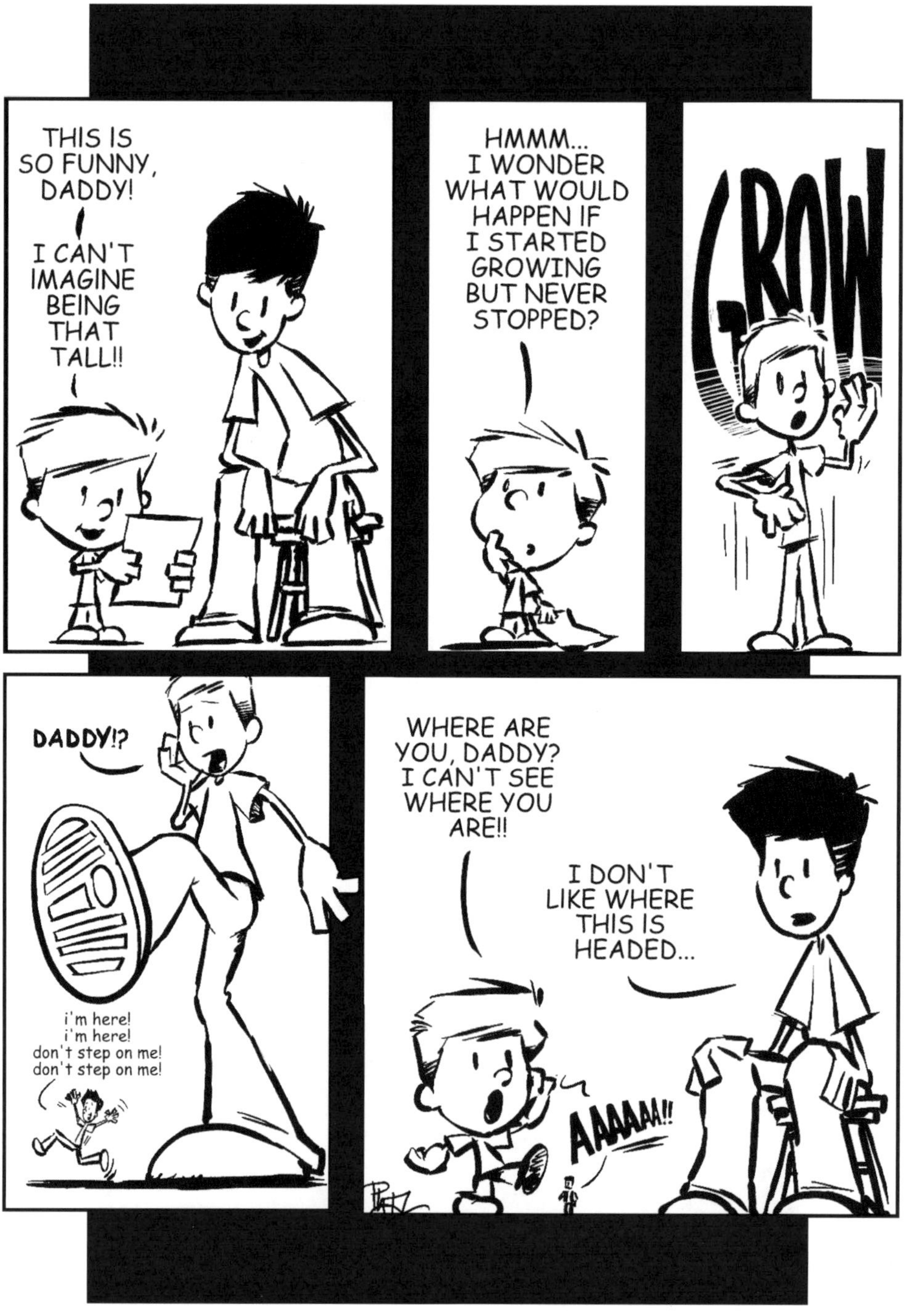
THIS IS SO FUNNY, DADDY!
I CAN'T IMAGINE BEING THAT TALL!!
HMMM... I WONDER WHAT WOULD HAPPEN IF I STARTED GROWING BUT NEVER STOPPED?
GROW
DADDY!?
i'm here! i'm here! don't step on me! don't step on me!
WHERE ARE YOU, DADDY? I CAN'T SEE WHERE YOU ARE!!
I DON'T LIKE WHERE THIS IS HEADED...
AAAAAA!!

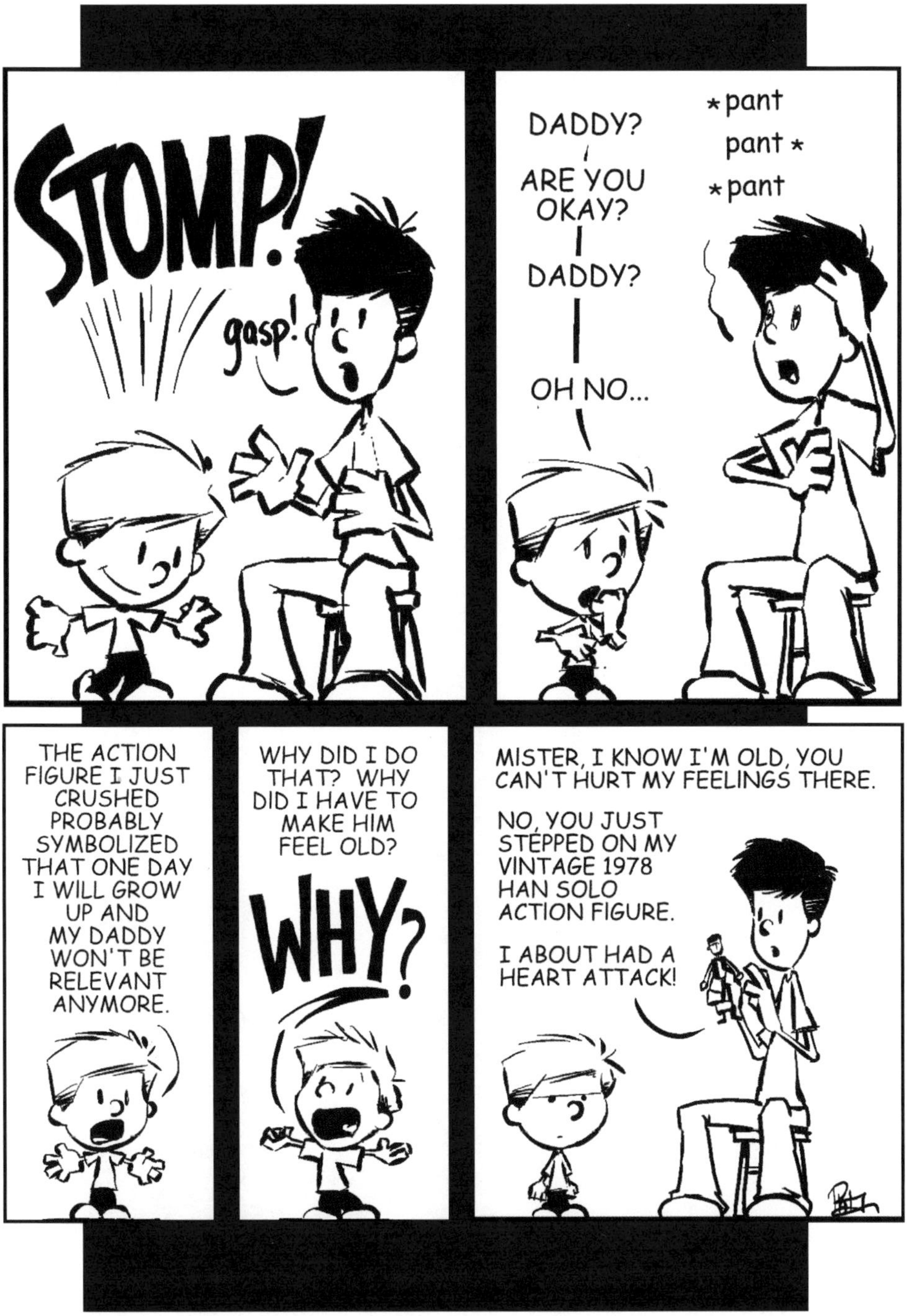
STOMP!
gasp!
DADDY?
ARE YOU OKAY?
DADDY?
OH NO...
*pant
pant*
*pant
THE ACTION FIGURE I JUST CRUSHED PROBABLY SYMBOLIZED THAT ONE DAY I WILL GROW UP AND MY DADDY WON'T BE RELEVANT ANYMORE.
WHY DID I DO THAT? WHY DID I HAVE TO MAKE HIM FEEL OLD?
WHY?
MISTER, I KNOW I'M OLD, YOU CAN'T HURT MY FEELINGS THERE.
NO, YOU JUST STEPPED ON MY VINTAGE 1978 HAN SOLO ACTION FIGURE.
I ABOUT HAD A HEART ATTACK!

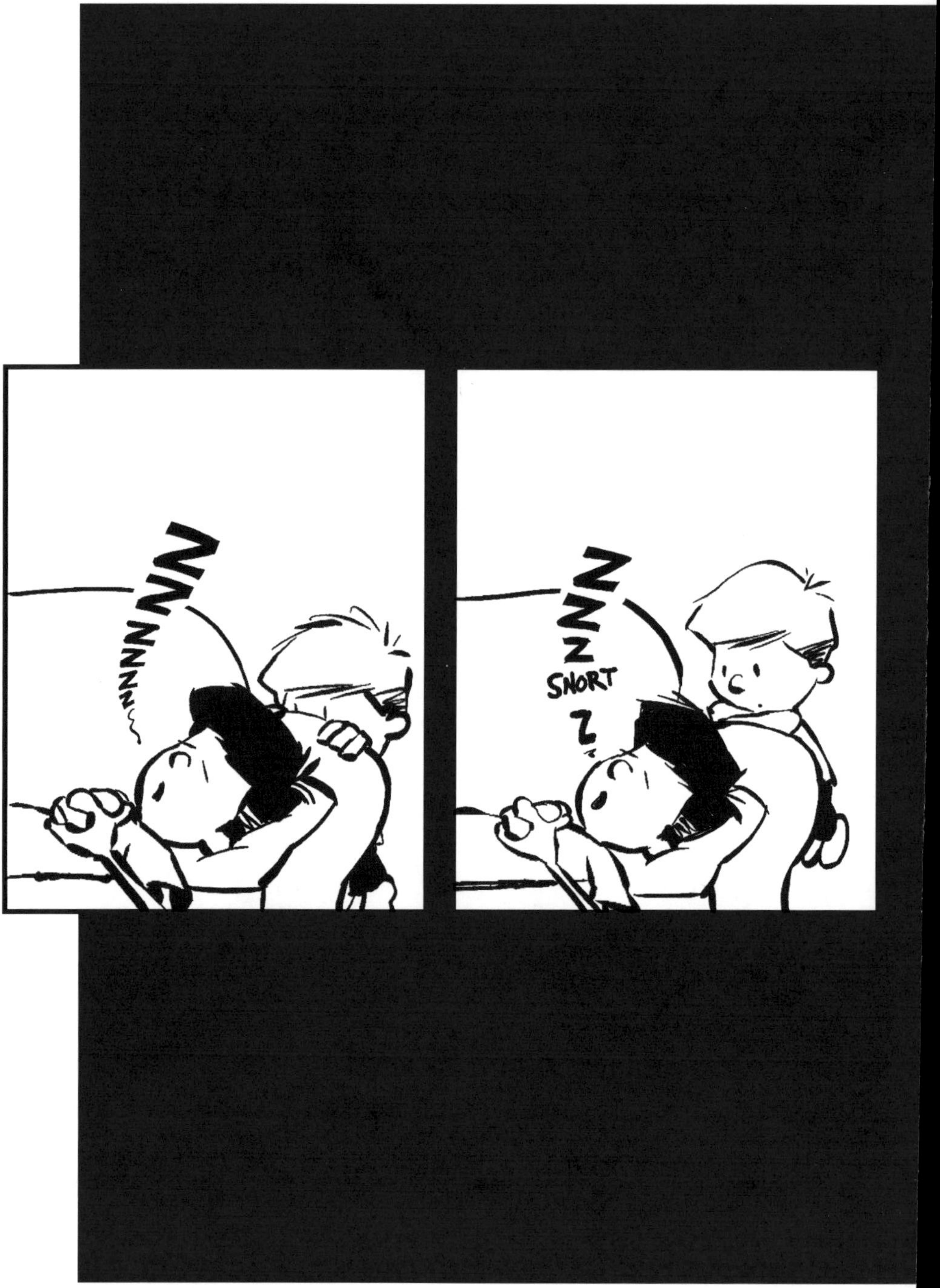
Z
Z
Z
SNORT
Z

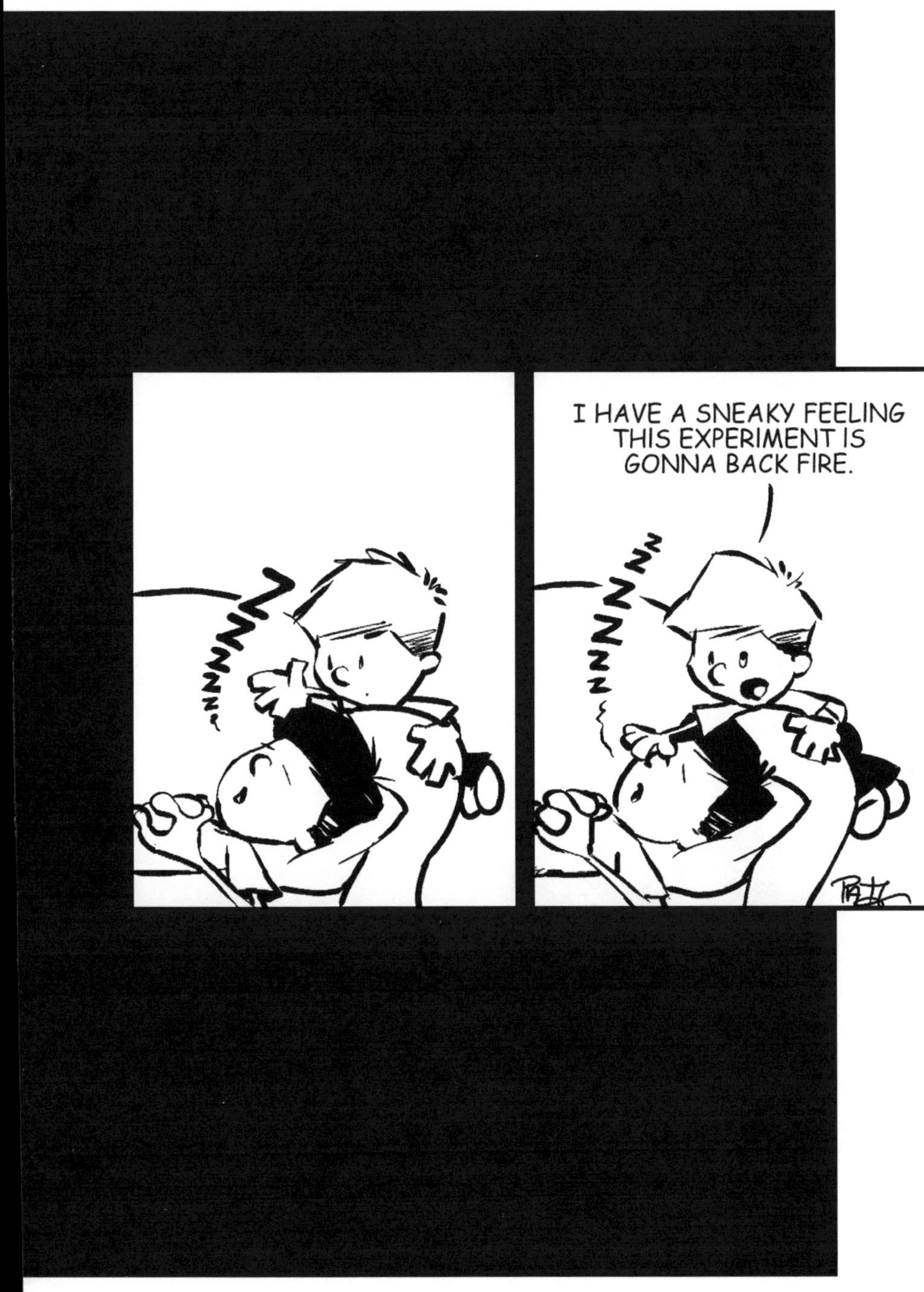
I HAVE A SNEAKY FEELING THIS EXPERIMENT IS GONNA BACK FIRE.

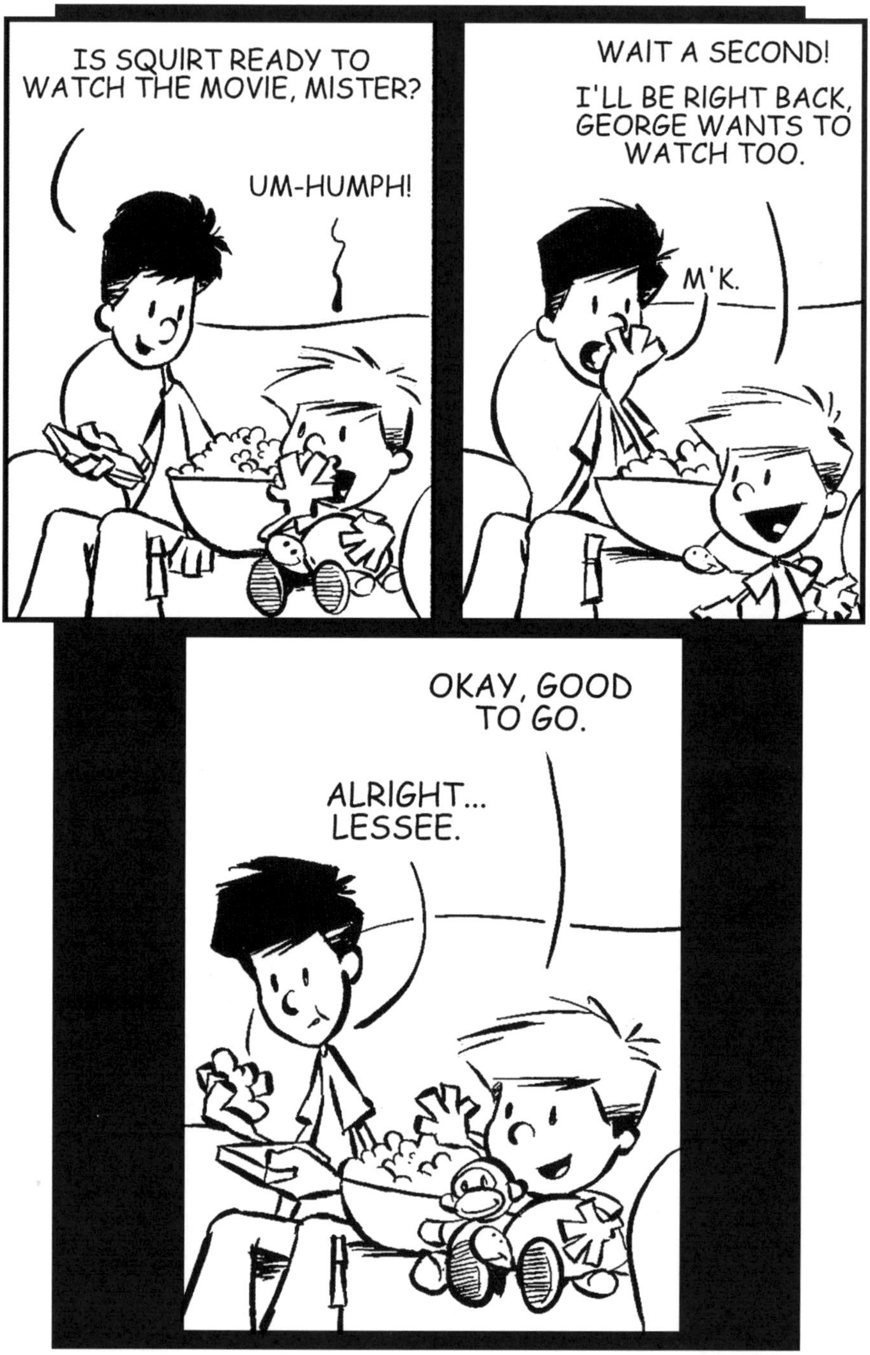
IS SQUIRT READY TO WATCH THE MOVIE, MISTER?
UM-HUMPH!
WAIT A SECOND!
I'LL BE RIGHT BACK, GEORGE WANTS TO WATCH TOO.
M'K.
OKAY, GOOD TO GO.
ALRIGHT... LESSEE.

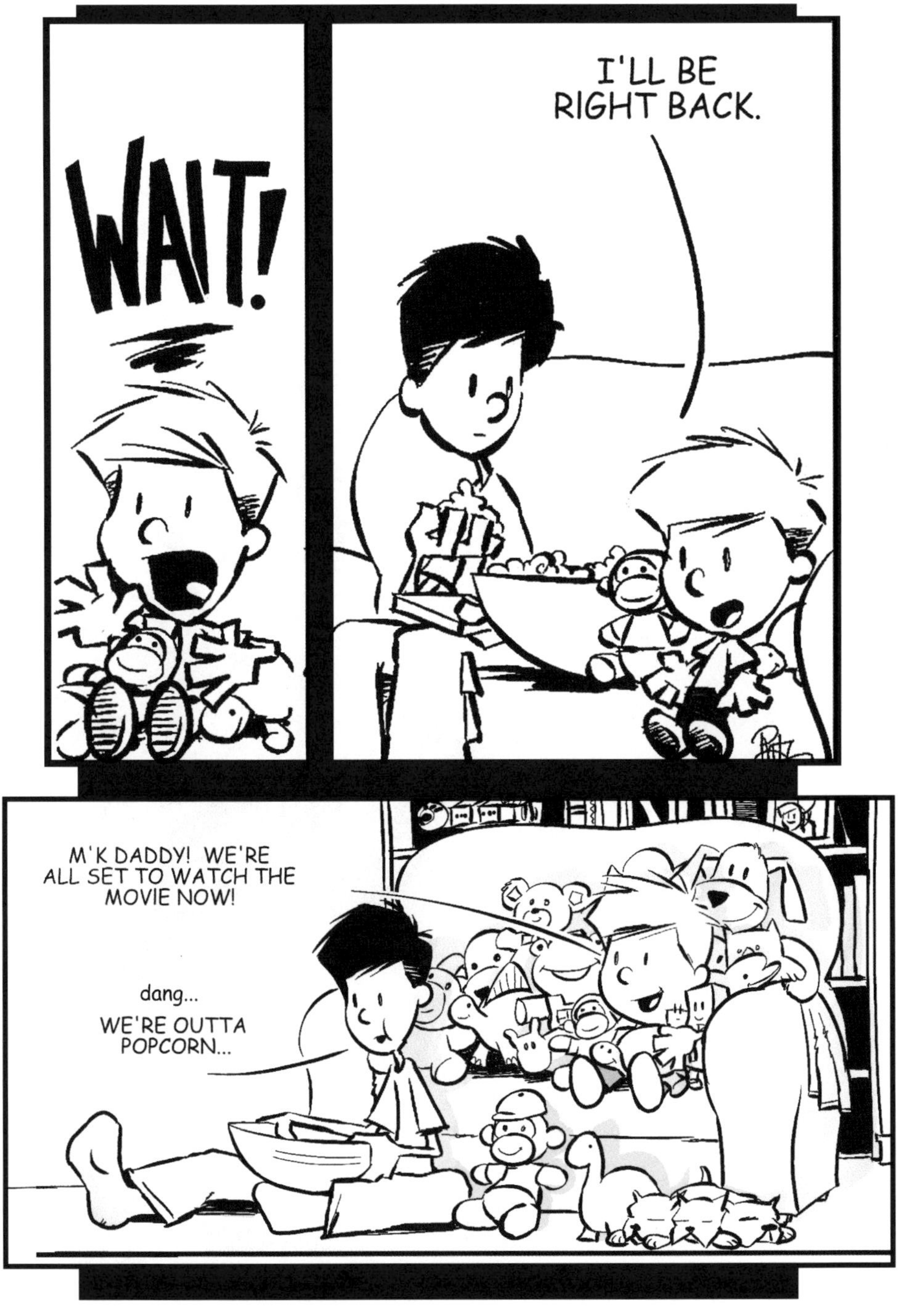
WAIT!
I'LL BE RIGHT BACK.
M'K DADDY! WE'RE ALL SET TO WATCH THE MOVIE NOW!
dang...
WE'RE OUTTA POPCORN...

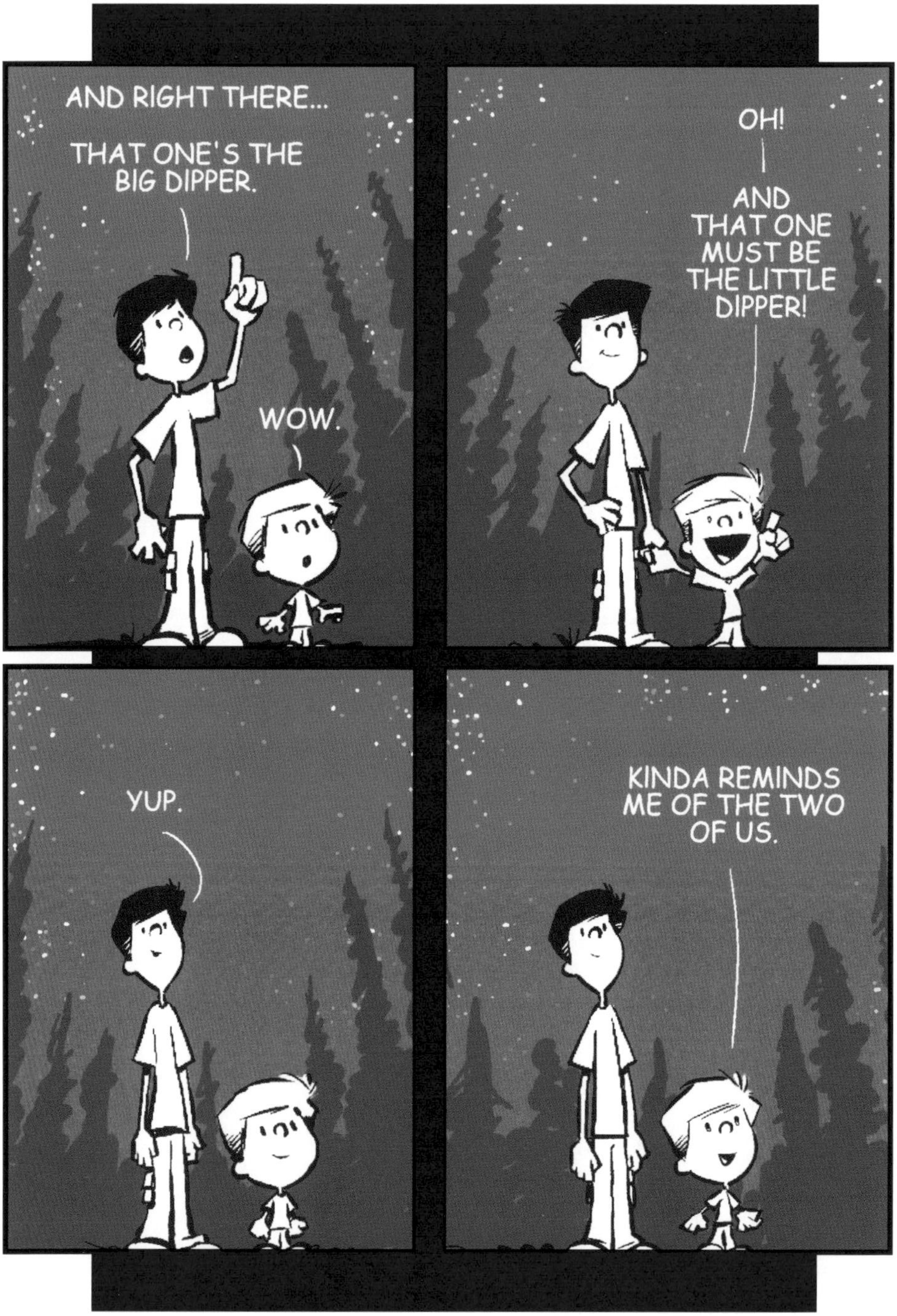
AND RIGHT THERE...
THAT ONE'S THE BIG DIPPER.
WOW.
OH!
AND THAT ONE MUST BE THE LITTLE DIPPER!
YUP.
KINDA REMINDS ME OF THE TWO OF US.

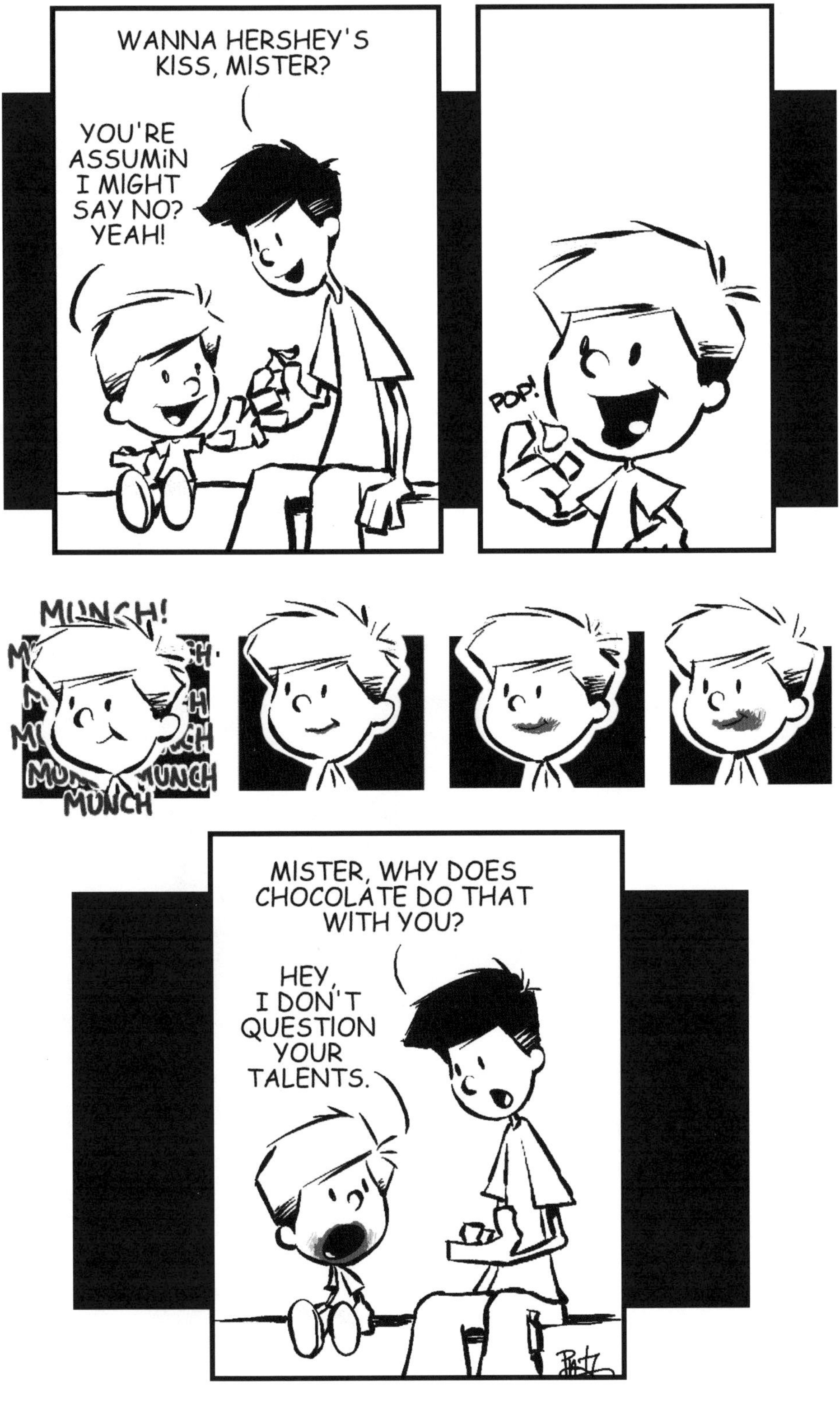

WANNA HERSHEY'S KISS, MISTER?
YOU'RE ASSUMiN I MIGHT SAY NO? YEAH!
POP!
MUNCH!
MUNCH
MUNCH
MISTER, WHY DOES CHOCOLATE DO THAT WITH YOU?
HEY, I DON'T QUESTION YOUR TALENTS.

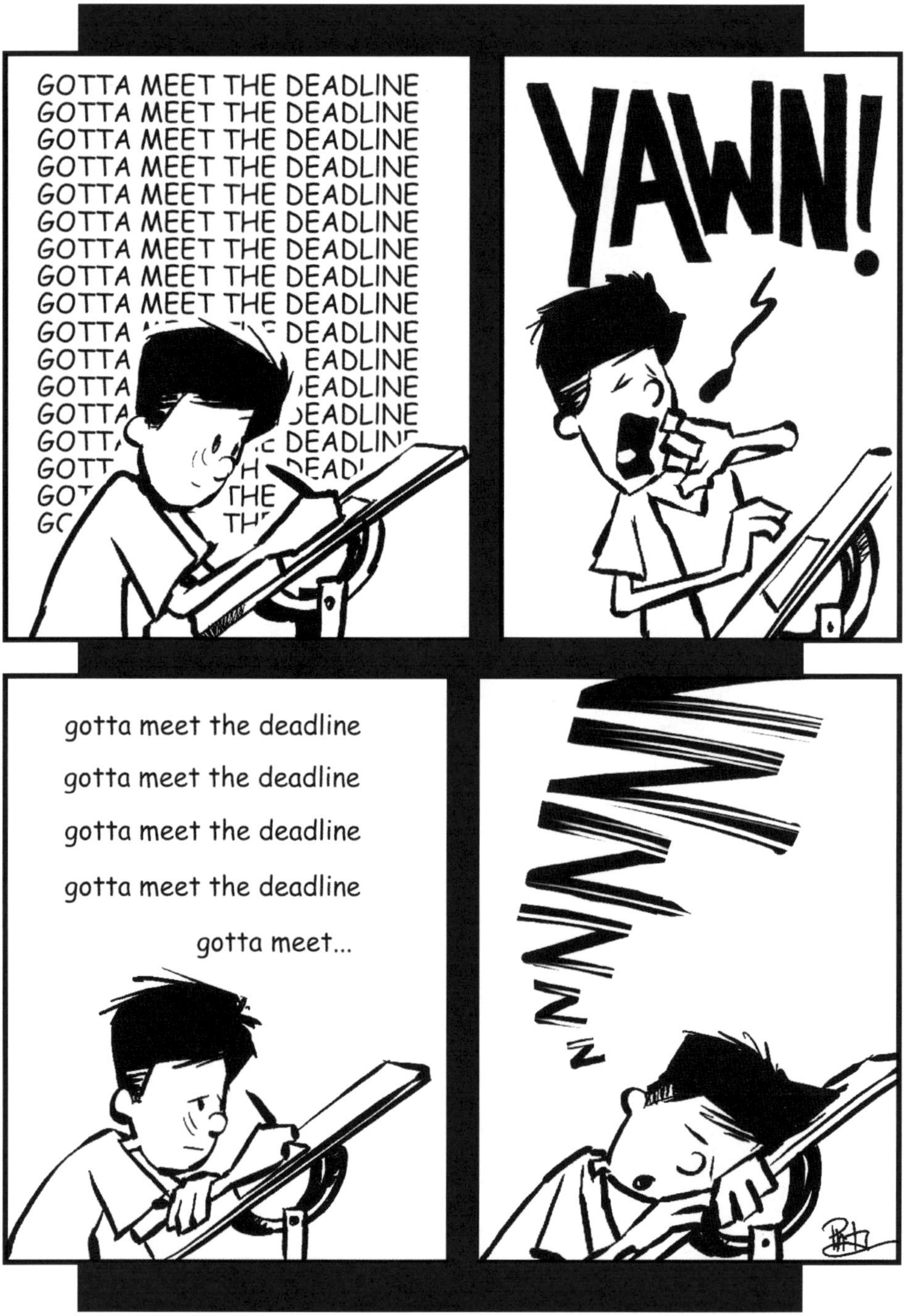
GOTTA MEET THE DEADLINE
GOTTA MEET THE DEADLINE
GOTTA MEET THE DEADLINE
GOTTA MEET THE DEADLINE
GOTTA MEET THE DEADLINE
GOTTA MEET THE DEADLINE
GOTTA MEET THE DEADLINE
GOTTA MEET THE DEADLINE
GOTTA MEET THE DEADLINE
YAWN!
gotta meet the deadline
gotta meet the deadline
gotta meet the deadline
gotta meet the deadline
gotta meet...

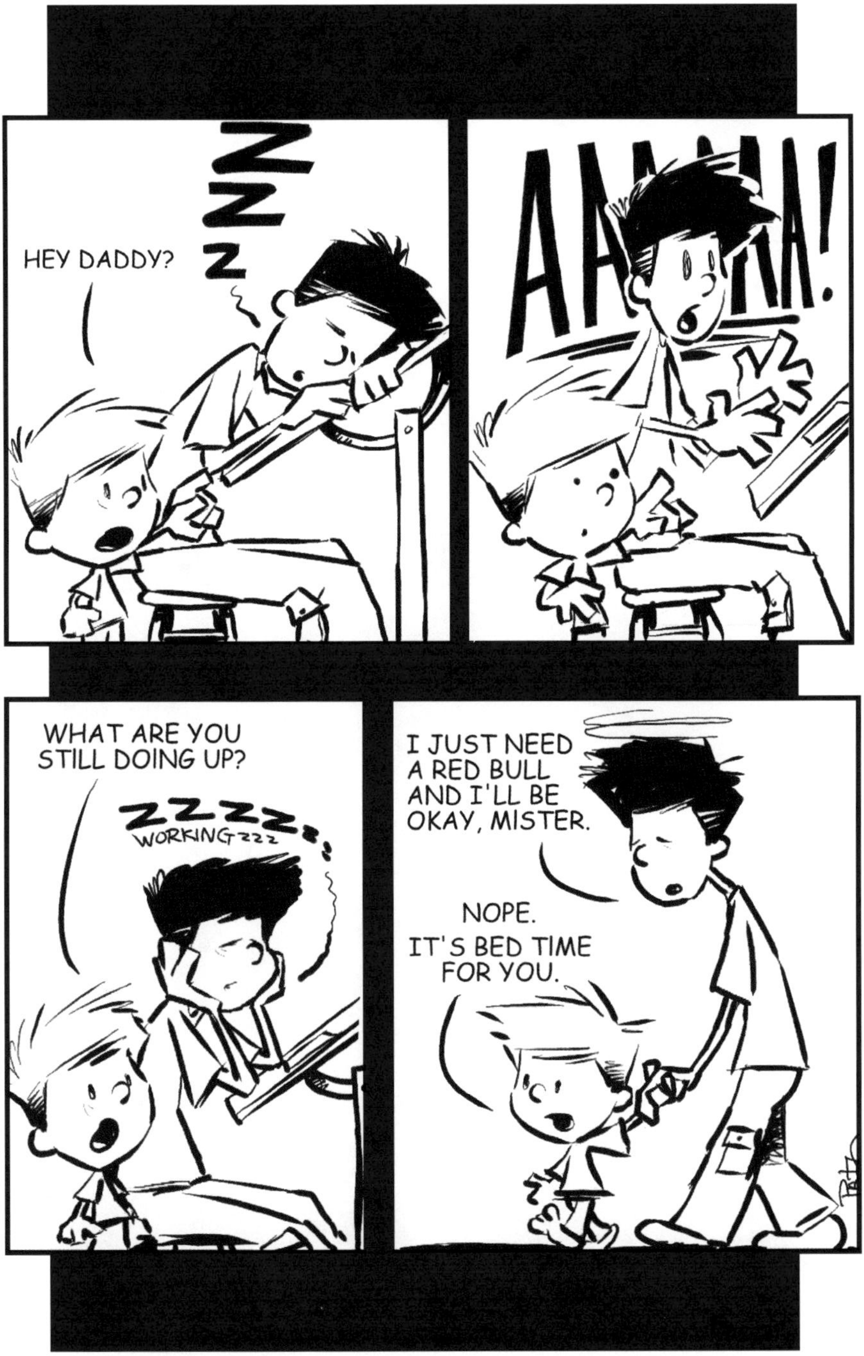
HEY DADDY?
ZZZ
AAAAA!
WHAT ARE YOU STILL DOING UP?
ZZZZZ WORKING ZZZ
I JUST NEED A RED BULL AND I'LL BE OKAY, MISTER.
NOPE. IT'S BED TIME FOR YOU.

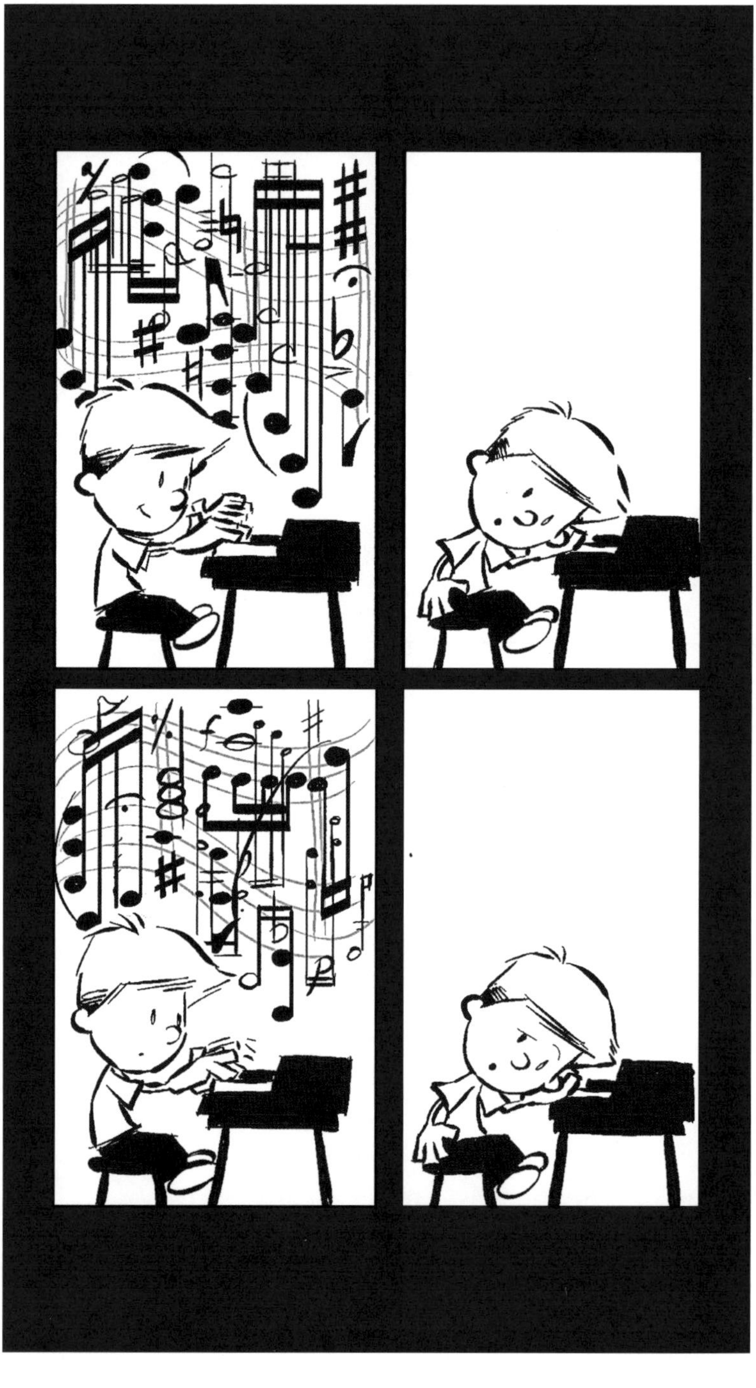

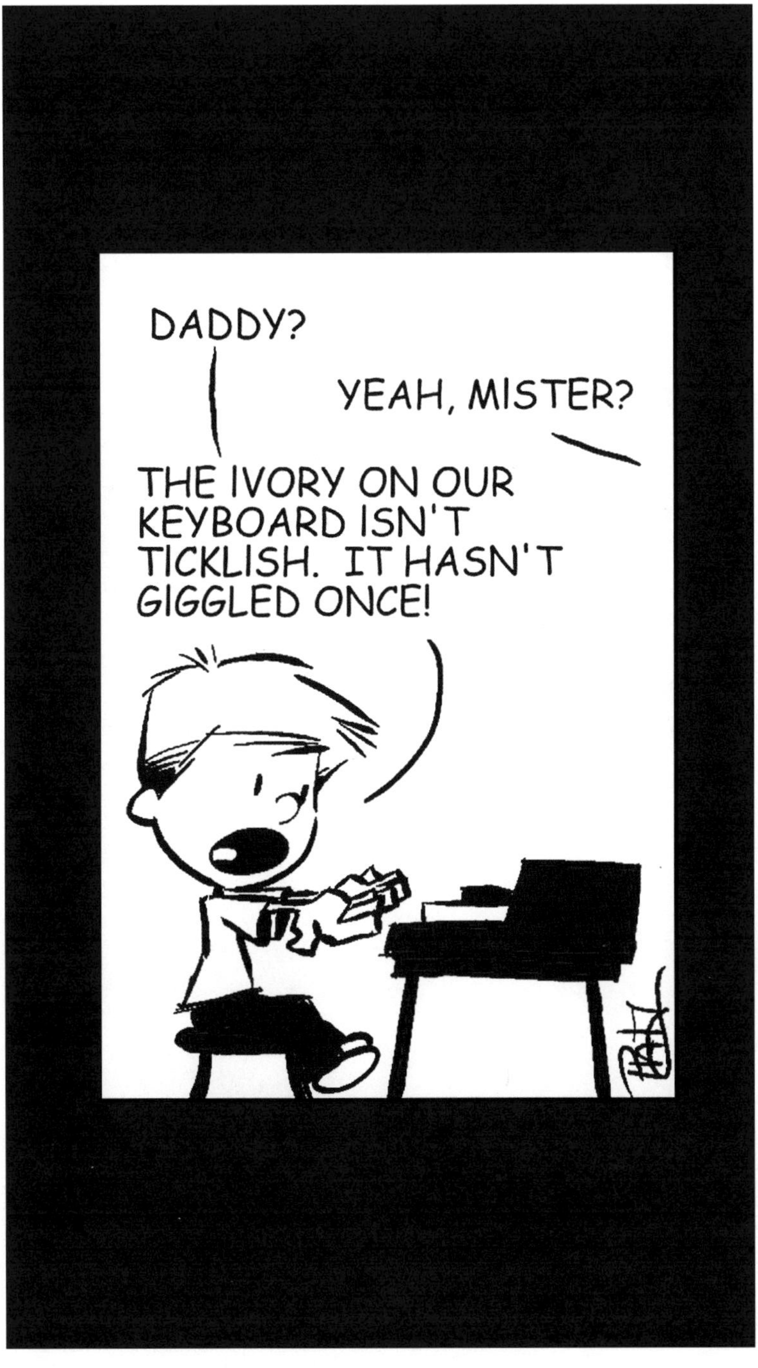
DADDY?
YEAH, MISTER?
THE IVORY ON OUR KEYBOARD ISN'T TICKLISH. IT HASN'T GIGGLED ONCE!

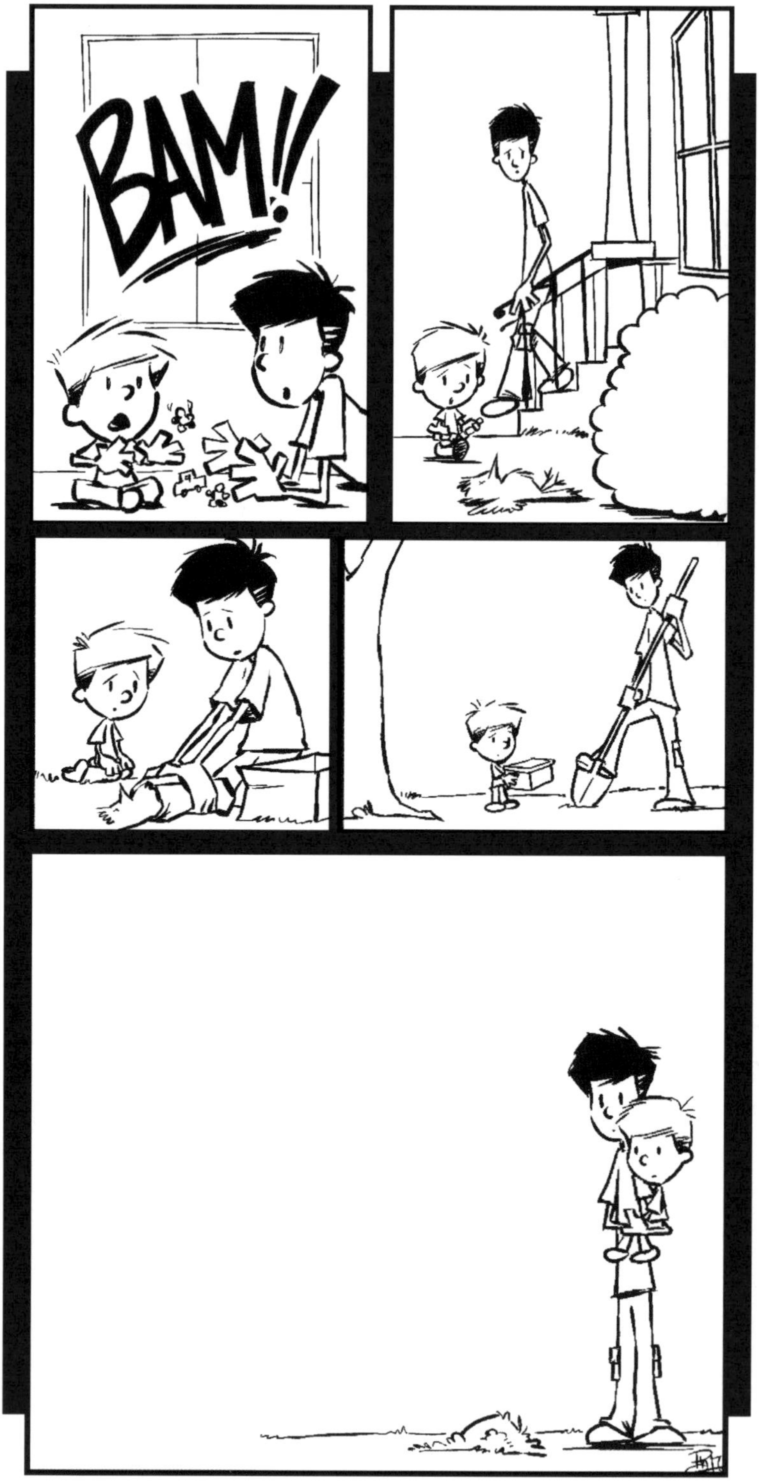
BAM!!

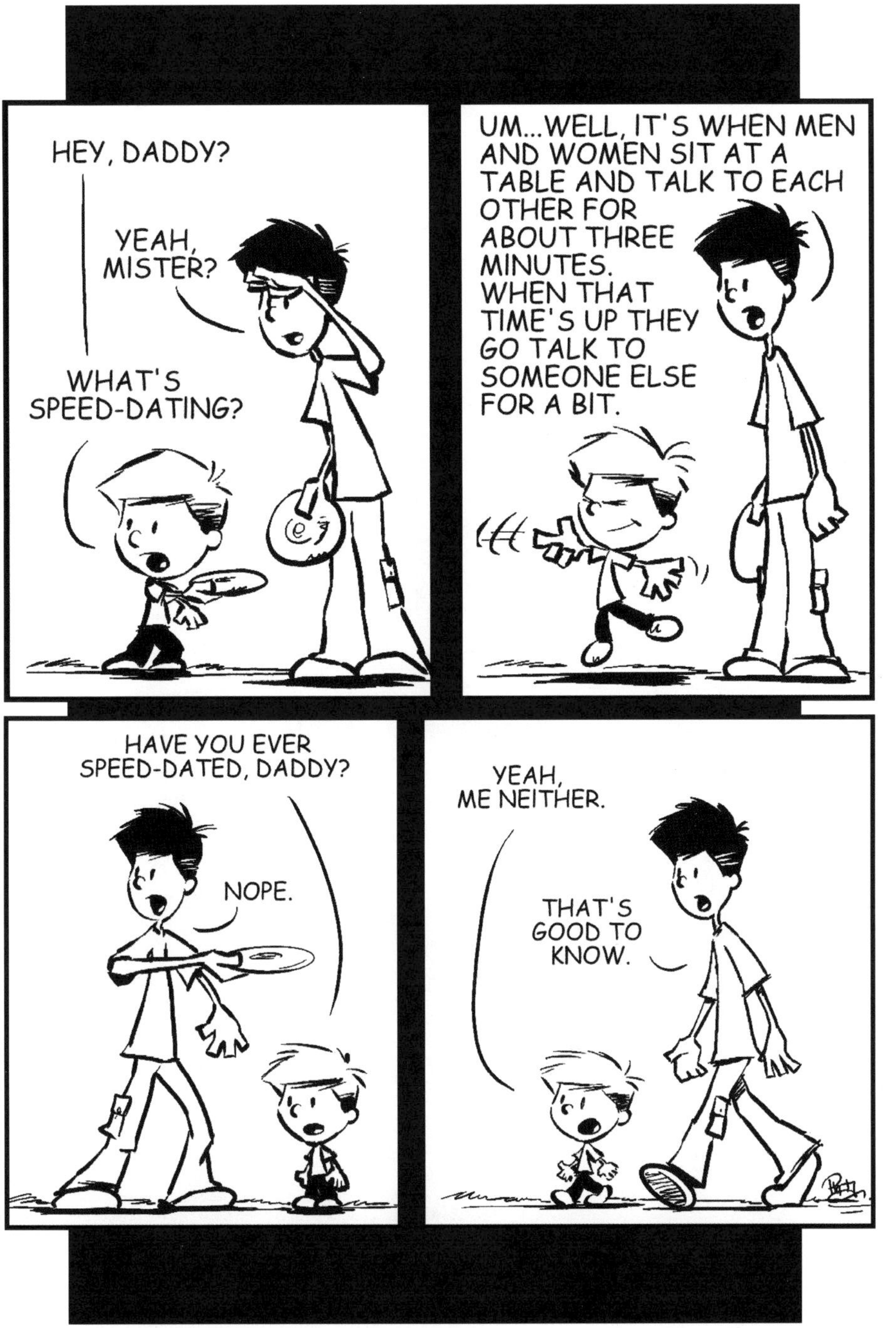
HEY, DADDY?
YEAH, MISTER?
WHAT'S SPEED-DATING?
UM...WELL, IT'S WHEN MEN AND WOMEN SIT AT A TABLE AND TALK TO EACH OTHER FOR ABOUT THREE MINUTES. WHEN THAT TIME'S UP THEY GO TALK TO SOMEONE ELSE FOR A BIT.
HAVE YOU EVER SPEED-DATED, DADDY?
NOPE.
YEAH, ME NEITHER.
THAT'S GOOD TO KNOW.

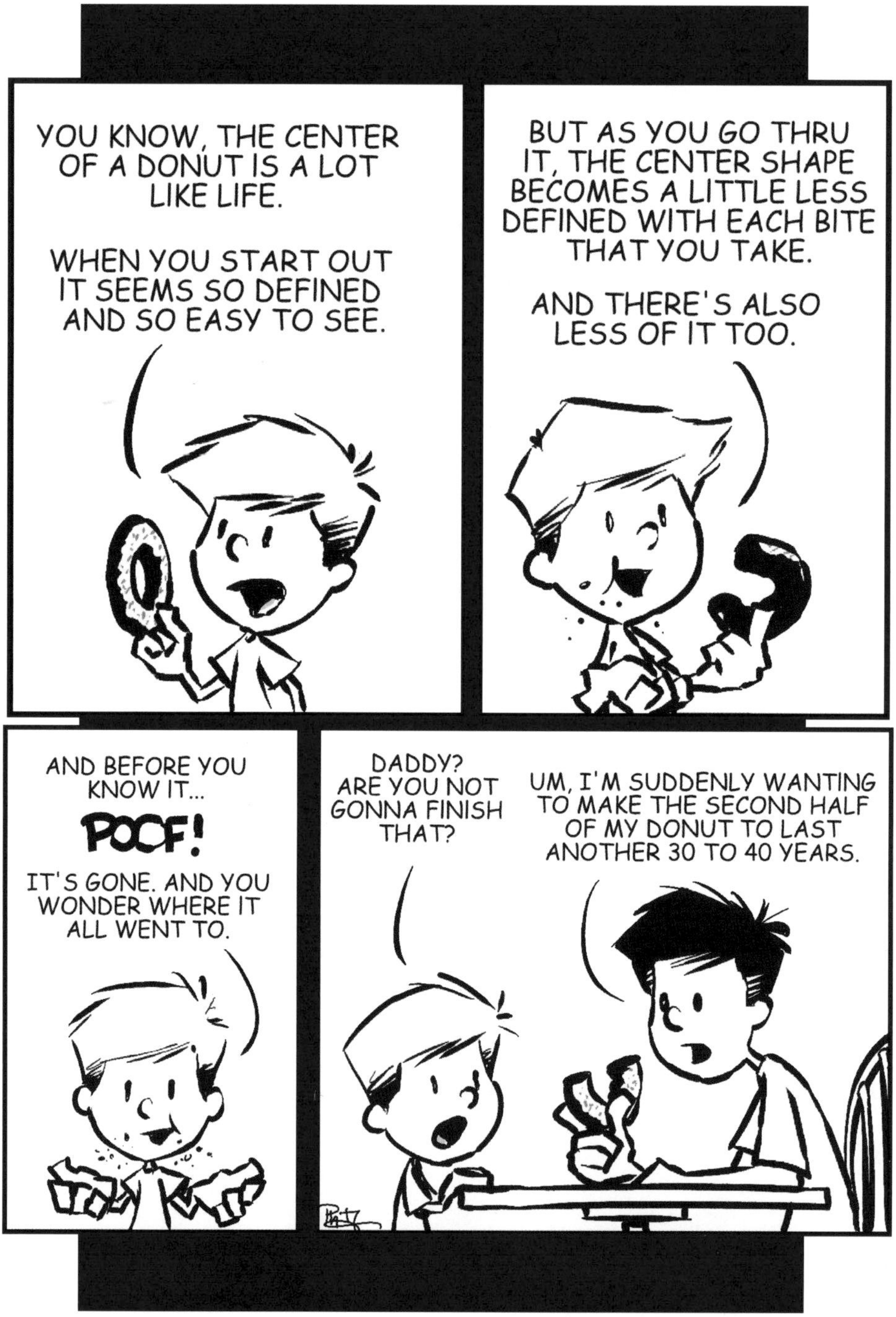
YOU KNOW, THE CENTER OF A DONUT IS A LOT LIKE LIFE.
WHEN YOU START OUT IT SEEMS SO DEFINED AND SO EASY TO SEE.
BUT AS YOU GO THRU IT, THE CENTER SHAPE BECOMES A LITTLE LESS DEFINED WITH EACH BITE THAT YOU TAKE.
AND THERE'S ALSO LESS OF IT TOO.
AND BEFORE YOU KNOW IT...
POOF!
IT'S GONE. AND YOU WONDER WHERE IT ALL WENT TO.
DADDY? ARE YOU NOT GONNA FINISH THAT?
UM, I'M SUDDENLY WANTING TO MAKE THE SECOND HALF OF MY DONUT TO LAST ANOTHER 30 TO 40 YEARS.

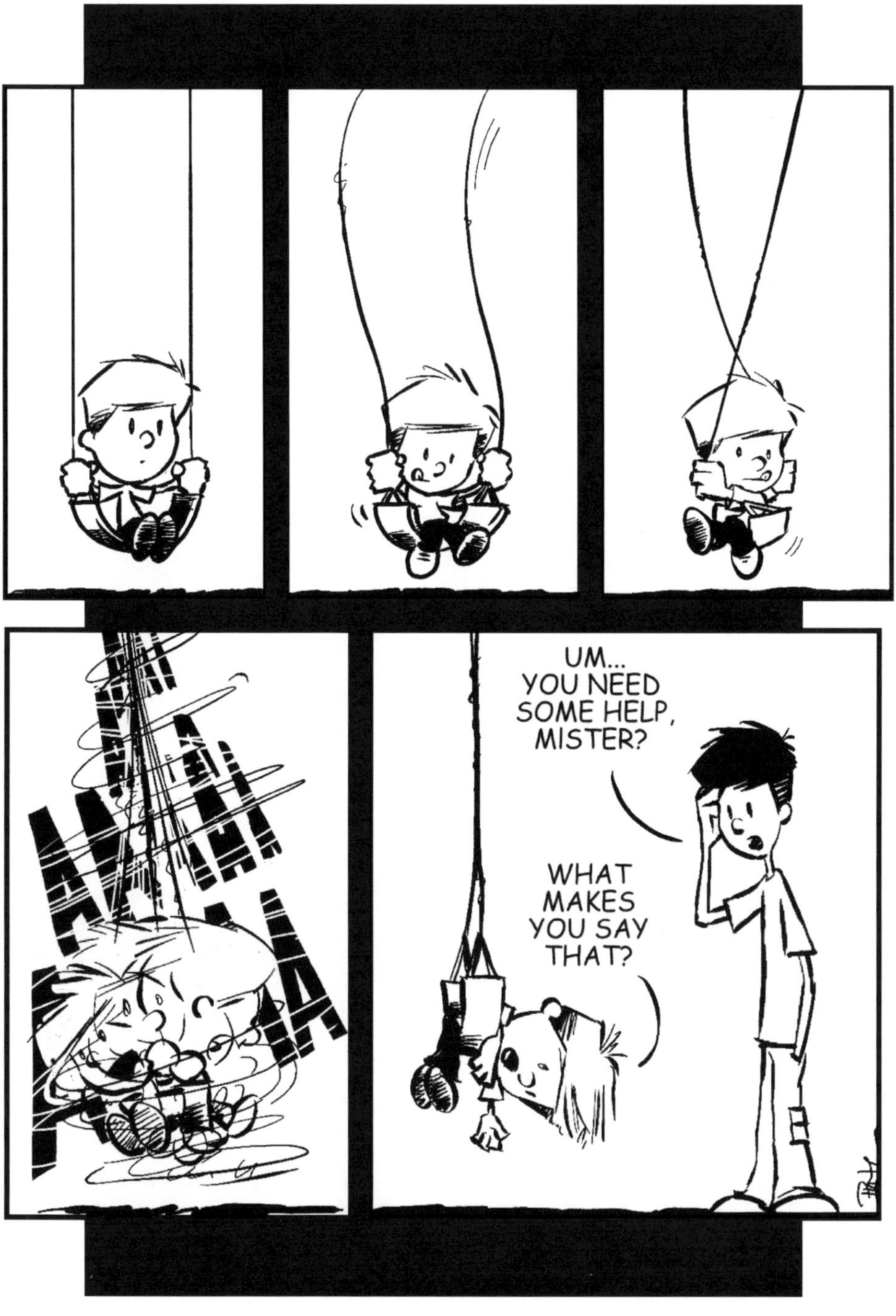
UM...
YOU NEED
SOME HELP,
MISTER?
WHAT
MAKES
YOU SAY
THAT?

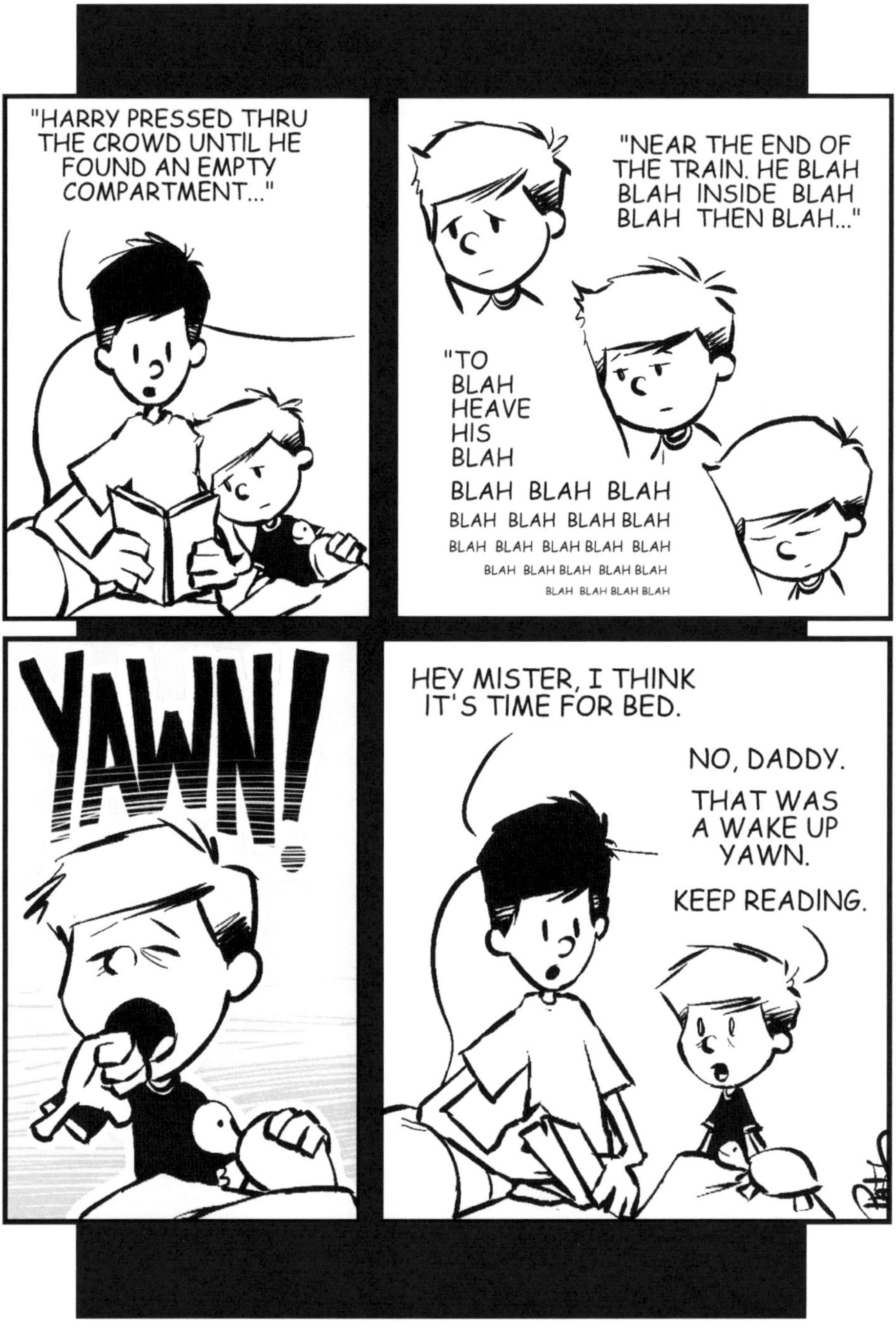
"HARRY PRESSED THRU THE CROWD UNTIL HE FOUND AN EMPTY COMPARTMENT..."
"NEAR THE END OF THE TRAIN. HE BLAH BLAH INSIDE BLAH BLAH THEN BLAH..."
"TO BLAH HEAVE HIS BLAH
BLAH BLAH BLAH
BLAH BLAH BLAH BLAH
BLAH BLAH BLAH BLAH BLAH
BLAH BLAH BLAH BLAH BLAH
BLAH BLAH BLAH BLAH
YAWN!
HEY MISTER, I THINK IT'S TIME FOR BED.
NO, DADDY.
THAT WAS A WAKE UP YAWN.
KEEP READING.

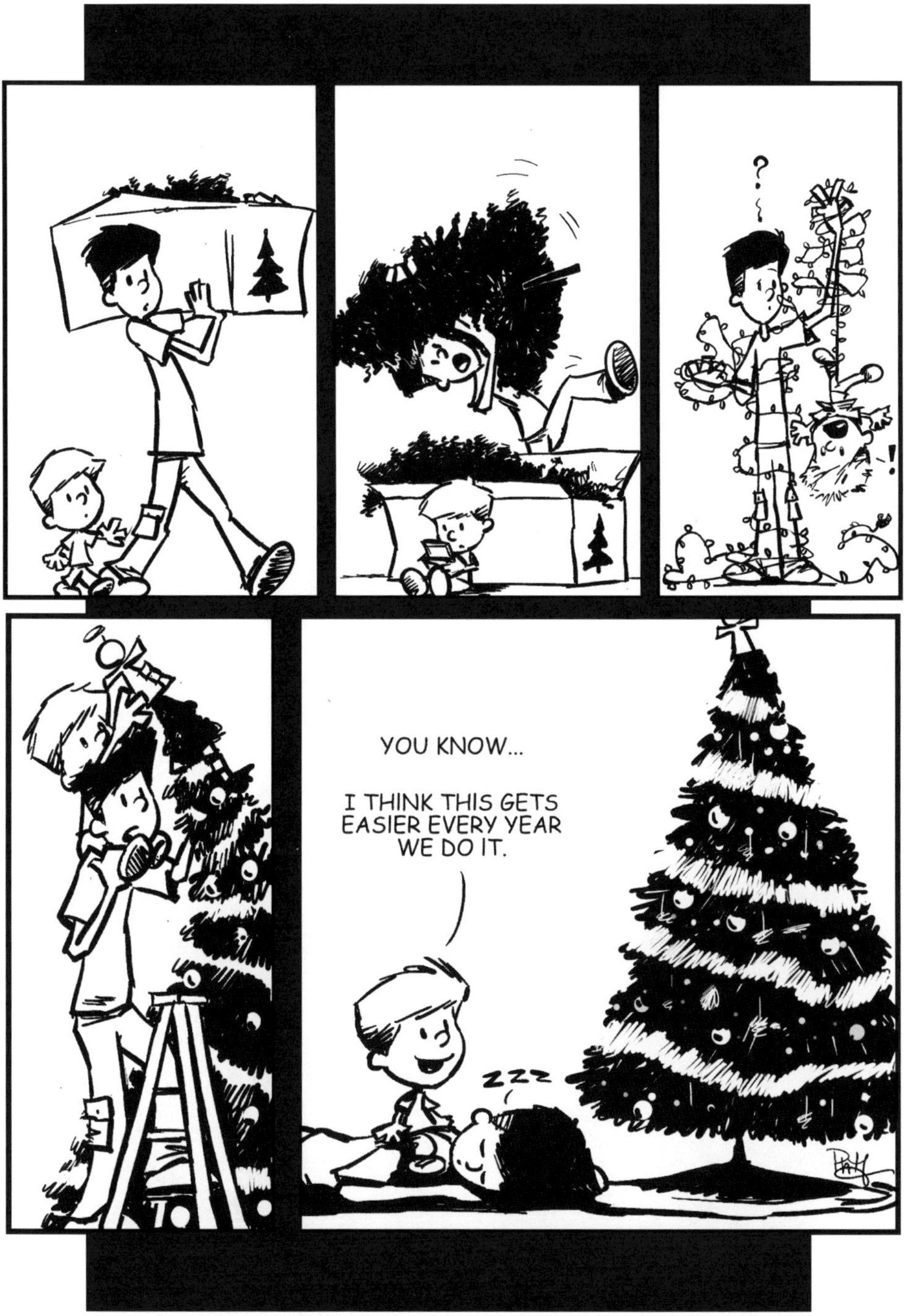
?
!
YOU KNOW...
I THINK THIS GETS EASIER EVERY YEAR WE DO IT.
ZZZ

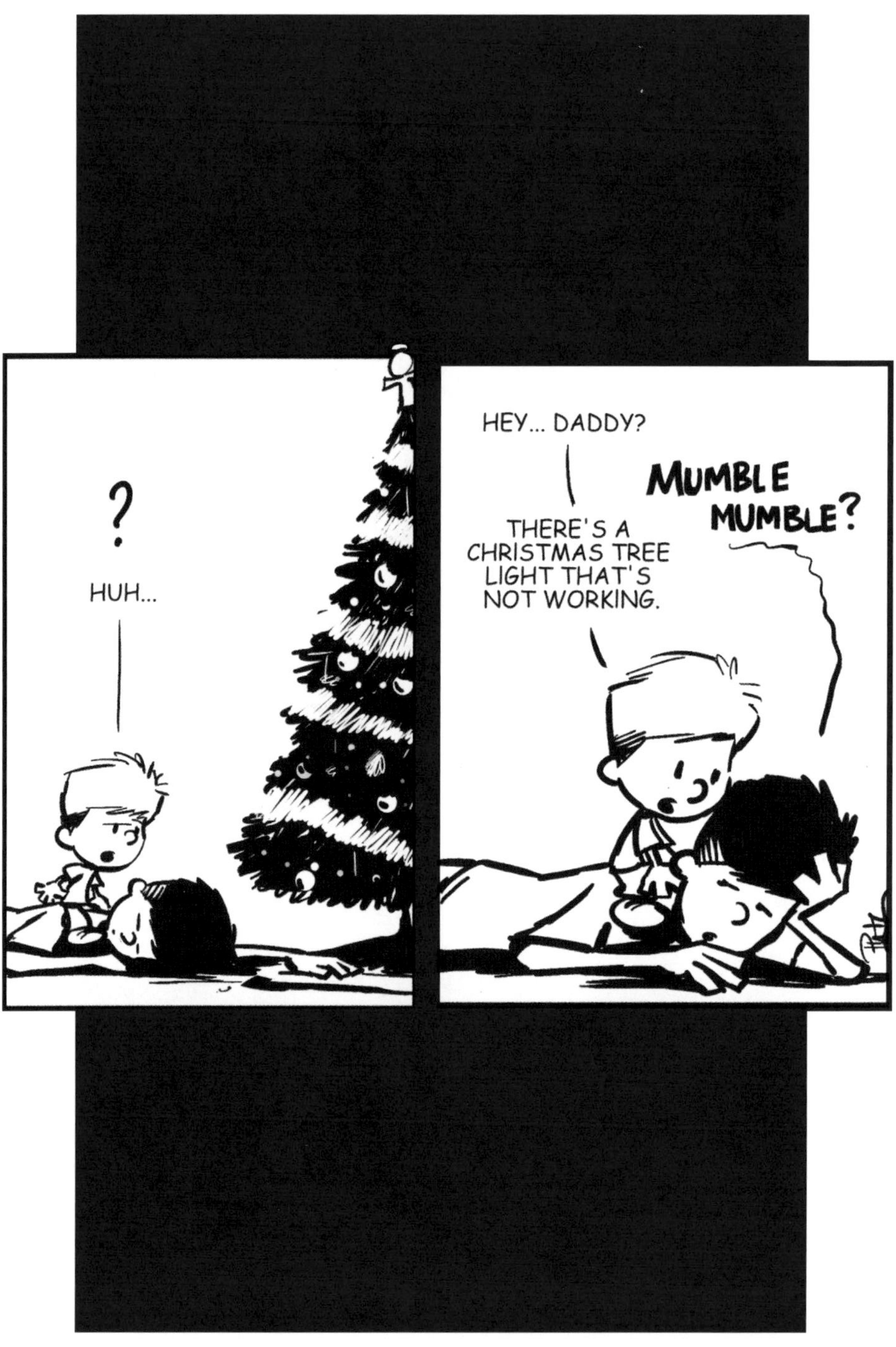
?
HUH...
HEY... DADDY?
THERE'S A CHRISTMAS TREE LIGHT THAT'S NOT WORKING.
MUMBLE MUMBLE?

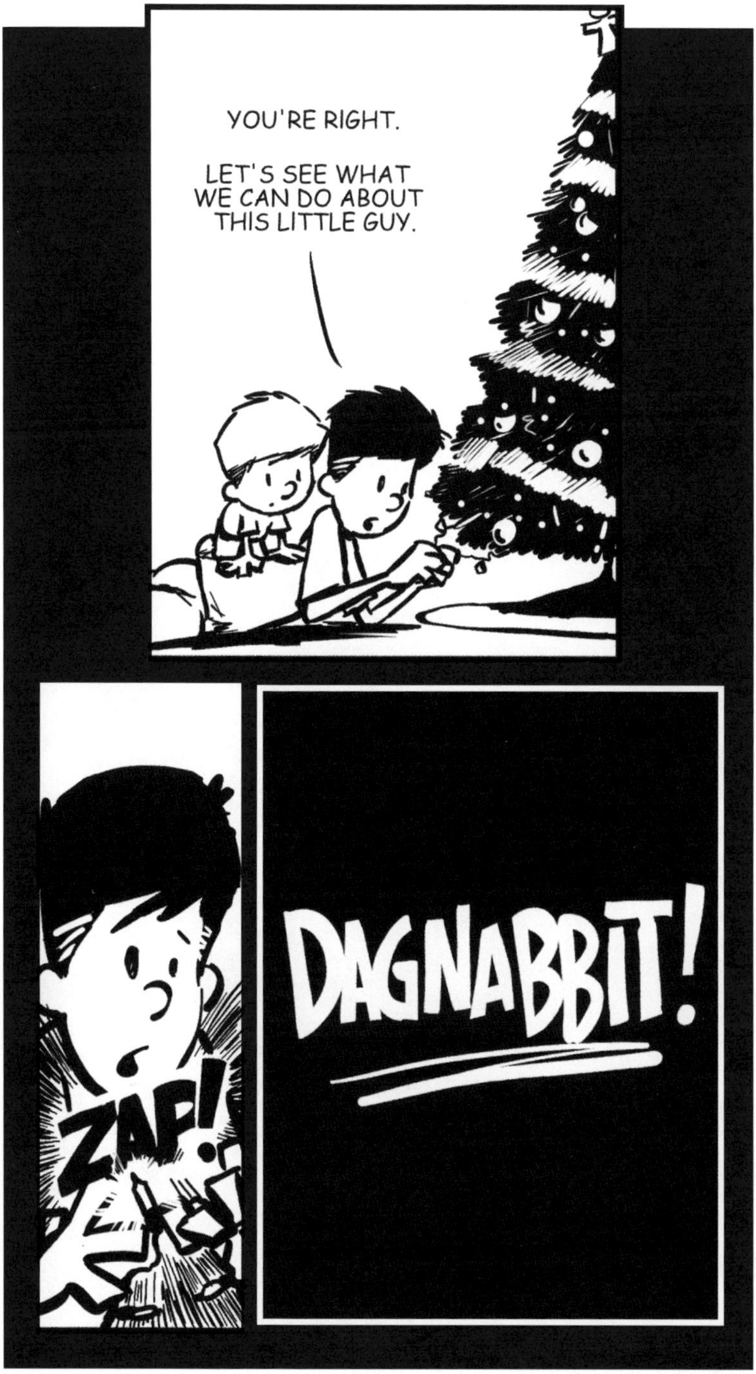

YOU'RE RIGHT.
LET'S SEE WHAT WE CAN DO ABOUT THIS LITTLE GUY.
ZAP!
DAGNABBIT!

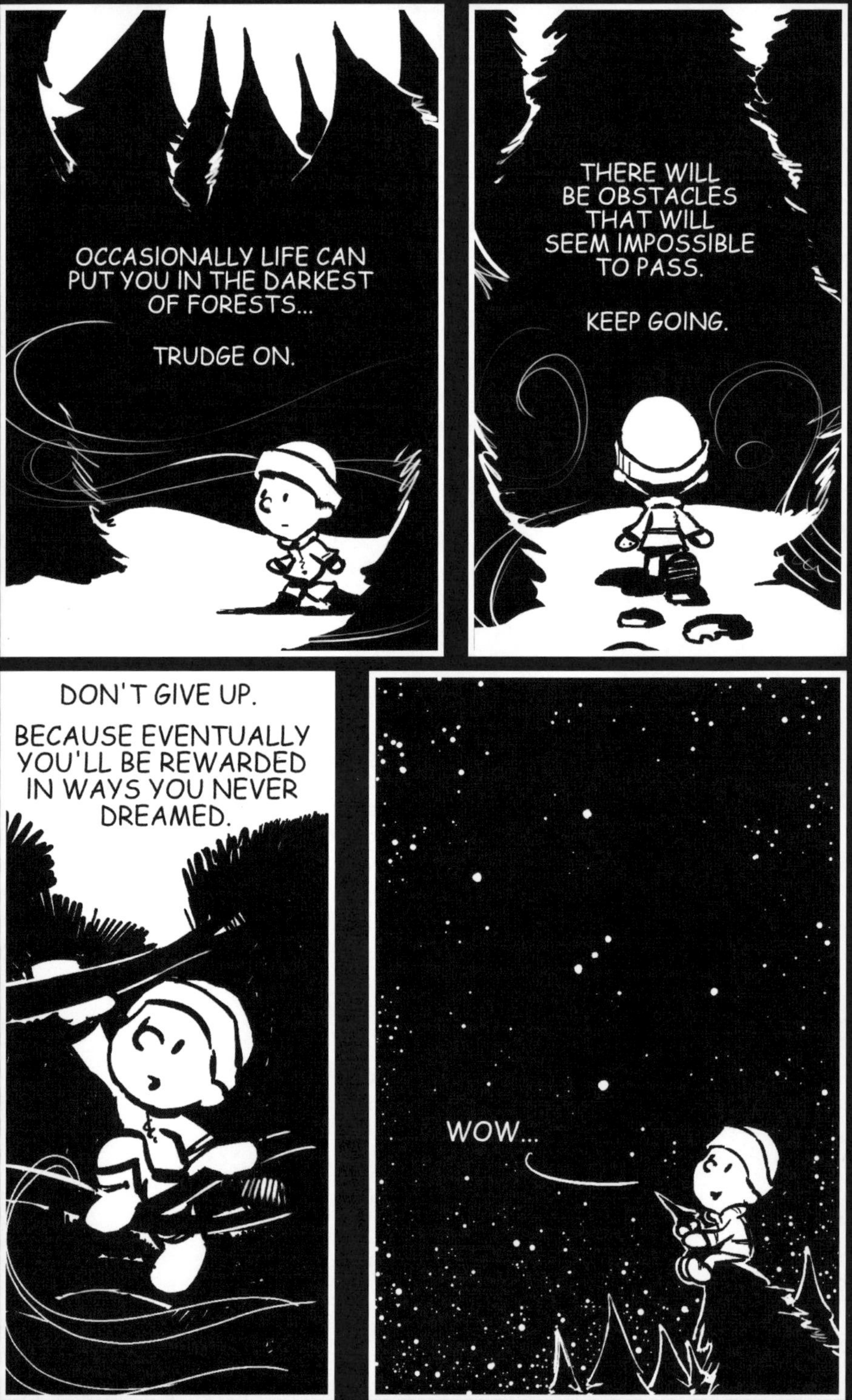
OCCASIONALLY LIFE CAN PUT YOU IN THE DARKEST OF FORESTS...
TRUDGE ON.
THERE WILL BE OBSTACLES THAT WILL SEEM IMPOSSIBLE TO PASS.
KEEP GOING.
DON'T GIVE UP.
BECAUSE EVENTUALLY YOU'LL BE REWARDED IN WAYS YOU NEVER DREAMED.
WOW...

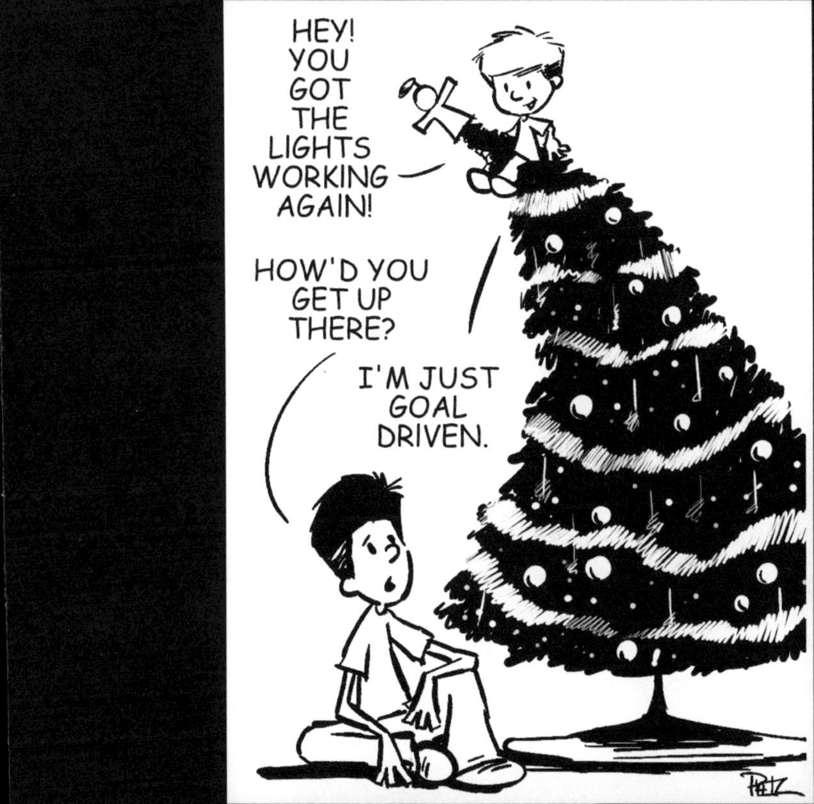
HEY! YOU GOT THE LIGHTS WORKING AGAIN!
HOW'D YOU GET UP THERE?
I'M JUST GOAL DRIVEN.
PIRTZ

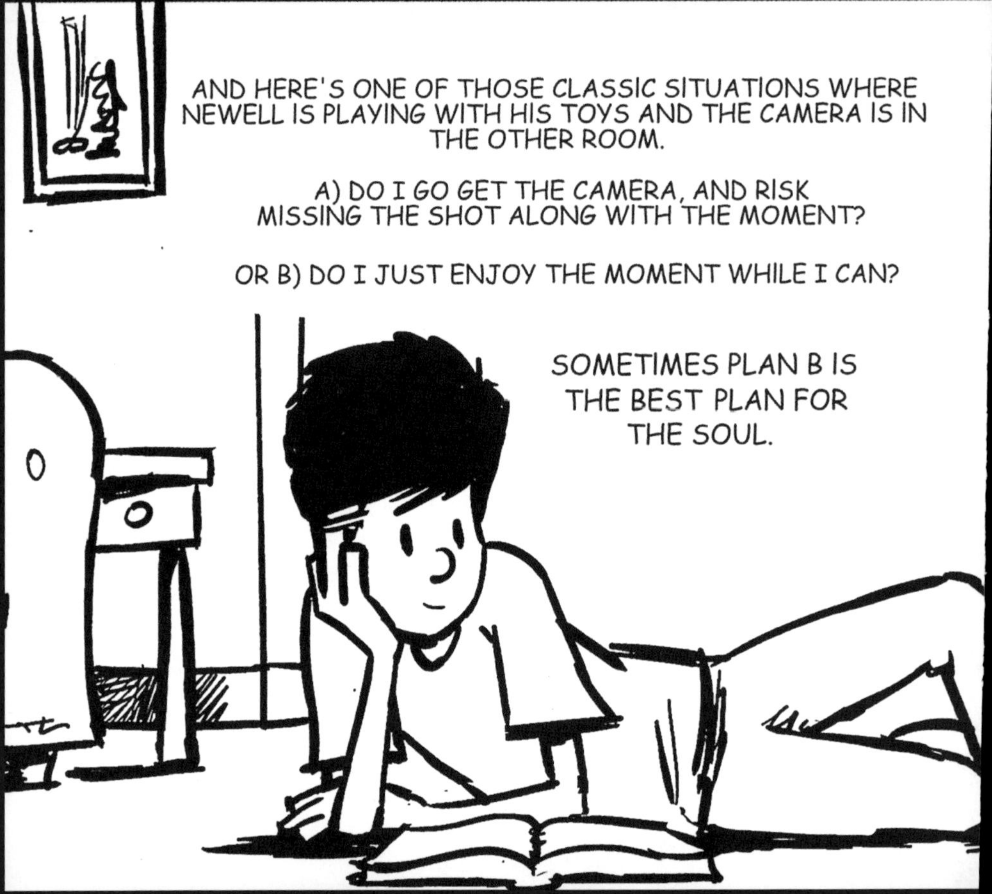
AND HERE'S ONE OF THOSE CLASSIC SITUATIONS WHERE NEWELL IS PLAYING WITH HIS TOYS AND THE CAMERA IS IN THE OTHER ROOM.
A) DO I GO GET THE CAMERA, AND RISK MISSING THE SHOT ALONG WITH THE MOMENT?
OR B) DO I JUST ENJOY THE MOMENT WHILE I CAN?
SOMETIMES PLAN B IS THE BEST PLAN FOR THE SOUL.

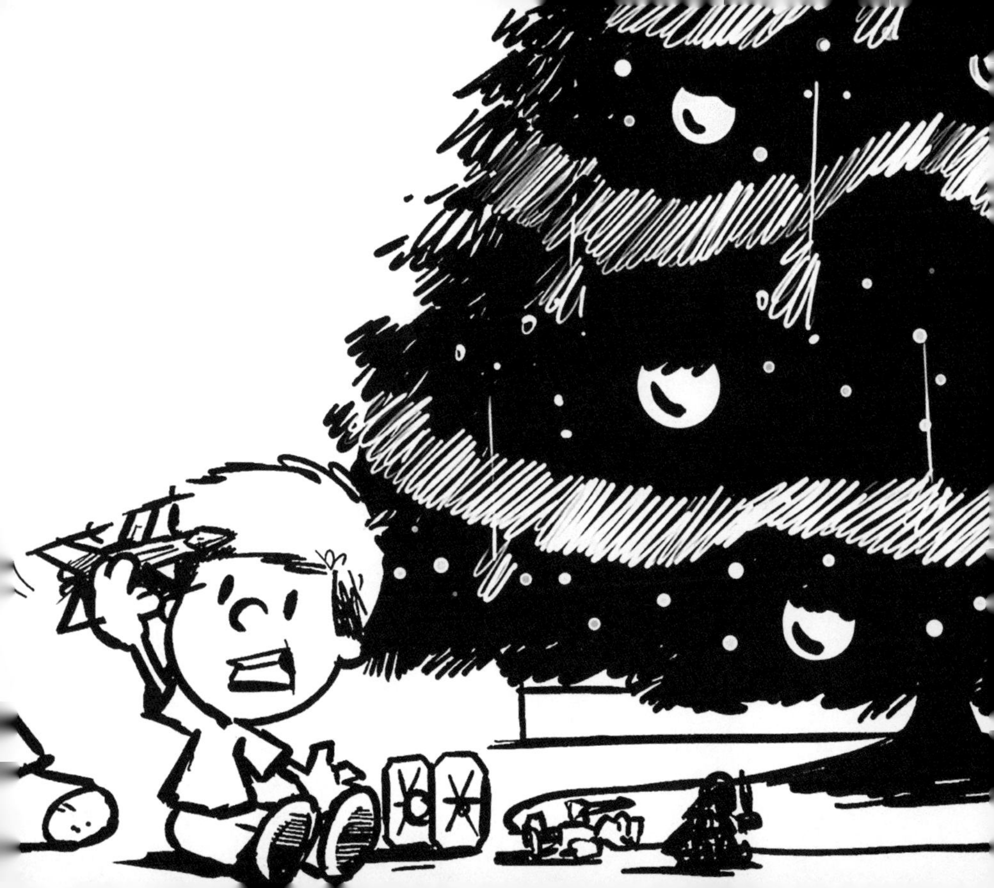

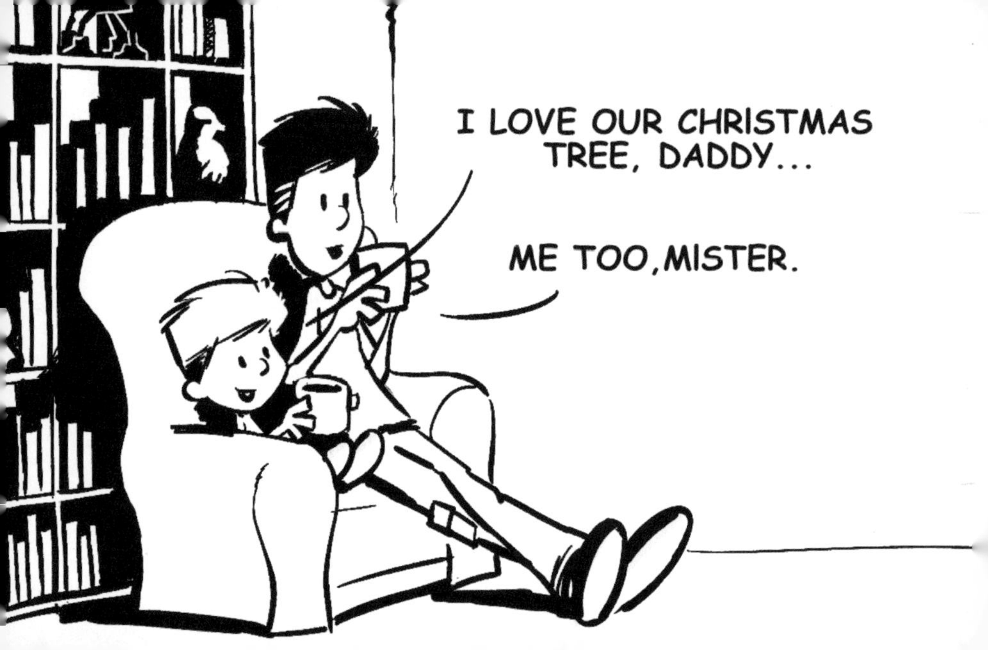
I LOVE OUR CHRISTMAS TREE, DADDY...
ME TOO, MISTER.

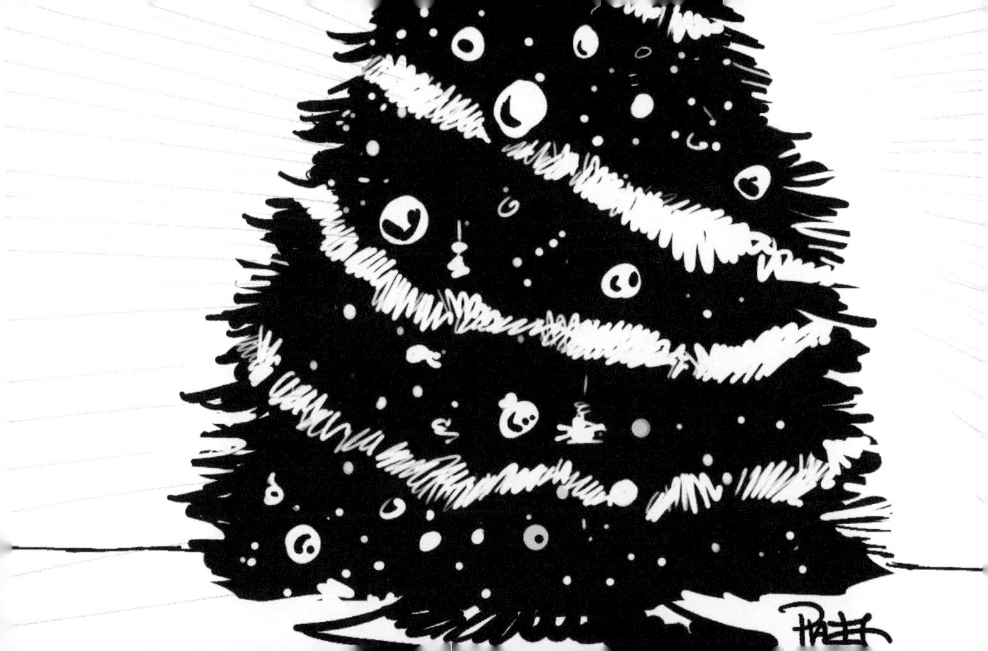

AFTERWARD

In "Dream", the fist collection of Mister & Me comics, there aren't too many times where you go beyond the world of Newell and his dad. Outside of the two of them there is the little girl, Clara, Newell's nemesis; Newell's teacher; A disgruntled TV star and his assistant; the troupe who does the Mister & Me show; and then there's...

Wait... I'm so wrong. Apparently it does go beyond just the two of them. So forget where I was going with that.

The point where I was headed is that in "Of Castles and Kings" we see that Newell's dad has a life outside of just being the father to his son. We see that he has friends that are apart of his life. And we see that he is on the cusp of finding out what it's like to date as a single-parent.

Parenting is an exhausting job—mind you—the best job in the world. But, as any parent can testify, an exhausting one.

Here's to all of my friends, and all the friends of dedicated parents, who help keep the laughter going.

Cheers.

JP

FAN ART

JON ESPARZA

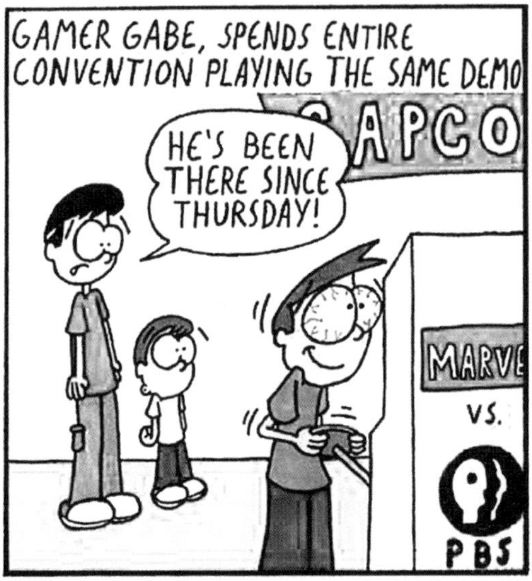
GAMER GABE, SPENDS ENTIRE
CONVENTION PLAYING THE SAME DEMO
HE'S BEEN THERE SINCE THURSDAY!
VS.
PBS

JASON MCKINNEY

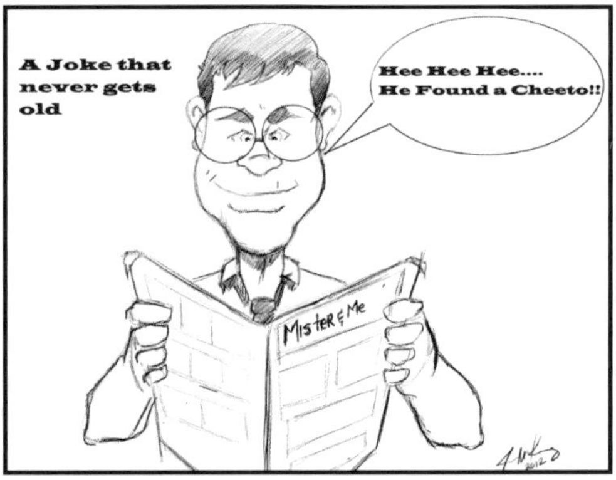
A Joke that never gets old
Hee Hee Hee.... He Found a Cheeto!!
Mister & Me

ACTOR CHAD TALLON AND HIS MISTER & ME SHIRT

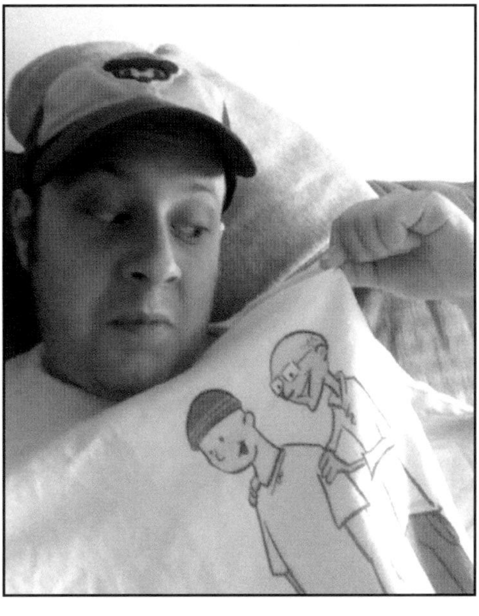

The adventures continue at
www.mister-and-me.com

And become a Mister & Me patron at
www.patreon.com/jasonplatt

CPSIA information can be obtained at www.ICGtesting.com
Printed in the USA
BVIW120652210620
581971BV00019B/360